Let Us Sing

לְכוּ נְרַנְּנָה

L'chu N'ran'nah

Blessings before and after the meal,

Z'mirot and songs

for Shabbat, Festivals, and other occasions

Editor: Barry Dov Walfish
Associate Editors: Mark Frydenberg, Aviva Richman
Artwork: Shoshana Walfish
Book Design: Joe Buchwald Gelles   Cover Design: Mark B. Frydenberg

Some translations, transliterations, and Hebrew text:
© *Siddur Chaveirim Kol Yisraeil* (Hoboken, NJ: Ktav, 2000). Used with permission of the authors.
Thanks to Shefa Gold for permission to publish "You are the Source of Life."
Thanks to Hannah Tiferet Siegel for permission to publish *V'achalta v'savata*.

ISBN 978-0-9664740-7-7

Contact us at bencher@birkat.org or visit www.birkat.org for more information or
to listen to or share your own audio recordings of some of the songs in this book.

To order: www.haggadahsrus.com 877-308-4175

♲ printed on recycled paper

Introduction

L'chu n'ran'nah! Come, let us sing! This phrase from the first of the Kabbalat Shabbat psalms invites us to honor and celebrate Shabbat with song and blessing. This bencher extends that invitation by presenting liturgies for the blessings after the meal, kiddush for Shabbat and Festivals, z'mirot, and popular songs, in an attractive user-friendly format.

What makes this bencher special?

It is easy to use and fully transliterated. This bencher uses the three-column linear format first introduced in *Siddur Chaveirim Kol Yisraeil*. Transliteration, Hebrew text, and translation appear side by side on each page. Raised dot symbols separate syllables in transliteration to make it easier to read.

It is fully egalitarian and inclusive. Women and men have equal status in all aspects of the liturgy, including invocations, blessing one's family, recalling our ancestors (including the matriarchs), and blessings for newborn daughters and bat mitzvah girls.

It provides alternatives. There are several benching options: full traditional, abbreviated traditional, and contemporary. Within the text, alternatives to the traditional text are indicated in square brackets.

It has a contemporary, faithful, gender-neutral translation. The translation stays close to the text, deviating only when necessary to address issues of gender, including masculine God language.

It is scholarly. An attempt has been made to produce as accurate a Hebrew text as possible, even if this means deviating occasionally from the text found in most benchers. The notes point to biblical and rabbinic sources and explain difficult passages.

The editors would like to thank Ben Dreyfus, Ray Scheindlin, and Miriam-Simma Walfish for helpful comments, and Mordechai Walfish, Tzemah Yoreh, and especially Yael Richardson for proofreading. We would also like to express our sincere gratitude to Shoshana Walfish for her lovely illustrations and to Joe Buchwald Gelles for his excellent work on the bencher's layout and design.

Iyar 5769/May 2009

Table of Contents

בִּרְכַּת הַמָּזוֹן
Blessings After the Meal ◆ Birkat HaMazon

- On Shabbat, Festivals, and joyous occasions, start with *Shir HaMaalot*, p. 2.
- On Shabbat, Festivals, Bar/Bat Mitzvah celebrations and other festive occasions, continue with the invitation, p. 4.
- At a wedding, begin with the invitation on p. 4; after the first four lines, continue on p. 5.
- At a *b'rit milah* or *simchat bat*, use the invitation on pp. 30-33.
- On all occasions (including when alone), continue with main part of *Birkat HaMazon*, pp. 6-25.
- At a wedding, follow this with *Sheva B'rachot*, pp. 26-28.
- Alternatives:
    - Abbreviated traditional *Birkat HaMazon*, pp. 34-36.
    - Three Short Prayers, p. 37.
    - "You are the Source of Everything" by Shefa Gold, pp. 38-39.
    - "V'achalta v'savata" by Hannah Tiferet Siegel, p. 40.
- Blessings before Foods, p. 41.
- *B'rachah Acharonah*, Blessings after Foods other than bread, pp. 42-44.

Birkat HaMazon · בִּרְכַּת הַמָּזוֹן

On Shabbat, festivals, or joyous occasions, begin here, with Psalm 126. At other times, begin with an invitation on page 4.

Shir ha·ma·a·lot.	שִׁיר הַמַּעֲלוֹת.	A song of ascents.
b'shuv A·do·nai	בְּשׁוּב יְיָ	When Adonai restores
et shi·vat Tzi·yon	אֶת שִׁיבַת צִיּוֹן	the fortunes of Zion,
ha·yi·nu k'chol·mim.	הָיִינוּ כְּחֹלְמִים.	we will be like dreamers.
Az yi·ma·lei s'chok pi·nu	אָז יִמָּלֵא שְׂחוֹק פִּינוּ	Then will our mouth fill with laughter
u·l'sho·nei·nu ri·nah.	וּלְשׁוֹנֵנוּ רִנָּה.	and our tongue with joyous song.
Az yo·m'ru va·go·yim	אָז יֹאמְרוּ בַגּוֹיִם	Then they will say among the nations,
Hig·dil A·do·nai la·a·sot im ei·leh.	הִגְדִּיל יְיָ לַעֲשׂוֹת עִם אֵלֶּה.	Great things has Adonai done for them.
Hig·dil A·do·nai la·a·sot i·ma·nu	הִגְדִּיל יְיָ לַעֲשׂוֹת עִמָּנוּ	Great things has Adonai done for us,
ha·yi·nu s'mei·chim.	הָיִינוּ שְׂמֵחִים.	we will rejoice.
Shu·vah A·do·nai et sh'vi·tei·nu	שׁוּבָה יְיָ אֶת שְׁבִיתֵנוּ	Return, Adonai, our fortunes
ka·a·fi·kim ba·Ne·gev.	כַּאֲפִיקִים בַּנֶּגֶב.	like streams in the Negev.
Ha·zo·r'im b'dim·ah	הַזֹּרְעִים בְּדִמְעָה	Those who sow in tears
b'ri·nah yik·tzo·ru.	בְּרִנָּה יִקְצֹרוּ.	with joyous song will reap.
Ha·loch yei·leich u·va·choh	הָלוֹךְ יֵלֵךְ וּבָכֹה	The one who walks along tearfully
no·sei me·shech ha·za·ra	נֹשֵׂא מֶשֶׁךְ הַזָּרַע	carrying the bag of seed
bo ya·vo v'ri·nah	בֹּא יָבֹא בְרִנָּה	will surely come with joyous song
no·sei a·lu·mo·tav.	נֹשֵׂא אֲלֻמֹּתָיו.	carrying sheaves of grain.

T'hi·lat A·do·nai y'da·ber pi,
vi·va·reich kol ba·sar
sheim kod·sho l'o·lam va·ed.
Va·a·nach·nu n'va·reich Yah
mei·a·tah v'ad o·lam ha·l'lu·yah.
Ho·du lA·do·nai ki tov,
ki l'o·lam chas·do.
Mi y'ma·leil g'vu·rot A·do·nai
yash·mi·a kol t'hi·la·to.

תְּהִלַּת יְיָ יְדַבֶּר פִּי,
וִיבָרֵךְ כָּל בָּשָׂר
שֵׁם קָדְשׁוֹ לְעוֹלָם וָעֶד.
וַאֲנַחְנוּ נְבָרֵךְ יָהּ
מֵעַתָּה וְעַד עוֹלָם הַלְלוּיָהּ.
הוֹדוּ לַייָ כִּי טוֹב,
כִּי לְעוֹלָם חַסְדּוֹ.
מִי יְמַלֵּל גְּבוּרוֹת יְיָ
יַשְׁמִיעַ כָּל תְּהִלָּתוֹ.

My mouth will speak Adonai's praise,
every creature will bless
Your holy Name forever and ever.
And we will bless Yah
from now until forever. Halleluyah.
Give thanks to God for God is good,
for God's kindness is forever.
Who can utter Adonai's mighty acts,
or make all God's praises heard?[1]

---

1. Psalms 145:21, 115:18, 118:1, 106:2.

When three or more have eaten together, the Leader invites the others to recite Birkat HaMazon with either a formal or informal invitation. At a B'rit Milah or Simchat Bat, begin on page 30. When praying individually, begin at Hazan et hakol, page 6.

Leader:

Cha·vei·rai n'va·reich.   **חֲבֵרַי נְבָרֵךְ.**   Friends, let us offer a blessing.

On more formal occasions, one may begin:

[G'vi·ro·tai v']ra·bo·tai n'va·reich.   **[גְּבִירוֹתַי וְ]רַבּוֹתַי נְבָרֵךְ.**   [Ladies and] Gentlemen, let us offer a blessing.

Group, then the Leader repeats:

Y'hi sheim A·do·nai m'vo·rach   יְהִי שֵׁם יְיָ מְבֹרָךְ   May Adonai's Name be praised
mei·a·tah v'ad o·lam.   מֵעַתָּה וְעַד עוֹלָם.   from now and beyond all time.

At a wedding or Sheva B'rachot, continue on p. 5.

[When fewer than ten have eaten together, do not say Eloheinu אֱלֹהֵינוּ *Our God.]*

Leader:

Bir·shut   בִּרְשׁוּת   With the permission of
[cha·vei·rai | kol ha·m'su·bin kan]   [חֲבֵרַי | כָּל הַמְסֻבִּין כָּאן]   [my friends | all those assembled here],
n'va·reich (E·lo·hei·nu)   נְבָרֵךְ (אֱלֹהֵינוּ)   let us bless (Our God,)
she·a·chal·nu mi·she·lo.   שֶׁאָכַלְנוּ מִשֶּׁלּוֹ.   whose food we have eaten.

Group, then the Leader repeats:

Ba·ruch (E·lo·hei·nu) she·a·chal·nu   בָּרוּךְ (אֱלֹהֵינוּ) שֶׁאָכַלְנוּ   Blessed is (our God,) whose food we have
mi·she·lo u·v'tu·vo cha·yi·nu.   מִשֶּׁלּוֹ וּבְטוּבוֹ חָיִינוּ.   eaten, and through whose goodness we live.

All together:

Ba·ruch hu u·va·ruch sh'mo.   בָּרוּךְ הוּא וּבָרוּךְ שְׁמוֹ.   Blessed is God, and blessed is The Name.

Proceed to page 6.

At a wedding or Sheva B'rachot, begin on p. 4, then continue here:

Leader:

D'vai ha·seir v'gam cha·ron,	דְּוַי הָסֵר וְגַם חָרוֹן,	Remove sorrow and also fury,
v'az i·leim b'shir ya·ron.	וְאָז אִלֵּם בְּשִׁיר יָרוֹן,	and then the voiceless shall sing a song.
n'chei·nu b'ma·g'lei tze·dek,	נְחֵנוּ בְּמַעְגְּלֵי צֶדֶק,	Guide us on righteous paths,
sh'eih bir·kat b'nei A·ha·ron.	שְׁעֵה בִּרְכַּת בְּנֵי אַהֲרֹן.	Accept the blessings of Aaron's children.

Bir·shut	בִּרְשׁוּת	With the permission of
[cha·vei·rai | kol ha·m'su·bin kan]	[חֲבֵרַי|כָּל הַמְסוּבִּין כָּאן]	[my friends | all those assembled here]
n'va·reich (E·lo·hei·nu)	נְבָרֵךְ אֱלֹהֵינוּ	Let us bless our God
she·ha·sim·chah bim·o·no	שֶׁהַשִּׂמְחָה בִּמְעוֹנוֹ	in whose Dwelling is Joy
v'she·a·chal·nu mi·she·lo.	וְשֶׁאָכַלְנוּ מִשֶּׁלּוֹ.	and of whose food we have eaten.

Group, then the Leader repeats:

Ba·ruch E·lo·hei·nu	בָּרוּךְ אֱלֹהֵינוּ	Blessed is our God
she·ha·sim·chah bim·o·no,	שֶׁהַשִּׂמְחָה בִּמְעוֹנוֹ,	in whose Dwelling is joy,
v'she·a·chal·nu mi·she·lo,	וְשֶׁאָכַלְנוּ מִשֶּׁלּוֹ,	whose food we have eaten,
u·v'tu·vo cha·yi·nu.	וּבְטוּבוֹ חָיִינוּ.	and through whose goodness we live.

All together:

Ba·ruch hu u·va·ruch sh'mo.	בָּרוּךְ הוּא וּבָרוּךְ שְׁמוֹ.	Blessed is God and blessed is The Name.

The First Blessing: Nourisher of All

Attributed to Moses, who composed it to thank God for the manna which sustained the Israelites as they wandered in the wilderness.

Ba·ruch A·tah A·do·nai,	**בָּרוּךְ** אַתָּה יְיָ,	Blessed are You, Adonai,
E·lo·hei·nu Me·lech ha·O·lam,	אֱלֹהֵינוּ מֶלֶךְ הָעוֹלָם,	our God, Ruler of the Universe,
ha·zan et ha·o·lam ku·lo b'tu·vo	הַזָּן אֶת הָעוֹלָם כֻּלּוֹ בְּטוּבוֹ	who sustains the world with goodness
b'chein b'che·sed u·v'ra·cha·mim.	בְּחֵן בְּחֶסֶד וּבְרַחֲמִים.	with favor, kindness, and mercy.
Hu no·tein le·chem l'chol ba·sar	הוּא נוֹתֵן לֶחֶם לְכָל בָּשָׂר	You give food to all creatures
ki l'o·lam chas·do.	כִּי לְעוֹלָם חַסְדּוֹ.	for Your kindness is everlasting.
U·v'tu·vo ha·ga·dol,	וּבְטוּבוֹ הַגָּדוֹל,	And because of Your great goodness,
ta·mid lo cha·sar la·nu	תָּמִיד לֹא חָסַר לָנוּ	never have we lacked
v'al yech·sar la·nu	וְאַל יֶחְסַר לָנוּ	and never will we lack
ma·zon l'o·lam va·ed.	מָזוֹן לְעוֹלָם וָעֶד.	food forever and ever.
Ba·a·vur sh'mo ha·ga·dol,	בַּעֲבוּר שְׁמוֹ הַגָּדוֹל,	For the sake of Your great Name,
ki hu zan u·m'far·neis la·kol,	כִּי הוּא זָן וּמְפַרְנֵס לַכֹּל,	for You nourish and keep all,
u·mei·tiv la·kol, u·mei·chin ma·zon	וּמֵטִיב לַכֹּל, וּמֵכִין מָזוֹן	and do good for all, and prepare food
l'chol b'ri·yo·tav a·sher ba·ra.	לְכָל בְּרִיּוֹתָיו אֲשֶׁר בָּרָא.	for all the living things You created.
Ba·ruch A·tah A·do·nai,	בָּרוּךְ אַתָּה יְיָ,	Blessed are You, Adonai,
ha·zan et ha·kol.	הַזָּן אֶת הַכֹּל.	who nourishes all.

The Second Blessing: For the Land and For the Food

Attributed to Joshua, who composed it upon entering the Land of Israel.

No·deh l'cha, A·do·nai E·lo·hei·nu,	נוֹדֶה לְּךָ, יְיָ אֱלֹהֵינוּ,	We thank You, Adonai our God,
al she·hin·chal·ta	עַל שֶׁהִנְחַלְתָּ	for giving
la·a·vo·tei·nu [u·l'i·mo·tei·nu]	לַאֲבוֹתֵינוּ [וּלְאִמּוֹתֵינוּ]	to our ancestors
e·retz chem·dah to·vah u·r'cha·vah,	אֶרֶץ חֶמְדָּה טוֹבָה וּרְחָבָה,	a land desirable, good, and spacious,
v'al she·ho·tzei·ta·nu,	וְעַל שֶׁהוֹצֵאתָנוּ,	for bringing us out,
A·do·nai E·lo·hei·nu, mei·eretz Mitz·ra·yim,	יְיָ אֱלֹהֵינוּ, מֵאֶרֶץ מִצְרַיִם,	Adonai our God, from the land of Egypt,
u·f'di·ta·nu mi·beit a·va·dim,	וּפְדִיתָנוּ מִבֵּית עֲבָדִים,	for freeing us from the house of slavery,
v'al b'rit·cha she·cha·tam·ta	וְעַל בְּרִיתְךָ שֶׁחָתַמְתָּ	for Your covenant that You sealed
[biv·sa·rei·nu | b'li·bei·nu],	[בִּבְשָׂרֵנוּ | בְּלִבֵּנוּ],	in our [flesh|hearts],[1]
v'al To·rat·cha she·li·mad·ta·nu,	וְעַל תּוֹרָתְךָ שֶׁלִּמַּדְתָּנוּ,	for the Torah that You taught us,
v'al chu·ke·cha she·ho·da·ta·nu,	וְעַל חֻקֶּיךָ שֶׁהוֹדַעְתָּנוּ,	for the laws which You made known to us,
v'al cha·yim chein va·che·sed	וְעַל חַיִּים חֵן וָחֶסֶד	for the life, favor, and kindness
she·cho·nan·ta·nu,	שֶׁחוֹנַנְתָּנוּ,	that You have granted us,
v'al a·chi·lat mazon	וְעַל אֲכִילַת מָזוֹן	and for the food
sha·A·tah zan u·m'far·neis	שָׁאַתָּה זָן וּמְפַרְנֵס	with which You nourish and sustain
o·ta·nu ta·mid,	אוֹתָנוּ תָּמִיד,	us always,
b'chol yom u·v'chol eit u·v'chol sha·ah.	בְּכָל יוֹם וּבְכָל עֵת וּבְכָל שָׁעָה.	every day, at all times, and in every hour.

1. Some, who feel that the traditional phrase "the Covenant sealed in our flesh" refers only to males, substitute the phrase "the Covenant sealed in our hearts" (cf. Deuteronomy 30:6).

Al ha·ni·sim, v'al ha·pur·kan,	עַל הַנִּסִּים, וְעַל הַפֻּרְקָן,	For the miracles, for the salvation,
v'al ha·g'vu·rot, v'al ha·t'shu·ot,	עַל הַגְּבוּרוֹת, וְעַל הַתְּשׁוּעוֹת,	for the mighty deeds, for the victories
v'al ha·mil·cha·mot	וְעַל הַמִּלְחָמוֹת	and for the battles
she·a·si·ta la·a·vo·tei·nu [u·l'·i·mo·tei·nu]	שֶׁעָשִׂיתָ לַאֲבוֹתֵינוּ [וּלְאִמּוֹתֵינוּ]	You performed for our ancestors
ba·ya·mim ha·heim ba·z'man ha·zeh.	בַּיָּמִים הָהֵם בַּזְּמַן הַזֶּה.	in those days, at this season [we thank You].

Biy·mei Ma·tit·ya·hu ben Yo·cha·nan,	בִּימֵי מַתִּתְיָהוּ בֶּן יוֹחָנָן,	In the days of Matityahu ben Yochanan,
ko·hein ga·dol, Chash·mo·nai u·va·nav,	כֹּהֵן גָּדוֹל, חַשְׁמוֹנַאי וּבָנָיו,	the High Priest, the Hasmonean and his sons,
k'she·am·dah mal·chut	כְּשֶׁעָמְדָה מַלְכוּת	when a wicked Hellenic government opposed
Ya·van ha·r'sha·ah al am·cha Yis·ra·eil	יָוָן הָרְשָׁעָה עַל עַמְּךָ יִשְׂרָאֵל	Your people Israel, [determined]
l'hash·ki·cham To·ra·te·cha,	לְהַשְׁכִּיחָם תּוֹרָתֶךָ,	to make them forget Your Torah,
u·l'ha·a·vi·ram mei·chu·kei r'tzo·ne·cha.	וּלְהַעֲבִירָם מֵחֻקֵּי רְצוֹנֶךָ.	and transgress the laws of Your will,
V'a·tah b'ra·cha·me·cha ha·ra·bim,	וְאַתָּה בְּרַחֲמֶיךָ הָרַבִּים,	You, in Your great mercy,
a·mad·ta la·hem b'eit tza·ra·tam,	עָמַדְתָּ לָהֶם בְּעֵת צָרָתָם,	stood by them in their time of distress,
rav·ta et ri·vam, dan·ta et di·nam,	רַבְתָּ אֶת רִיבָם, דַּנְתָּ אֶת דִּינָם,	You championed their cause, defended their rights,
na·kam·ta et nik·ma·tam.	נָקַמְתָּ אֶת נִקְמָתָם.	and avenged their injustice.
ma·sar·ta gi·bo·rim b'yad cha·la·shim,	מָסַרְתָּ גִבּוֹרִים בְּיַד חַלָּשִׁים,	You delivered the strong into the hands of the weak,
v'ra·bim b'yad m'a·tim,	וְרַבִּים בְּיַד מְעַטִּים,	the many into the hands of the few,
u·t'mei·im b'yad t'ho·rim,	וּטְמֵאִים בְּיַד טְהוֹרִים,	the impure into the hands of the pure,
u·r'sha·im b'yad tza·di·kim,	וּרְשָׁעִים בְּיַד צַדִּיקִים,	the wicked into the hands of the righteous,
v'zei·dim b'yad	וְזֵדִים בְּיַד	and the arrogant into the hands
os·kei To·ra·te·cha.	עוֹסְקֵי תוֹרָתֶךָ.	of the students of your Torah.
U·l'cha a·si·ta	וּלְךָ עָשִׂיתָ	You made for Yourself
sheim ga·dol v'ka·dosh b'o·la·me·cha,	שֵׁם גָּדוֹל וְקָדוֹשׁ בְּעוֹלָמֶךָ,	a great and holy name in Your world,

u·l'am·cha Yis·ra·eil a·si·ta	וּלְעַמְּךָ יִשְׂרָאֵל עָשִׂיתָ	and for Your people Israel You performed
t'shu·ah g'do·lah	תְּשׁוּעָה גְדוֹלָה	a great act of salvation
u·fur·kan k'ha·yom ha·zeh.	וּפֻרְקָן כְּהַיּוֹם הַזֶּה.	and deliverance [unrivaled] unto this day.
V'a·char kein ba·u va·ne·cha	וְאַחַר כֵּן בָּאוּ בָנֶיךָ	Afterwards, Your children came
lid·vir bei·te·cha,	לִדְבִיר בֵּיתֶךָ,	to the inner sanctum of Your house,
u·fi·nu et hei·cha·le·cha,	וּפִנּוּ אֶת הֵיכָלֶךָ,	cleansed Your Temple,
v'ti·ha·ru et mik·da·she·cha,	וְטִהֲרוּ אֶת מִקְדָּשֶׁךָ,	purified Your sanctuary,
v'hid·li·ku nei·rot b'chatz·rot kod·she·cha,	וְהִדְלִיקוּ נֵרוֹת בְּחַצְרוֹת קָדְשֶׁךָ,	lit candles in Your holy courtyards,
v'ka·v'u sh'mo·nat y'mei Cha·nu·kah ei·lu	וְקָבְעוּ שְׁמוֹנַת יְמֵי חֲנֻכָּה אֵלּוּ	and set these eight days of Chanukah
l'ho·dot u·l'ha·leil l'shim·cha ha·ga·dol.	לְהוֹדוֹת וּלְהַלֵּל לְשִׁמְךָ הַגָּדוֹל.	for giving thanks and praise to Your great Name.

On Purim:

Biy·mei Mor·d'chai v'Es·teir	בִּימֵי מָרְדְּכַי וְאֶסְתֵּר	In the days of Mordechai and Esther
b'Shu·shan ha·bi·rah,	בְּשׁוּשַׁן הַבִּירָה,	in the fortress city of Shushan,
k'she·a·mad a·lei·hem Ha·man ha·ra·sha,	כְּשֶׁעָמַד עֲלֵיהֶם הָמָן הָרָשָׁע,	when there arose against them the wicked Haman,
bi·keish l'hash·mid,	בִּקֵּשׁ לְהַשְׁמִיד,	who wanted to annihilate,
la·ha·rog u·l'a·beid et kol ha·Y'hu·dim,	לַהֲרֹג וּלְאַבֵּד אֶת כָּל הַיְּהוּדִים,	murder, and destroy all the Jews,
mi·na·ar v'ad za·kein, taf v'na·shim,	מִנַּעַר וְעַד זָקֵן, טַף וְנָשִׁים,	young and old, children and women,
b'yom e·chad, bish·lo·shah a·sar	בְּיוֹם אֶחָד, בִּשְׁלֹשָׁה עָשָׂר	on one day, on the thirteenth [day]
l'cho·desh sh'neim a·sar, hu cho·desh A·dar,	לְחֹדֶשׁ שְׁנֵים עָשָׂר, הוּא חֹדֶשׁ אֲדָר,	of the twelfth month, the month of Adar,
u·sh'la·lam la·voz,	וּשְׁלָלָם לָבוֹז,	and plunder their property,
v'A·tah b'ra·cha·me·cha ha·ra·bim	וְאַתָּה בְּרַחֲמֶיךָ הָרַבִּים	You, in Your great mercy,
hei·far·ta et a·tza·to,	הֵפַרְתָּ אֶת עֲצָתוֹ,	frustrated his plan,
v'kil·kal·ta et ma·cha·shav·to,	וְקִלְקַלְתָּ אֶת מַחֲשַׁבְתּוֹ,	and ruined his plot,
va·ha·shei·vo·ta g'mu·lo b'ro·sho,	וַהֲשֵׁבוֹתָ גְּמוּלוֹ בְּרֹאשׁוֹ,	and caused it to backfire on him,
v'ta·lu o·to v'et ba·nav al ha·eitz.	וְתָלוּ אוֹתוֹ וְאֶת בָּנָיו עַל הָעֵץ.	and he and his sons were hanged on the gallows.

V'al ha·kol, A·do·nai E·lo·hei·nu,
a·nach·nu mo·dim lach
u·m'var·chim o·tach.
Yit·ba·rach shim·cha
b'fi chol chai
ta·mid l'o·lam va·ed.
Ka·ka·tuv, v'a·chal·ta
v'sa·va·ta, u·vei·rach·ta
et A·do·nai E·lo·he·cha
al ha·a·retz ha·to·vah
a·sher na·tan lach.
Ba·ruch A·tah A·do·nai,
al ha·a·retz v'al ha·ma·zon.

וְעַל הַכּל, יְיָ אֱלֹהֵינוּ,
אֲנַחְנוּ מוֹדִים לָךְ
וּמְבָרְכִים אוֹתָךְ.
יִתְבָּרַךְ שִׁמְךָ
בְּפִי כָל חַי
תָּמִיד לְעוֹלָם וָעֶד.
כַּכָּתוּב, וְאָכַלְתָּ
וְשָׂבָעְתָּ, וּבֵרַכְתָּ
אֶת יְיָ אֱלֹהֶיךָ
עַל הָאָרֶץ הַטּבָה
אֲשֶׁר נָתַן לָךְ.
בָּרוּךְ אַתָּה יְיָ,
עַל הָאָרֶץ וְעַל הַמָּזוֹן.

For all these things, Adonai our God,
we thank You
and bless You.
May Your Name be blessed,
by the mouth of all the living
always, forever and ever.
As it is written, "You shall eat
and be satisfied and bless
Adonai Your God
for the good land
which God gave you."[2]
Blessed are You, Adonai,
for the land and for the food.

---

2. Deuteronomy 8:10.

The Third Blessing: In Mercy, God Rebuilds Jerusalem

Boneh v'Rachamav Y'rushalayim בּוֹנֶה בְּרַחֲמָיו יְרוּשָׁלָיִם

Attributed to David and Solomon, asking for the rebuilding of Jerusalem.

Ra·cheim, A·do·nai E·lo·hei·nu,	רַחֵם, יְיָ אֱלֹהֵינוּ,	Have mercy, Adonai our God,
al Yis·ra·eil a·me·cha,	עַל יִשְׂרָאֵל עַמֶּךָ,	on Israel, Your people,
v'al Y'ru·sha·la·yim i·re·cha,	וְעַל יְרוּשָׁלַיִם עִירֶךָ,	and on Jerusalem, Your city,
v'al Tzi·yon mish·kan k'vo·de·cha,	וְעַל צִיּוֹן מִשְׁכַּן כְּבוֹדֶךָ,	and on Zion, home of Your glory,
v'al mal·chut beit Da·vid	וְעַל מַלְכוּת בֵּית דָּוִד	and on the dynasty of the House of David,
m'shi·che·cha,	מְשִׁיחֶךָ,	Your anointed,
v'al ha·ba·yit ha·ga·dol v'ha·ka·dosh	וְעַל הַבַּיִת הַגָּדוֹל וְהַקָּדוֹשׁ	and on the great and holy Temple
she·nik·ra shim·cha a·lav.	שֶׁנִּקְרָא שִׁמְךָ עָלָיו.	which is named after you.
E·lo·hei·nu, A·vi·nu, r'ei·nu,	אֱלֹהֵינוּ, אָבִינוּ, רְעֵנוּ,	Our God, our Parent, care for us,
zu·nei·nu, par·n'sei·nu, v'chal·k'lei·nu,	זוּנֵנוּ, פַּרְנְסֵנוּ, וְכַלְכְּלֵנוּ,	nourish us, sustain us, support us,
v'har·vi·chei·nu, v'har·vach la·nu,	וְהַרְוִיחֵנוּ, וְהַרְוַח לָנוּ,	relieve us, and grant us relief,
A·do·nai E·lo·hei·nu,	יְיָ אֱלֹהֵינוּ,	Adonai our God,
m'hei·rah mi·kol tza·ro·tei·nu.	מְהֵרָה מִכָּל צָרוֹתֵינוּ.	quickly from all our troubles.
V'na, al tatz·ri·chei·nu,	וְנָא, אַל תַּצְרִיכֵנוּ,	Let us depend,
A·do·nai E·lo·hei·nu,	יְיָ אֱלֹהֵינוּ,	Adonai our God,
lo liy·dei mat·nat ba·sar va·dam,	לֹא לִידֵי מַתְּנַת בָּשָׂר וָדָם,	neither on the gifts of flesh and blood,
v'lo liy·dei hal·va·a·tam,	וְלֹא לִידֵי הַלְוָאָתָם,	nor on their loans,
Ki im l'ya·d'cha, ha·m'lei·ah,	כִּי אִם לְיָדְךָ, הַמְּלֵאָה,	but rather on Your hand, full,

ha·p'tu·chah, ha·g'du·shah, v'ha·r'cha·vah,
she·lo nei·vosh
v'lo ni·ka·leim l'o·lam va·ed.

הַפְּתוּחָה, הַגְּדוּשָׁה וְהָרְחָבָה,
שֶׁלֹּא נֵבוֹשׁ
וְלֹא נִכָּלֵם לְעוֹלָם וָעֶד.

open, abundant,[1] and generous,
so we shall neither be ashamed
nor humiliated for ever and ever.

---

1. *Ha·g'du·shah* הַגְּדוּשָׁה means abundant. Many siddurim and birkonim have *ha·k'do·shah* הַקְּדוֹשָׁה (holy), but the context requires a synonym for full, open, and generous.

On Shabbat:

R'tzeih v'ha·cha·li·tzei·nu,
A·do·nai E·lo·hei·nu, b'mitz·vo·te·cha
u·v'mitz·vat yom ha·sh'vi·i,
ha·Shab·bat ha·ga·dol v'ha·ka·dosh ha·zeh.

רְצֵה וְהַחֲלִיצֵנוּ,
יְיָ אֱלֹהֵינוּ, בְּמִצְוֹתֶיךָ
וּבְמִצְוַת יוֹם הַשְּׁבִיעִי,
הַשַּׁבָּת הַגָּדוֹל וְהַקָּדוֹשׁ הַזֶּה.

May it please You to strengthen us,
Adonai, our God, with Your Commandments
and the mitzvah of the seventh day,
this Sabbath, great and holy.

Ki yom zeh ga·dol
v'ka·dosh hu l'fa·ne·cha,
lish·bot bo v'la·nu·ach bo
b'a·ha·vah k'mitz·vat r'tzo·ne·cha.
bir·tzon·cha ha·nach la·nu,
A·do·nai E·lo·hei·nu,
she·lo t'hi tza·rah v'ya·gon
va·a·na·chah b'yom m'nu·cha·tei·nu.

כִּי יוֹם זֶה גָּדוֹל
וְקָדוֹשׁ הוּא לְפָנֶיךָ,
לִשְׁבָּת בּוֹ וְלָנוּחַ בּוֹ
בְּאַהֲבָה כְּמִצְוַת רְצוֹנֶךָ.
בִּרְצוֹנְךָ הָנַח לָנוּ,
יְיָ אֱלֹהֵינוּ,
שֶׁלֹּא תְהִי צָרָה וְיָגוֹן
וַאֲנָחָה בְּיוֹם מְנוּחָתֵנוּ.

For this day is great
and holy before You,
to refrain from work on it and to rest on it
with love as commanded by Your will.
By Your will, grant us rest,
Adonai our God,
that there be no trouble, sorrow,
or sighing on our day of rest.

V'har·ei·nu, A·do·nai E·lo·hei·nu,
b'ne·cha·mat Tzi·yon i·re·cha,

וְהַרְאֵנוּ, יְיָ אֱלֹהֵינוּ,
בְּנֶחָמַת צִיּוֹן עִירֶךָ,

And may we see, Adonai our God,
the comfort of Zion, Your city,

u·v'·vin·yan Y'ru·sha·la·yim	וּבְנְיַן יְרוּשָׁלַיִם	and the building of Jerusalem,
ir kod·she·cha,	עִיר קׇדְשֶׁךָ,	Your holy city,
ki A·tah hu ba·al ha·y'shu·ot	כִּי אַתָּה הוּא בַּעַל הַיְשׁוּעוֹת	for You are the supreme Savior
u·va·al ha·ne·cha·mot.	וּבַעַל הַנֶּחָמוֹת.	and Consoler.

On Rosh Chodesh and festivals:

E·lo·hei·nu vei·lo·hei	אֱלֹהֵינוּ וֵאלֹהֵי	Our God, and God
a·vo·tei·nu [v'i·mo·tei·nu],	אֲבוֹתֵינוּ [וְאִמּוֹתֵינוּ],	of our ancestors,
ya·a·leh, v'ya·vo, v'ya·gi·a,	יַעֲלֶה, וְיָבֹא, וְיַגִּיעַ,	let ascend, come, arrive,
v'yei·ra·eh, v'yei·ra·tzeh, v'yi·sha·ma,	וְיֵרָאֶה, וְיֵרָצֶה, וְיִשָּׁמַע,	appear, be accepted, be heard,
v'yi·pa·keid, v'yi·za·cheir	וְיִפָּקֵד, וְיִזָּכֵר	be recollected, and be remembered
zich·ro·nei·nu u·fik·do·nei·nu,	זִכְרוֹנֵנוּ וּפִקְדוֹנֵנוּ,	our remembrance and recollection,
v'zich·ron a·vo·tei·nu [v'i·mo·tei·nu],	וְזִכְרוֹן אֲבוֹתֵינוּ [וְאִמּוֹתֵינוּ],	the remembrance of our ancestors,
v'zich·ron Ma·shi·ach	וְזִכְרוֹן מָשִׁיחַ	the remembrance of the Messiah
ben Da·vid av·de·cha,	בֶּן דָּוִד עַבְדֶּךָ,	son of David, Your servant,
v'zich·ron Y'ru·sha·la·yim	וְזִכְרוֹן יְרוּשָׁלַיִם	the remembrance of Jerusalem
ir kod·she·cha,	עִיר קׇדְשֶׁךָ,	Your holy city,
v'zich·ron kol a·m'cha	וְזִכְרוֹן כָּל עַמְּךָ	and the remembrance of all Your people
beit Yis·ra·eil l'·fa·ne·cha,	בֵּית יִשְׂרָאֵל לְפָנֶיךָ,	the House of Israel before You,
lif·lei·tah, l'to·vah,	לִפְלֵיטָה, לְטוֹבָה,	for survival, for goodness,

l'chein u·l'che·sed u·l'ra·cha·mim, *l'cha·yim u·l'sha·lom, b'yom*	לְחֵן וּלְחֶסֶד וּלְרַחֲמִים, לְחַיִּים וּלְשָׁלוֹם, בְּיוֹם	for grace, for kindness, and for mercy, for life and for peace, on this day of

Select the appropriate occasion:

Shavuot:	Pesach:	Sh'mini Atzeret/Simchat Torah:	Sukkot:	Rosh Hashanah:	Rosh Chodesh:
חַג הַשָּׁבוּעוֹת הַזֶּה.	חַג הַמַּצּוֹת הַזֶּה.	הַשְּׁמִינִי חַג הָעֲצֶרֶת הַזֶּה.	חַג הַסֻּכּוֹת הַזֶּה.	הַזִּכָּרוֹן הַזֶּה.	רֹאשׁ הַחֹדֶשׁ הַזֶּה.
the Festival of Weeks.	the Festival of Matzot.	the eighth day Festival of Assembly.	the Festival of Sukkot.	Remembrance.	the New Moon.
Chag ha·Sha·vu·ot ha·zeh.	*Chag ha·Ma·tzot ha·zeh.*	*ha·Sh'mi·ni Chag ha·A·tze·ret ha·zeh.*	*Chag ha·Suk·kot ha·zeh.*	*ha·Zi·ka·ron ha·zeh.*	*Rosh ha·Cho·desh ha·zeh.*

| *Zoch·rei·nu, A·do·nai E·lo·hei·nu,*
bo l'to·vah,
u·fok·dei·nu vo liv·ra·chah,
v'ho·shi·ei·nu vo l'cha·yim.
U·vid·var y'shu·ah v'ra·cha·mim,
chus v'cho·nei·nu,
v'ra·cheim a·lei·nu, v'ho·shi·ei·nu,
ki Ei·le·cha ei·nei·nu,
ki Eil me·lech
cha·nun v'ra·chum A·tah. | זָכְרֵנוּ, יְיָ אֱלֹהֵינוּ,
בּוֹ לְטוֹבָה,
וּפָקְדֵנוּ בּוֹ לִבְרָכָה,
וְהוֹשִׁיעֵנוּ בּוֹ לְחַיִּים.
וּבִדְבַר יְשׁוּעָה וְרַחֲמִים,
חוּס וְחָנֵּנוּ,
וְרַחֵם עָלֵינוּ, וְהוֹשִׁיעֵנוּ,
כִּי אֵלֶיךָ עֵינֵינוּ,
כִּי אֵל מֶלֶךְ
חַנּוּן וְרַחוּם אָתָּה. | Remember us, Adonai our God,
this day for good,
recall us this day for blessing,
save us this day for life.
With salvation and mercy,
spare us, be gracious to us,
have pity on us, and save us,
for our eyes are upon You,
for You are a gracious and merciful
Divine Ruler. |

At all other times, continue here:

U·v'neih Y'ru·sha·la·yim,
ir ha·ko·desh, bim·hei·rah v'ya·mei·nu.
Ba·ruch A·tah A·do·nai,
bo·neh v'ra·cha·mav Y'ru·sha·la·yim. A·mein.

וּבְנֵה יְרוּשָׁלַיִם,
עִיר הַקֹּדֶשׁ, בִּמְהֵרָה בְיָמֵינוּ.
בָּרוּךְ אַתָּה יְיָ,
בּוֹנֶה בְרַחֲמָיו יְרוּשָׁלַיִם. אָמֵן.

Rebuild Jerusalem,
the holy city, speedily in our days.
Blessed are You, Adonai,
who rebuilds in mercy Jerusalem. Amen.

The Fourth Blessing: The Good One, Who Does Good to All

HaTov, v'HaMeitiv LaKol הַטּוֹב, וְהַמֵּטִיב לַכֹּל

The essence of the fourth blessing refers to God's goodness. It was composed by the court of Rabban Gamaliel the elder, who lived in the first half of the first century C.E. and was a grandson of Hillel.

Ba·ruch A·tah A·do·nai,	בָּרוּךְ אַתָּה יְיָ,	Blessed are You, Adonai,
E·lo·hei·nu Me·lech ha·O·lam,	אֱלֹהֵינוּ מֶלֶךְ הָעוֹלָם,	our God, Ruler of the Universe,
Ha·Eil A·vi·nu, Mal·kei·nu,	הָאֵל אָבִינוּ, מַלְכֵּנוּ,	The God who is Our Parent, our Ruler,
a·di·rei·nu, bo·r'ei·nu, go·a·lei·nu,	אַדִירֵנוּ, בּוֹרְאֵנוּ, גּוֹאֲלֵנוּ,	our Mighty One, our Creator, our Redeemer,
yo·tz'rei·nu, k'do·shei·nu, k'dosh Ya·a·kov,	יוֹצְרֵנוּ, קְדוֹשֵׁנוּ, קְדוֹשׁ יַעֲקֹב,	our Maker, our Holy One, the Holy One of Jacob,
Ro·ei·nu ro·eih Yis·ra·eil,	רוֹעֵנוּ רוֹעֵה יִשְׂרָאֵל,	our Shepherd, Shepherd of Israel,
ha·Me·lech ha·tov, v'ha·mei·tiv la·kol,	הַמֶּלֶךְ הַטּוֹב, וְהַמֵּטִיב לַכֹּל,	the Good Ruler, who does good to all,
she·b'chol yom va·yom hu hei·tiv,	שֶׁבְּכָל יוֹם וָיוֹם הוּא הֵטִיב,	who day after day has done good,
hu mei·tiv, hu yei·tiv la·nu.	הוּא מֵטִיב, הוּא יֵיטִיב לָנוּ.	does good, and will do good for us.
Hu g'ma·la·nu, hu go·m'lei·nu,	הוּא גְמָלָנוּ, הוּא גוֹמְלֵנוּ,	God has rewarded us, rewards us,
hu yig·m'lei·nu la·ad	הוּא יִגְמְלֵנוּ לָעַד	and will reward us forever with
l'chein u·l'che·sed u·l'ra·cha·mim,	לְחֵן וּלְחֶסֶד וּלְרַחֲמִים,	favor, kindness, and mercy,
u·l're·vach ha·tza·lah v'hatz·la·chah,	וּלְרֶוַח הַצָּלָה וְהַצְלָחָה,	relief, rescue, and success,
b'ra·chah viy·shu·ah,	בְּרָכָה וִישׁוּעָה,	blessing and deliverance,
ne·cha·mah, par·na·sah v'chal·ka·lah,	נֶחָמָה, פַּרְנָסָה וְכַלְכָּלָה,	consolation, sustenance, and support,
v'ra·cha·mim, v'cha·yim, v'sha·lom	וְרַחֲמִים, וְחַיִּים וְשָׁלוֹם	mercy, life, and peace
v'chol tov, u·mi·kol tov	וְכָל טוֹב, וּמִכָּל טוֹב	and everything good, and who of all good things
l'o·lam al y'cha·s'rei·nu.	לְעוֹלָם אַל יְחַסְּרֵנוּ.	may never deprive us.

Ha·ra·cha·man, hu yim·loch a·lei·nu l'o·lam va·ed.	הָרַחֲמָן, הוּא יִמְלֹךְ עָלֵינוּ לְעוֹלָם וָעֶד.	Merciful One, may You rule over us now and forever.
Ha·ra·cha·man, hu yit·ba·rach ba·sha·ma·yim u·va·a·retz.	הָרַחֲמָן, הוּא יִתְבָּרַךְ בַּשָּׁמַיִם וּבָאָרֶץ.	Merciful One, may You be praised in the heavens and on earth.
Ha·ra·cha·man, hu yish·ta·bach l'dor do·rim, v'yit·pa·ar ba·nu l'nei·tzach n'tza·chim, v·yit·ha·dar ba·nu la·ad u·l'ol'mei o·la·mim.	הָרַחֲמָן, הוּא יִשְׁתַּבַּח לְדוֹר דּוֹרִים, וְיִתְפָּאַר בָּנוּ לְנֵצַח נְצָחִים, וְיִתְהַדַּר בָּנוּ לָעַד וּלְעוֹלְמֵי עוֹלָמִים.	Merciful One, may You be praised from generation to generation, glorified through us for all eternity, and beautified through us forever and for all time.
Ha·ra·cha·man, hu y'far·n'sei·nu b'cha·vod.	הָרַחֲמָן, הוּא יְפַרְנְסֵנוּ בְּכָבוֹד.	Merciful One, may You sustain us with honor.
Ha·ra·cha·man, hu yish·bor u·lei·nu mei·al tza·va·rei·nu v'hu yo·li·chei·nu ko·m'mi·yut l'ar·tzei·nu.	הָרַחֲמָן, הוּא יִשְׁבּוֹר עֻלֵנוּ מֵעַל צַוָּארֵנוּ וְהוּא יוֹלִיכֵנוּ קוֹמְמִיּוּת לְאַרְצֵנוּ.	Merciful One, may You break the yoke from our necks, and lead us upright to our land.
Ha·ra·cha·man, hu yish·lach b'ra·chah m'ru·bah ba·ba·yit ha·zeh, v'al shul·chan zeh she·a·chal·nu a·lav.	הָרַחֲמָן, הוּא יִשְׁלַח בְּרָכָה מְרֻבָּה בַּבַּיִת הַזֶּה, וְעַל שֻׁלְחָן זֶה שֶׁאָכַלְנוּ עָלָיו.	Merciful One, may You send abundant blessing to this house, and upon this table at which we have eaten.
Ha·ra·cha·man, hu yish·lach la·nu et Ei·li·ya·hu ha·Na·vi, za·chur la·tov, viy·va·ser la·nu b'so·rot to·vot y'shu·ot v'ne·cha·mot.	הָרַחֲמָן, הוּא יִשְׁלַח לָנוּ אֶת אֵלִיָּהוּ הַנָּבִיא, זָכוּר לַטּוֹב, וִיבַשֶּׂר לָנוּ בְּשׂוֹרוֹת טוֹבוֹת יְשׁוּעוֹת וְנֶחָמוֹת.	Merciful One, may You send us Elijah the Prophet, of blessed memory, and may he bring us good news of deliverance and comfort.

We offer blessings for the special guests at our table:

For one's own family at home:

Ha·ra·cha·man, hu y'va·reich o·ti	הָרַחֲמָן, הוּא יְבָרֵךְ אוֹתִי	Merciful One, may You bless me,
[v'et i·shi | v'et ish·ti |	[וְאֶת אִישִׁי | וְאֶת אִשְׁתִּי |	[and my husband | and my wife |
v'et do·di | v'et zar·i]	וְאֶת דּוֹדִי | וְאֶת זַרְעִי]	and my beloved | and my children]
v'et kol a·sher li . . .	וְאֶת כָּל אֲשֶׁר לִי . . .	and all that is mine . . .

For one's hosts [or parents]:

Ha·ra·cha·man, hu y'va·reich et	הָרַחֲמָן, הוּא יְבָרֵךְ אֶת	Merciful One, may You bless
[a·vi mo·ri]	[אָבִי מוֹרִי]	[my father, my teacher,]
ba·al ha·ba·yit ha·zeh,	בַּעַל הַבַּיִת הַזֶּה,	the master of this household,
v'et [i·mi mo·ra·ti]	וְאֶת [אִמִּי מוֹרָתִי]	and [my mother, my teacher,]
ba·a·lat ha·ba·yit ha·zeh,	בַּעֲלַת הַבַּיִת הַזֶּה,	the mistress of this household,
o·tam v'et bei·tam v'et zar·am	אוֹתָם וְאֶת בֵּיתָם וְאֶת זַרְעָם	them, their household and their children
v'et kol a·sher la·hem,	וְאֶת כָּל אֲשֶׁר לָהֶם,	and all that is theirs,
o·ta·nu v'et kol a·sher la·nu . . .	אוֹתָנוּ וְאֶת כָּל אֲשֶׁר לָנוּ . . .	us and all that is ours . . .

In a large group:

Ha·ra·cha·man, hu y'va·reich	הָרַחֲמָן, הוּא יְבָרֵךְ	Merciful One, may You bless
et kol ha·m'su·bin kan,	אֶת כָּל הַמְסֻבִּין כָּאן,	all those who are gathered here,
o·tam v'et bei·tam v'et zar·am	אוֹתָם וְאֶת בֵּיתָם וְאֶת זַרְעָם	them, their household and their children
v'et kol a·sher la·hem,	וְאֶת כָּל אֲשֶׁר לָהֶם,	and all that is theirs,
o·ta·nu v'et kol a·sher la·nu . . .	אוֹתָנוּ וְאֶת כָּל אֲשֶׁר לָנוּ . . .	us and all that is ours . . .

... k'mo [she·nit·ba·r'chu i·mo·tei·nu
Sa·rah, Riv·kah, Ra·cheil, v'Lei·ah
hei·tiv, to·vat, tov, tov,
u·ch'mo] she·nit·ba·r'chu a·vo·tei·nu
Av·ra·ham, Yitz·chak, v'Ya·a·kov,
ba·kol, mi·kol, kol,
kein y'va·reich o·ta·nu ku·la·nu ya·chad
biv·ra·chah sh'lei·mah,
v'no·mar A·mein.

... כְּמוֹ [שֶׁנִּתְבָּרְכוּ אִמּוֹתֵינוּ
שָׂרָה, רִבְקָה, רָחֵל, וְלֵאָה
הֵיטִיב, טֹבַת, טוֹב ,טוֹב,
וּכְמוֹ] שֶׁנִּתְבָּרְכוּ אֲבוֹתֵינוּ
אַבְרָהָם, יִצְחָק, וְיַעֲקֹב,
בַּכֹּל, מִכֹּל, כֹּל,
כֵּן יְבָרֵךְ אוֹתָנוּ כֻּלָּנוּ יַחַד
בִּבְרָכָה שְׁלֵמָה,
וְנֹאמַר אָמֵן.

... as [You have blessed our mothers
Sarah, Rebecca, Rachel, and Leah
"well, goodly, better, and good,"[1]
and as] You have blessed our fathers
Abraham, Isaac, and Jacob
"in all, from all, with all things,"
so may You bless us, all of us, together
with a complete blessing,
and let us say Amen.

---

1. Adding the Matriarchs. The phrase *bakol, mikol, kol* בַּכֹּל, מִכֹּל, כֹּל refers to three biblical verses describing God's blessings to Abraham, Isaac, and Jacob, as follows: Abraham: Genesis 24:1 (God blessed Abraham *bakol* בַּכֹּל — with all things); Isaac: Genesis 27:33 (*mikol* מִכֹּל — from all things, he shall be blessed); Jacob: Genesis 33:11(God provided me with *kol* כֹּל — all things).

הֵיטִיב, טֹבַת, טוֹב ,טוֹב — Rather than break this relationship by adding the names of the Matriarchs immediately after those of the Patriarchs, we have followed the recent innovation of adding a parallel phrase including

references to biblical verses with variations of the word *tov* טוֹב (good) to refer to the Matriarchs: Sarah: Genesis 12:16 (And [Pharaoh] treated Abram well *heitiv* הֵיטִיב — for Sarai's sake); Rebecca: Genesis 24:16 (And she was *tovat mareh m'od* טֹבַת מַרְאֶה מְאֹד — very pretty to look upon); Rachel: Genesis 29:19 (And Laban said, It is *tov* טוֹב — better that I give her to you [Jacob] than to another man...); Leah: Genesis 30:20 (And Leah said, God has given me *zeved tov* זֶבֶד טוֹב — a good dowry).

So as not to interrupt the familiar rhythm when reciting the traditional blessing, the additional phrases naming the Matriarchs appear first.

Ba·ma·rom y'la·m'du
a·lei·hem v'a·lei·nu
z'chut she·t'hi l'mish·me·ret sha·lom.
v'ni·sa v'ra·chah mei·eit A·do·nai
u·tz'da·kah mei·E·lo·hei yish·ei·nu
v'nim·tza chein v'sei·chel tov
b'ei·nei E·lo·him v'a·dam.

בַּמָּרוֹם יְלַמְּדוּ
עֲלֵיהֶם וְעָלֵינוּ
זְכוּת שֶׁתְּהִי לְמִשְׁמֶרֶת שָׁלוֹם.
וְנִשָּׂא בְרָכָה מֵאֵת יְיָ
וּצְדָקָה מֵאֱלֹהֵי יִשְׁעֵנוּ
וְנִמְצָא חֵן וְשֵׂכֶל טוֹב
בְּעֵינֵי אֱלֹהִים וְאָדָם.

On high, may they plead
on their behalf and on ours
for an enduring peace.
May we receive a blessing from Adonai
and justice from our saving God
and may we find favor and success
in the eyes of God and humanity.

For a Bat Mitzvah:

Ha·ra·cha·man, hu y'va·reich
et ha·ba·chu·rah bat ha·mitz·vah
v'et kol b'nei mish·pach·tah.

הָרַחֲמָן, הוּא יְבָרֵךְ
אֶת הַבְּחוּרָה בַּת הַמִּצְוָה
וְאֶת כָּל בְּנֵי מִשְׁפַּחְתָּה.

Merciful One, may You bless
the Bat Mitzvah girl
and all her family.

For a Bar Mitzvah:

Ha·ra·cha·man, hu y'va·reich
et ha·ba·chur bar ha·mitz·vah
v'et kol b'nei mish·pach·to.

הָרַחֲמָן, הוּא יְבָרֵךְ
אֶת הַבָּחוּר בַּר הַמִּצְוָה
וְאֶת כָּל בְּנֵי מִשְׁפַּחְתּוֹ.

Merciful One, may You bless
the Bar Mitzvah boy
and all his family.

At a wedding celebration:

Ha·ra·cha·man, hu y'va·reich
et he·cha·tan v'et ha·ka·lah
v'et kol b'nei mish·p'cho·tei·hem.

הָרַחֲמָן, הוּא יְבָרֵךְ
אֶת הֶחָתָן וְאֶת הַכַּלָּה
וְאֶת כָּל בְּנֵי מִשְׁפָּחוֹתֵיהֶם.

Merciful One, may You bless
the groom and the bride[1]
and all their families.

1. See note 3 on page 28 for constructing alternative formulations.

Following a B'rit Milah or Simchat Bat, offer the special blessings on page 32 or 33 then continue below when appropriate:

We offer blessings for special days in the Jewish calendar.

On Shabbat:

Ha·ra·cha·man, hu yan·chi·lei·nu
yom she·ku·lo Shab·bat
u·m'nu·chah l'cha·yei ha·o·la·mim.

הָרַחֲמָן, הוּא יַנְחִילֵנוּ
יוֹם שֶׁכֻּלוֹ שַׁבָּת
וּמְנוּחָה לְחַיֵּי הָעוֹלָמִים.

Merciful One, may You grant us
a day that is all Shabbat
and rest reflecting eternal life.

On Rosh Chodesh:

Ha·ra·cha·man, hu y'cha·deish
a·lei·nu et ha·cho·desh ha·zeh
l'to·vah v'liv·ra·chah.

הָרַחֲמָן, הוּא יְחַדֵּשׁ
עָלֵינוּ אֶת הַחֹדֶשׁ הַזֶּה
לְטוֹבָה וְלִבְרָכָה.

Merciful One, may You renew
for us this month
for goodness and blessing.

On Pesach, Shavuot, and Sukkot:

Ha·ra·cha·man, hu yan·chi·lei·nu
yom she·ku·lo tov.

הָרַחֲמָן, הוּא יַנְחִילֵנוּ
יוֹם שֶׁכֻּלוֹ טוֹב.

Merciful One, may You grant us
a day that is all good.

On Rosh Hashanah:

Ha·ra·cha·man, hu y'cha·deish
a·lei·nu et ha·sha·nah ha·zot
l'to·vah v'liv·ra·chah.

הָרַחֲמָן, הוּא יְחַדֵּשׁ
עָלֵינוּ אֶת הַשָּׁנָה הַזֹּאת
לְטוֹבָה וְלִבְרָכָה.

Merciful One, may You renew
for us this year
for goodness and blessing.

On Sukkot:

Ha·ra·cha·man, hu ya·kim la·nu
et suk·kat Da·vid ha·no·fe·let.

הָרַחֲמָן, הוּא יָקִים לָנוּ
אֶת סֻכַּת דָּוִד הַנּוֹפֶלֶת.

Merciful One, may You restore for us
the fallen sukkah of David.

We offer blessings for those who are in our prayers. There is a custom of inviting participants to offer additional blessings at this point, following the pattern of the traditional prayers to the Merciful One.

Ha·ra·cha·man, hu y'va·rech et ha·a·retz ha·zot v'ya·gein a·le·ha.	הָרַחֲמָן, הוּא יְבָרֵךְ אֶת הָאָרֶץ הַזֹּאת וְיָגֵן עָלֶיהָ.	Merciful One, may you bless this country and protect it.
Ha·ra·cha·man, hu yi·tein ru·ach a·cha·vah b'toch am Yis·ra·eil.	הָרַחֲמָן, הוּא יִתֵּן רוּחַ אַחֲוָה בְּתוֹךְ עַם יִשְׂרָאֵל.	Merciful One, may you instill a spirit of tolerance in the Jewish people.
Ha·ra·cha·man, hu y'va·reich et M'di·nat Yis·ra·eil im Y'ru·sha·la·yim ir ha·ko·desh vi·vi·eim lig·u·lah sh'lei·mah.	הָרַחֲמָן, הוּא יְבָרֵךְ אֶת מְדִינַת יִשְׂרָאֵל עִם יְרוּשָׁלַיִם עִיר הַקֹּדֶשׁ וִיבִיאֵם לִגְאֻלָּה שְׁלֵמָה.	Merciful One, may You bless the State of Israel with the holy city of Jerusalem and bring them to complete redemption.
Ha·ra·cha·man, hu yash·kin sha·lom bein b'nei [Yitz·chak | Sa·rah] u·vein b'nei [Yish·ma·eil | Ha·gar].	הָרַחֲמָן, הוּא יַשְׁכִּין שָׁלוֹם בֵּין בְּנֵי [יִצְחָק | שָׂרָה] וּבֵין בְּנֵי [יִשְׁמָעֵאל | הָגָר].	Merciful One, may You instill peace between the children of [Isaac | Sarah] and the children of [Ishmael | Hagar].
Ha·ra·cha·man, hu y'va·reich et cha·ya·lei Tz'va Ha·ga·nah l'Yis·ra·eil v'ya·gein a·lei·hem.	הָרַחֲמָן, הוּא יְבָרֵךְ אֶת חַיָּלֵי צְבָא הֲגַנָּה לְיִשְׂרָאֵל וְיָגֵן עֲלֵיהֶם.	Merciful One, may you bless the soldiers of the Israel Defense Forces and protect them from harm.
Ha·ra·cha·man, hu y'va·reich et a·chei·nu v'nei Yis·ra·eil ha·n'tu·nim b'tza·rah v'yo·tzi·eim mei·a·fei·lah l'o·rah.	הָרַחֲמָן, הוּא יְבָרֵךְ אֶת אַחֵינוּ בְּנֵי יִשְׂרָאֵל הַנְּתוּנִים בְּצָרָה וְיוֹצִיאֵם מֵאֲפֵלָה לְאוֹרָה.	Merciful One, may you bless our fellow Jews who are in dire straits and take them out of darkness unto light.

Ha·ra·cha·man, hu y'za·kei·nu
liy·mot ha·ma·shi·ach
u·l'cha·yei ha·o·lam ha·ba.

הָרַחֲמָן, הוּא יְזַכֵּנוּ
לִימוֹת הַמָּשִׁיחַ
וּלְחַיֵּי הָעוֹלָם הַבָּא.

Merciful One, may You find us worthy
of the Messianic era
and life in the World to Come.

On Shabbat, Rosh Chodesh, festivals, and festive occasions:

מִגְדּוֹל יְשׁוּעוֹת מַלְכּוֹ,

God is a Tower of Victory for the king,[1]

Mig·dol y'shu·ot mal·ko,

On all other days:

מַגְדִּיל יְשׁוּעוֹת מַלְכּוֹ,

God grants great victories to the king[2]

Mag·dil y'shu·ot mal·ko,

---

v'o·seh che·sed lim·shi·cho,
l'Da·vid u·l'zar·o ad o·lam.
O·seh sha·lom bim·ro·mav
hu ya·a·seh sha·lom a·lei·nu
v'al kol Yis·ra·eil
[v'al kol yo·sh'vei tei·veil]
v'im·ru a·mein.

וְעֹשֶׂה חֶסֶד לִמְשִׁיחוֹ,
לְדָוִד וּלְזַרְעוֹ עַד עוֹלָם.
עֹשֶׂה שָׁלוֹם בִּמְרוֹמָיו
הוּא יַעֲשֶׂה שָׁלוֹם עָלֵינוּ
וְעַל כָּל יִשְׂרָאֵל
[וְעַל כָּל יוֹשְׁבֵי תֵבֵל]
וְאִמְרוּ אָמֵן.

showing kindness to God's anointed one,
to David and his descendants forever.
May the Maker of peace in the heavens
make peace for us
and for all Israel
[and for all who dwell on earth]
and say Amen.

1. 2 Samuel 22:51
2. Psalms 18:51

Y'ru et A·do·nai, k'do·shav,	יְראוּ אֶת יְיָ, קְדוֹשָׁיו,	Fear Adonai, holy ones,
ki ein mach·sor li·rei·av.	כִּי אֵין מַחְסוֹר לִירֵאָיו.	for those who fear You are not deprived.
K'fi·rim ra·shu v'ra·ei·vu	כְּפִירִים רָשׁוּ וְרָעֵבוּ	Young lions may feel want or hunger
v'do·r'shei A·do·nai	וְדוֹרְשֵׁי יְיָ	but those who seek Adonai
lo yach·s'ru chol tov.	לֹא יַחְסְרוּ כָל טוֹב.	will not lack anything that is good.[1]
Ho·du lA·do·nai ki tov,	הוֹדוּ לַייָ כִּי טוֹב,	Give thanks to Adonai who is good,
ki l'o·lam chas·do.	כִּי לְעוֹלָם חַסְדּוֹ.	for Your kindness is forever.[2]
Po·tei·ach et ya·de·cha	פּוֹתֵחַ אֶת יָדֶךָ	You open Your hand,
u·mas·bi·a l'chol chai ra·tzon.	וּמַשְׂבִּיעַ לְכָל חַי רָצוֹן.	and satisfy the desire of every living thing.[3]
Ba·ruch ha·ge·ver	בָּרוּךְ הַגֶּבֶר	Blessed are they
a·sher yiv·tach bA·do·nai,	אֲשֶׁר יִבְטַח בַּייָ,	who trust in Adonai,
v'ha·yah A·do·nai miv·ta·cho.	וְהָיָה יְיָ מִבְטַחוֹ.	Adonai will be their refuge.[4]
[Lu y'hi:] Na·ar ha·yi·ti gam za·kan·ti	[לוּ יְהִי:] נַעַר הָיִיתִי גַּם זָקַנְתִּי	[May it be:][5] A youth I was, now I have grown old,
v'lo ra·i·ti tza·dik ne·e·zav,	וְלֹא רָאִיתִי צַדִּיק נֶעֱזָב,	I have not seen the righteous forsaken
v'zar·o m'va·keish la·chem.	וְזַרְעוֹ מְבַקֶּשׁ לָחֶם.	nor their children begging bread.[6]
A·do·nai oz l'a·mo yi·tein,	יְיָ עֹז לְעַמּוֹ יִתֵּן,	God will give strength to The People,
A·do·nai y'va·reich et a·mo va·sha·lom.	יְיָ יְבָרֵךְ אֶת עַמּוֹ בַשָּׁלוֹם.	God will bless The People with peace.[7]

---

1. Psalms 34:10-11   2. Psalms 136:1   3. Psalms 145:16   4. Jeremiah 17:7

5. The verse that follows seems to present the view that truly righteous people are rewarded in this world and therefore, anyone who is suffering and lacking bread is not right-eous and deserves this fate. For this reason some people omit it or say it silently. It is possible, however, to see this verse as a utopian vision of a world in which all people will be able to say, "A youth I was, now I have grown old, but I have not seen the righteous forsaken, nor their children begging bread" (Psalms 37:25). Preceding this sentence with the phrase "May it be" and reciting it aloud affirms the belief and hope that such a world can exist. Some may prefer to use the alternative on the following page.

6. Psalms 37:25   7. Psalms 29:11

Some may wish to follow the custom of liberal congregations in Germany, reciting the following instead of Naar hayiti:

A·chal·nu v'sa·va·nu,	אָכַלְנוּ וְשָׂבַעְנוּ,	We have eaten and are satisfied,
ach al nit·a·leim	אַךְ אַל נִתְעַלֵּם	but let us not ignore
mi·tzor·chei rei·ei·nu	מִצָּרְכֵי רֵעֵינוּ	the needs of our fellow human beings
v'e·al tei·a·tam·nah oz·nei·nu	וְאַל תֵּאָטַמְנָה אָזְנֵינוּ	and let us not block our ears
mi·tza·a·ka·tam l'ma·zon.	מִצַּעֲקָתָם לְמָזוֹן.	to their cries for food.
P'kach ei·nei·nu	פְּקַח עֵינֵינוּ	Open our eyes
u·f'tach l'va·vei·nu	וּפְתַח לְבָבֵינוּ	and open our hearts
v'nit·chal'kah b'mat·no·te·cha	וְנִתְחַלְּקָה בְּמַתְּנוֹתֶיךָ	so that we may share your gifts
l'ma·an chi·sul ha·ra'av	לְמַעַן חִסּוּל הָרָעָב	in order to eliminate poverty
v'ha·mach·sor mei·o·la·mei·nu.	וְהַמַּחְסוֹר מֵעוֹלָמֵנוּ.	and need from our world.

Conclude with:

A·do·nai oz l'a·mo yi·tein,	יְיָ עֹז לְעַמּוֹ יִתֵּן,	May God give strength to The People,
A·do·nai y'va·reich et a·mo va·sha·lom.	יְיָ יְבָרֵךְ אֶת עַמּוֹ בַשָּׁלוֹם.	May God bless The People with peace.

Recite the Sheva B'rachot following Birkat HaMazon, in the presence of a recently married couple. Just as a minyan is required for a wedding cere-mony, ten adults should be present to offer these blessings as well. Birkat HaMazon is recited over a cup of wine. The seventh blessing is recited over a second cup, which has been held during the recitation of all the b'rachot. After the seven blessings are recited, wine from each cup is poured into a third cup from which the couple drink.

Ba·ruch A·tah A·do·nai,	1. בָּרוּךְ אַתָּה יְיָ,	Blessed are You, Adonai,
E·lo·hei·nu Me·lech ha·O·lam,	אֱלֹהֵינוּ מֶלֶךְ הָעוֹלָם,	our God, Ruler of the Universe,
she·ha·kol ba·ra lich·vo·do.	שֶׁהַכֹּל בָּרָא לִכְבוֹדוֹ.	who created all for God's glory.
Ba·ruch A·tah A·do·nai,	2. בָּרוּךְ אַתָּה יְיָ,	Blessed are You, Adonai,
E·lo·hei·nu Me·lech ha·O·lam,	אֱלֹהֵינוּ מֶלֶךְ הָעוֹלָם,	our God, Ruler of the Universe,
yo·tzeir ha·a·dam.	יוֹצֵר הָאָדָם.	who formed the human being.
Ba·ruch A·tah A·do·nai,	3. בָּרוּךְ אַתָּה יְיָ,	Blessed are You, Adonai,
E·lo·hei·nu Me·lech ha·O·lam,	אֱלֹהֵינוּ מֶלֶךְ הָעוֹלָם,	our God, Ruler of the Universe,
a·sher ya·tzar et ha·a·dam b'tzal·mo,	אֲשֶׁר יָצַר אֶת הָאָדָם בְּצַלְמוֹ,	who formed the human being in Your image,
b'tze·lem d'mut tav·ni·to,	בְּצֶלֶם דְּמוּת תַּבְנִיתוֹ,	in the image of the likeness of Your form,
v'hit·kin lo mi·me·nu	וְהִתְקִין לוֹ מִמֶּנּוּ	and established from it
bin·yan a·dei ad.	בִּנְיָן עֲדֵי עַד.	an everlasting structure.
Ba·ruch A·tah A·do·nai,	בָּרוּךְ אַתָּה יְיָ,	Blessed are You, Adonai,
yo·tzeir ha·a·dam.	יוֹצֵר הָאָדָם.	who formed the human being.

4. Sos ta·sis v'ta·geil ha·a·ka·rah
b'ki·butz ba·ne·ha
l'to·chah b'sim·chah.
Ba·ruch A·tah A·do·nai,
m'sa·mei·ach Tzi·yon b'va·ne·ha.

.4 שׂוֹשׂ תָּשִׂישׂ וְתָגֵל הָעֲקָרָה
בְּקִבּוּץ בָּנֶיהָ
לְתוֹכָהּ בְּשִׂמְחָה.
בָּרוּךְ אַתָּה יְיָ,
מְשַׂמֵּחַ צִיּוֹן בְּבָנֶיהָ.

May the barren one[1] joyfully rejoice and exult
in the gathering of her children
into her midst in happiness.
Blessed are You, Adonai,
who brings Zion happiness through her children.

5. Sa·mei·ach t'sa·mach
rei·im ha·a·hu·vim
k'sa·mei·cha·cha y'tzir·cha
b'Gan Ei·den mi·ke·dem.
Ba·ruch A·tah A·do·nai,
m'sa·mei·ach cha·tan v'cha·lah.

.5 שַׂמֵּחַ תְּשַׂמַּח
רֵעִים הָאֲהוּבִים
כְּשַׂמֵּחֲךָ יְצִירְךָ
בְּגַן עֵדֶן מִקֶּדֶם.
בָּרוּךְ אַתָּה יְיָ,
מְשַׂמֵּחַ חָתָן וְכַלָּה.

Bring great joy
to these beloved companions
as You brought joy to Your creature[2]
in the Garden of Eden long ago.
Blessed are You Adonai,
who brings happiness to the groom and bride.[3]

---

1. i.e., Zion

2. God, in fashioning Eve and bringing her to Adam, made him very happy.

3. Some couples may choose to replace the terms *chatan* and *kalah* in the 5th and 6th blessings with combinations of *chatan* and *kalah* that reflect their own genders, or the inclusive phrases *rei·im ahuvim / rei·ot ahuvot* (loving companions).

		6.
Ba·ruch A·tah A·do·nai,	בָּרוּךְ אַתָּה יְיָ,	Blessed are You, Adonai,
E·lo·hei·nu Me·lech ha·O·lam,	אֱלֹהֵינוּ מֶלֶךְ הָעוֹלָם,	our God, Ruler of the Universe,
a·sher ba·ra sa·son v'sim·chah,	אֲשֶׁר בָּרָא שָׂשׂוֹן וְשִׂמְחָה,	who created joy and happiness,
cha·tan v'cha·lah,	חָתָן וְכַלָּה,	groom and bride,
gi·lah, ri·nah, di·tzah v'ched·vah,	גִּילָה, רִנָּה, דִּיצָה וְחֶדְוָה,	exultation, song, gladness, and delight,
a·ha·vah v'a·cha·vah v'sha·lom v'rei·ut.	אַהֲבָה וְאַחֲוָה וְשָׁלוֹם וְרֵעוּת.	love and harmony, peace and companionship.
M'hei·rah A·do·nai E·lo·hei·nu yi·sha·ma	מְהֵרָה יְיָ אֱלֹהֵינוּ יִשָּׁמַע	Soon, Adonai our God, let there be heard
b'a·rei Y'hu·dah	בְּעָרֵי יְהוּדָה	in the cities of Judah
u·v'chu·tzot Y'ru·sha·la·yim	וּבְחֻצוֹת יְרוּשָׁלַיִם	and in the streets of Jerusalem
kol sa·son v·kol sim·chah,	קוֹל שָׂשׂוֹן וְקוֹל שִׂמְחָה,	the sound of joy, the sound of happiness,
kol cha·tan v'kol ka·lah,	קוֹל חָתָן וְקוֹל כַּלָּה,	the voice of the groom, the voice of the bride,
kol mitz·ha·lot [ka·lot va·]cha·ta·nim	קוֹל מִצְהֲלוֹת [כַּלּוֹת וַ]חֲתָנִים	the sound of couples' jubilation
mei·chu·pa·tam	מֵחֻפָּתָם	from the wedding canopy,
[u·n'a·rot] u·n'a·rim	[וּנְעָרוֹת] וּנְעָרִים	and of [maidens and] youths
mi·mish·teih n'gi·na·tam.	מִמִּשְׁתֵּה נְגִינָתָם.	from their song-filled feasts.
Ba·ruch A·tah A·do·nai,	בָּרוּךְ אַתָּה יְיָ,	Blessed are You Adonai,
m'sa·mei·ach cha·tan im ha·ka·lah.	מְשַׂמֵּחַ חָתָן עִם הַכַּלָּה.	who brings happiness to both groom and bride.

		7.
Ba·ruch A·tah A·do·nai,	בָּרוּךְ אַתָּה יְיָ,	Blessed are You, Adonai,
E·lo·hei·nu Me·lech ha·O·lam,	אֱלֹהֵינוּ מֶלֶךְ הָעוֹלָם,	our God, Ruler of the Universe,
bo·rei p'ri ha·ga·fen.	בּוֹרֵא פְּרִי הַגָּפֶן.	Creator of the fruit of the vine.

Use these special invitations when reciting the blessings after the meal at a boy's circumcision or a girl's naming ceremony.

Leader:

Cha·vei·rai n'va·reich.

חֲבֵרַי נְבָרֵךְ.

Friends, let us offer a blessing.

Group, then the Leader repeats:

Y'hi sheim A·do·nai m'vo·rach
mei·a·tah v'ad o·lam.

יְהִי שֵׁם יְיָ מְבֹרָךְ
מֵעַתָּה וְעַד עוֹלָם.

May Adonai's Name be praised
from now and beyond all time.

Leader:

No·deh l'shim·cha b'toch e·mu·nai,
b'ru·chim a·tem lA·do·nai.

נוֹדֶה לְשִׁמְךָ בְּתוֹךְ אֱמוּנַי,
בְּרוּכִים אַתֶּם לַיְיָ.

We praise Your Name among the faithful,
blessed are you to Adonai.

Leader:

Bir·shut Eil a·yom v'no·ra,
mis·gav l'i·tot ba·tza·rah,
Eil ne·zar big·vu·rah,
a·dir ba·ma·rom A·do·nai.

בִּרְשׁוּת אֵל אָיוֹם וְנוֹרָא,
מִשְׂגָּב לְעִתּוֹת בַּצָּרָה,
אֵל נֶאְזָר בִּגְבוּרָה,
אַדִּיר בַּמָרוֹם יְיָ.

With permission of the awesome and revered God,
the refuge in times of trouble,
God, girded with strength,
Adonai, who is might on high.

Group:

No·deh l'shim·cha b'toch e·mu·nai,
b'ruchim a·tem lA·do·nai.

נוֹדֶה לְשִׁמְךָ בְּתוֹךְ אֱמוּנַי,
בְּרוּכִים אַתֶּם לַיְיָ.

We praise Your Name among the faithful,
blessed are you to Adonai.

Leader:

Bir·shut ha·To·rah ha·k'do·shah,
t'horah hi, v'gam p'ru·shah,
tzi·vah la·nu mo·ra·shah

בִּרְשׁוּת הַתּוֹרָה הַקְּדוֹשָׁה,
טְהוֹרָה הִיא וְגַם פְּרוּשָׁה,
צִוָּה לָנוּ מוֹרָשָׁה

With the permission of the holy Torah,
which is pure, and explicit,
commanded to us as a heritage

Mo·sheh e·ved A·do·nai.	מֹשֶׁה עֶבֶד יְיָ	by Moses, servant of God.

Group:

No·deh l'shim·cha b'toch e·mu·nai,	נוֹדֶה לְשִׁמְךָ בְּתוֹךְ אֱמוּנֵי,	We praise Your Name among the faithful,
b'ruchim a·tem lA·do·nai.	בְּרוּכִים אַתֶּם לַייָ.	blessed are you to Adonai.

Leader:

Bir·shut ha·Ko·ha·nim ha·L'vi·im,	בִּרְשׁוּת הַכֹּהֲנִים הַלְוִים,	With the permission of the Kohanim of the tribe of Levi,
ek·ra lEi·lo·hei ha·Iv·riyim,	אֶקְרָא לֵאלֹהֵי הָעִבְרִיִּים,	I call upon the God of the Hebrews
a·ho·de·nu b'chol i·yim,	אֲהוֹדֶנּוּ בְּכָל אִיִּים,	I will praise God in all far away lands,
a·va·r'chah et A·do·nai.	אֲבָרְכָה אֶת יְיָ.	I will bless Adonai.

Group:

No·deh l'shim·cha b'toch e·mu·nai,	נוֹדֶה לְשִׁמְךָ בְּתוֹךְ אֱמוּנֵי,	We praise Your Name among the faithful,
b'ruchim a·tem lA·do·nai.	בְּרוּכִים אַתֶּם לַייָ.	blessed are you to Adonai.

Leader:

Bir·shut cha·vei·rai,	בִּרְשׁוּת חֲבֵרַי,	With the permission of my friends,
ef·t'chah b'shir pi u·s'fa·tai,	אֶפְתְּחָה בְּשִׁיר פִּי וּשְׂפָתַי,	I will open in song my mouth and lips
v'to·mar·nah atz·mo·tai:	וְתֹאמַרְנָה עַצְמוֹתַי:	Let my every bone declare:
Ba·ruch ha·ba b'sheim A·do·nai.	בָּרוּךְ הַבָּא בְּשֵׁם יְיָ.	"Blessed is the one who comes in the name of Adonai."[1]

Group:

No·deh l'shim·cha b'toch e·mu·nai,	נוֹדֶה לְשִׁמְךָ בְּתוֹךְ אֱמוּנֵי,	We praise Your Name among the faithful,
b'ruchim a·tem lA·do·nai.	בְּרוּכִים אַתֶּם לַייָ.	blessed are you to Adonai.

---

1. Psalms 118:26

Continue with בִּרְשׁוּת Bir'shut (With the permission of . . .) on page 4 until בְּעֵינֵי אֱלֹהִים וְאָדָם B'einei Elohim v'adam (In the eyes of God and humanity) on page 20, and then recite the appropriate additional verses for a boy or girl on the following pages.

Ha·ra·cha·man hu y'va·reich   הָרַחֲמָן הוּא יְבָרֵךְ   May the Merciful One bless

a·vi ha·ye·led v'i·mo,   אֲבִי הַיֶּלֶד וְאִמּוֹ,   the father and mother of the child;

v'yiz·ku l'ga·d'lo   וְיִזְכּוּ לְגַדְּלוֹ   may they be privileged to raise him,

u·l'cha·n'cho u·l'cha·k'mo.   וּלְחַנְּכוֹ וּלְחַכְּמוֹ.   educate him, and teach him wisdom.

Mi·yom ha·sh'mi·ni va·hal·ah   מִיּוֹם הַשְּׁמִינִי וָהָלְאָה   From this eighth day on

yei·ra·tzeh da·mo   יֵרָצֶה דָמוֹ   may his blood be accepted

vi·hi A·do·nai E·lo·hav i·mo.   וִיהִי יְיָ אֱלֹהָיו עִמּוֹ.   and may Adonai his God be with him.

Ha·ra·cha·man hu y'va·reich   הָרַחֲמָן הוּא יְבָרֵךְ   May the Merciful One bless

ba·al b'rit ha·mi·lah,   בַּעַל בְּרִית הַמִּילָה,   the master of the circumcision ritual [the sandak],

a·sher sas la·a·sot tze·dek b'gi·lah,   אֲשֶׁר שָׂשׂ לַעֲשׂוֹת צֶדֶק בְּגִילָה,   who rejoiced in performing this righteous act in joy;

vi·sha·leim pa·o·lo   וִישַׁלֵּם פָּעֳלוֹ   may his deed be rewarded,

u·mas·kur·to k'fu·lah,   וּמַשְׂכֻּרְתּוֹ כְּפוּלָה,   his recompense doubled,

v'yit·nei·hu l'ma·lah l'ma·lah.   וְיִתְּנֵהוּ לְמַעְלָה לְמָעְלָה.   and may God place him ever higher.

Ha·ra·cha·man hu y'va·reich   הָרַחֲמָן הוּא יְבָרֵךְ   May the Merciful One bless

rach ha·ni·mol lish·mo·nah,   רַךְ הַנִּמּוֹל לִשְׁמוֹנָה,   the tender child, just circumcised on the eighth day,

v'yih·yu ya·dav v'li·bo   וְיִהְיוּ יָדָיו וְלִבּוֹ   may his hands and his heart

la·Eil e·mu·nah,   לָאֵל אֱמוּנָה,   be faithful to God,

v'yiz·keh lir·ot p'nei ha·Sh'chi·nah   וְיִזְכֶּה לִרְאוֹת פְּנֵי הַשְּׁכִינָה   and may he merit seeing the Divine Presence

sha·losh p'a·mim ba·sha·nah.   שָׁלֹשׁ פְּעָמִים בַּשָּׁנָה.   three times a year.

Ha·ra·cha·man hu y'va·reich	הָרַחֲמָן הוּא יְבָרֵךְ	May the Merciful One bless
ha·mal b'sar ha·or·lah,	הַמָּל בְּשַׂר הָעָרְלָה,	the one who cut the uncircumcised flesh,
u·fa·ra, u·ma·tzatz d'mei ha·mi·lah.	וּפָרַע וּמָצַץ דְּמֵי הַמִּילָה.	split the membrane and drew off some blood.
ha·ya·rei v'rach ha·lei·vav	הַיָּרֵא וְרַךְ הַלֵּבָב	The work of a timid or fainthearted one
a·vo·da·to p'su·lah,	עֲבוֹדָתוֹ פְּסוּלָה,	would be invalid
im sh'losh ei·leh	אִם שְׁלֹשׁ אֵלֶּה	if these three acts
lo ya·a·seh lah.	לֹא יַעֲשֶׂה לָהּ.	were not performed.[1]

For a girl:

Ha·ra·cha·man hu y'va·reich et	הָרַחֲמָן הוּא יְבָרֵךְ אֶת	May the Merciful One bless
a·vi ha·yal·dah v'i·mah,	אֲבִי הַיַּלְדָה וְאִמָּהּ,	the child's father and mother,
v'yiz·ku l'ga·d'lah	וְיִזְכּוּ לְגַדְּלָהּ	may they be privileged to raise her,
u·l'cha·n'chah u·l'cha·k'mah,	וּלְחַנְּכָהּ וּלְחַכְּמָהּ,	educate her, and bring her to wisdom,
viy·hi A·do·nai E·lo·he·ha i·mah.	וִיהִי יְיָ אֱלֹהֶיהָ עִמָּהּ.	and may Adonai, her God, be with her.

Ha·ra·cha·man hu y'va·reich	הָרַחֲמָן הוּא יְבָרֵךְ	May the Merciful One bless
et ha·ra·kah ha·no·le·det,	אֶת הָרַכָּה הַנּוֹלֶדֶת,	this new born baby girl,
v'yih·yu ya·de·ha v'li·bah	וְיִהְיוּ יָדֶיהָ וְלִבָּהּ	may her hands and her heart
la·Eil e·mu·nah,	לָאֵל אֱמוּנָה,	be faithful to her God,
v'tiz·keh lir·ot p'nei ha·Sh'chi·nah	וְתִזְכֶּה לִרְאוֹת פְּנֵי הַשְּׁכִינָה	and may she merit to see the Divine Presence
sha·losh p'a·mim ba·sha·nah.	שָׁלֹשׁ פְּעָמִים בַּשָּׁנָה.	three times a year.

Return to page 20.

---

1. See Exodus 21:11. The verse is cited in full, even though the masculine *lo* is required in this context instead of *lah*.

This abbreviated version contains the essence of the four traditional blessings (for land, food, Jerusalem, and God's goodness) in the Grace after Meals.

On Shabbat and Festivals, begin with Shir HaMaalot, page 2.
On other days, begin with the Zimmun (invitation), page 4; then continue here.

Ba·ruch A·tah A·do·nai,	**בָּרוּךְ** אַתָּה יְיָ,	Blessed are You, Adonai,
E·lo·hei·nu Me·lech ha·O·lam,	אֱלֹהֵינוּ מֶלֶךְ הָעוֹלָם,	our God, Ruler of the Universe,
ha·zan et ha·o·lam ku·lo b'tu·vo	הַזָּן אֶת הָעוֹלָם כֻּלוֹ בְּטוּבוֹ	who sustains the world with goodness
b'chein b'che·sed u·v'ra·cha·mim.	בְּחֵן בְּחֶסֶד וּבְרַחֲמִים.	with favor, kindness, and mercy.
Hu no·tein le·chem l'chol ba·sar	הוּא נוֹתֵן לֶחֶם לְכָל בָּשָׂר	You give food to all creatures
ki l'o·lam chas·do.	כִּי לְעוֹלָם חַסְדּוֹ.	for Your kindness is everlasting.
U·v'tu·vo ha·ga·dol,	וּבְטוּבוֹ הַגָּדוֹל,	And because of Your great goodness,
ta·mid lo cha·sar la·nu	תָּמִיד לֹא חָסַר לָנוּ	never have we lacked
v'al yech·sar la·nu	וְאַל יֶחְסַר לָנוּ	and never will we lack
ma·zon l'o·lam va·ed.	מָזוֹן לְעוֹלָם וָעֶד.	food forever and ever.
Ba·a·vur sh'mo ha·ga·dol,	בַּעֲבוּר שְׁמוֹ הַגָּדוֹל,	For the sake of Your great Name,
ki hu zan u·m'far·neis la·kol,	כִּי הוּא זָן וּמְפַרְנֵס לַכֹּל,	for You nourish and keep all,
u·mei·tiv la·kol, u·mei·chin ma·zon	וּמֵטִיב לַכֹּל, וּמֵכִין מָזוֹן	and do good for all, and prepare food
l'chol b'ri·yo·tav a·sher ba·ra.	לְכֹל בְּרִיּוֹתָיו אֲשֶׁר בָּרָא.	for all the living things You created.
Ba·ruch A·tah A·do·nai,	בָּרוּךְ אַתָּה יְיָ,	Blessed are You, Adonai,
ha·zan et ha·kol.	הַזָּן אֶת הַכֹּל.	who nourishes all.

No·deh l'cha, A·do·nai E·lo·hei·nu,
al she·hin·chal·ta
la·a·vo·tei·nu [u·l'i·mo·tei·nu],
e·retz chem·dah to·vah u·r'cha·vah,
b'rit v'To·rah, cha·yim u·ma·zon.

Yit·ba·rach shim·cha
b'fi chol chai ta·mid
l'o·lam va·ed.
Ka·ka·tuv, v'a·chal·ta v'sa·va·ta,
u·vei·rach·ta et A·do·nai E·lo·he·cha
al ha·a·retz ha·to·vah a·sher na·tan lach.
Ba·ruch A·tah A·do·nai,
al ha·a·retz v'al ha·ma·zon.

נוֹדֶה לְךָ, יְיָ אֱלֹהֵינוּ,
עַל שֶׁהִנְחַלְתָּ
לַאֲבוֹתֵינוּ [וּלְאִמּוֹתֵינוּ],
אֶרֶץ חֶמְדָּה טוֹבָה וּרְחָבָה,
בְּרִית וְתוֹרָה חַיִּים וּמָזוֹן.

יִתְבָּרַךְ שִׁמְךָ
בְּפִי כָל חַי תָּמִיד
לְעוֹלָם וָעֶד.
כַּכָּתוּב, וְאָכַלְתָּ וְשָׂבָעְתָּ,
וּבֵרַכְתָּ אֶת יְיָ אֱלֹהֶיךָ
עַל הָאָרֶץ הַטֹּבָה אֲשֶׁר נָתַן לָךְ.
בָּרוּךְ אַתָּה יְיָ,
עַל הָאָרֶץ וְעַל הַמָּזוֹן.

We thank You, Adonai our God,
for giving
to our ancestors
a land beautiful, good, and spacious,
a covenant, a Torah, life and nourishment.

Blessed be Your Name
through the mouths of all living things always,
forever and ever.
As it is written, "You shall eat and be sated
and bless Adonai Your God
for the good land which God gave you."[1]
Blessed are You, Adonai,
for the land and for the food.

1. Psalms 8:10

For Shabbat:	For Yom Tov:	On Rosh Hashanah:	On Rosh Chodesh:
וּרְצֵה וְהַחֲלִיצֵנוּ בְּיוֹם הַשַּׁבָּת הַזֶּה.	וְשַׂמְּחֵנוּ בְּיוֹם הֶחָג הַזֶּה.	וְזָכְרֵנוּ לְטוֹבָה בְּיוֹם הַזִּכָּרוֹן הַזֶּה.	וְחַדֵּשׁ עָלֵינוּ אֶת הַחֹדֶשׁ הַזֶּה לְטוֹבָה וְלִבְרָכָה.
May it please You to strengthen us on this Sabbath day.	Cause us to rejoice on this Festival.	Remember us for good on this Day of Remembrance.	Renew this month for us for good and for blessing.
U·r'tseih v'ha·cha·li·tsei·nu b'yom ha·shab·bat ha·zeh.	V'sa·m'chei·nu b'yom ha·chag ha·zeh.	V'zoch·rei·nu l'tovah b'yom ha·zi·ka·ron ha·zeh.	V'cha·deish a·lei·nu et ha·cho·desh ha·zeh l'to·vah v'liv·ra·chah.

נוֹדֶה לְךָ עַל הַנִּסִּים וְעַל הַפֻּרְקָן שֶׁעָשִׂיתָ לַאֲבוֹתֵינוּ [וּלְאִמּוֹתֵינוּ] בַּיָּמִים הָהֵם בַּזְּמַן הַזֶּה.

No·deh l'cha al ha·ni·sim v'al ha·pur·kan she·a·si·ta la·a·vo·tei·nu [u·l'i·mo·tei·nu] ba·ya·mim ha·heim ba·z'man ha·zeh.

We thank You for the miracles and the salvation that you wrought for our ancestors in those days at this season.

U·v'neih Y'ru·sha·la·yim ir ha·ko·desh	**וּבְנֵה** יְרוּשָׁלַיִם עִיר הַקֹּדֶשׁ	Build up Jerusalem, the holy city
bim·hei·rah v'ya·mei·nu.	בִּמְהֵרָה בְיָמֵינוּ.	speedily in our days.
Ba·ruch A·tah A·do·nai,	בָּרוּךְ אַתָּה יְיָ,	Blessed are You, Adonai,
bo·neh v'ra·cha·mav Y'ru·sha·la·yim.	בּוֹנֶה בְרַחֲמָיו יְרוּשָׁלָיִם.	who builds in mercy Jerusalem.
A·mein.	אָמֵן.	Amen.

Ba·ruch A·tah A·do·nai,	**בָּרוּךְ** אַתָּה יְיָ,	Blessed are You, Adonai
E·lo·hei·nu Me·lech ha·O·lam,	אֱלֹהֵינוּ מֶלֶךְ הָעוֹלָם,	our God, Ruler of the Universe,
ha·Me·lech ha·tov, v'ha·mei·tiv la·kol,	הַמֶּלֶךְ הַטּוֹב, וְהַמֵּטִיב לַכֹּל,	the Good Ruler, who is good to all,
u'mi·kol tov	וּמִכָּל טוֹב	and of all good things
l'o·lam al y'chas·rei·nu.	לְעוֹלָם אַל יְחַסְּרֵנוּ.	may You never deprive us.

O·seh sha·lom bim·ro·mav,	**עֹשֶׂה שָׁלוֹם** בִּמְרוֹמָיו,	May the Maker of peace on high
hu ya·a·seh sha·lom,	הוּא יַעֲשֶׂה שָׁלוֹם,	make peace
a·lei·nu v'al kol Yis·ra·eil,	עָלֵינוּ וְעַל כָּל יִשְׂרָאֵל,	for us, and for all Israel,
v'im·ru a·mein.	וְאִמְרוּ אָמֵן.	and say Amen.

A·do·nai oz l'a·mo yi·tein,	**יְיָ עֹז** לְעַמּוֹ יִתֵּן,	May God give strength to The People,
A·do·nai y'va·reich et a·mo va·sha·lom.	יְיָ יְבָרֵךְ אֶת עַמּוֹ בַשָּׁלוֹם.	May God bless The People with peace.

Alternatives

The following alternatives may be considered to the full or abbreviated versions of Birkat HaMazon.
One may recite the Aramaic *B'rich Rachamana* and sing the English *kavvanah* by Shefa Gold.
One may also recite the Sephardic *Mah sheachalnu*, or one of the contemporary English alternatives by Shefa Gold and Hannah Tiferet Siegel.

B'rich ra·cha·ma·na,	בְּרִיךְ רַחֲמָנָא,	Blessed is the Merciful One,
[Mal·ka d'al·ma],	[מַלְכָּא דְעָלְמָא],	[Ruler of the Universe],
Ma·reih d'hai pi·ta.	מָרֵיה דְּהַאי פִּתָּא.	Provider of this bread.[1]

---

1. Talmud B'rachot 40b. According to Rav, reciting this formula is equivalent to reciting the first blessing of Birkat HaMazon. Though 'provider' is not an accurate translation of *mareih* (lit. Master of), it does convey the sentiment expressed in the first paragraph of Birkat HaMazon.

You are the Source of Life for all that is, and Your blessing flows through me.

— SHEFA GOLD

Mah she·a·chal·nu yih·yeh l'sov·ah,	מַה שֶׁאָכַלְנוּ יִהְיֶה לְשָׂבְעָה,	May what we have eaten be for satisfaction,
u·mah she·sha·ti·nu yih·yeh lir·fu·ah,	וּמַה שֶׁשָׁתִינוּ יִהְיֶה לִרְפוּאָה,	may what we have drunk be for health,
u·mah she·ho·tar·nu yih·yeh liv·ra·chah.	וּמַה שֶׁהוֹתַרְנוּ יִהְיֶה לִבְרָכָה.	may what we have left over be for a blessing.
Ho·du lA·do·nai ki tov	הוֹדוּ לַיְיָ כִּי טוֹב	Give thanks to Adonai who is good
ki l'o·lam chas·do.	כִּי לְעוֹלָם חַסְדוֹ.	for the One's kindness is eternal.

— SEPHARDIC TRADITION

A contemporary version of Birkat HaMazon by Shefa Gold. The refrain is recited with gusto and much table thumping.

First Blessing:
Nourisher of all

Yai da dai . . .
You are the source of everything,
It is because of you we sing.
You nourish the world with goodness and sustain it with grace,
We find you in the dust and in the vastness of space,
We taste you in the food we eat and see you in our friends,
You strengthen our rejoicing with a love that never ends.
Ba·ruch A·tah A·do·nai E·lo·hei·nu [Me·lech | Ru·ach] ha·O·lam,
Yai da dai . . . Ha·zan et ha·kol.

בָּרוּךְ אַתָּה יְיָ, אֱלֹהֵינוּ [מֶלֶךְ | רוּחַ] הָעוֹלָם,
הַזָּן אֶת הַכֹּל. . . .

Second Blessing:
For the land and for the food

You are the source of everything,
It is because of you we sing,
We thank you for the rain that falls upon the fertile ground,
And for all the plants and animals that in your world abound,
We fill our cups to overflow from the River of your Love,
We dig our roots into your soil and grow our leaves above.
Ba·ruch A·tah A·do·nai E·lo·hei·nu [Me·lech | Ru·ach] ha·O·lam,
Yai da dai . . . Al ha·a·retz v'al ha·ma·zon.

בָּרוּךְ אַתָּה יְיָ, אֱלֹהֵינוּ [מֶלֶךְ | רוּחַ] הָעוֹלָם,
עַל הָאָרֶץ וְעַל הַמָּזוֹן. . . .

Third Blessing:
In mercy, God rebuilds Jerusalem

You are the source of everything, it is because of you we sing,
You fill our eyes with visions of a Heaven here on earth,
Inspiring us to meet the challenge of our own re-birth,
We won't sit around and wait for Meschiach-time to start,
Your compassion builds Jerusalem in Israel and our hearts.
Ba·ruch A·tah A·do·nai E·lo·hei·nu [Me·lech | Ru·ach] ha·O·lam,
Yai da dai . . . Bo·neh v'ra·cha·mav Y'ru·sha·la·yim.

בָּרוּךְ אַתָּה יְיָ, אֱלֹהֵינוּ [מֶלֶךְ|רוּחַ] הָעוֹלָם,
בּוֹנֵה בְרַחֲמָיו יְרוּשָׁלָיִם. . . .

Fourth Blessing:
The good One, doing good to all

You are the source of everything, it is because of you we sing,
And even when it seems we've reached the end of our rope,
Your presence in our hearts reminds us not to lose all hope,
The knowledge of your goodness brings a light into our home,
Your presence gives us faith to wander into the unknown.
Ba·ruch A·tah A·do·nai E·lo·hei·nu [Me·lech | Ru·ach] ha·O·lam,
Yai da dai . . . Ha·tov v'ha·mei·tiv la·kol.

בָּרוּךְ אַתָּה יְיָ, אֱלֹהֵינוּ [מֶלֶךְ|רוּחַ] הָעוֹלָם,
הַטּוֹב וְהַמֵּטִיב לַכֹּל. . . .

Conclusion: Harachaman

Ha·ra·cha·man, Ha·ra·cha·man . . .

Bless this place and all who have shared our meal, May the food we eat strengthen the love we feel,
Bless the One who blesses us with peace, May our will to do your work increase,
Bless the child who searches for You in vain, May the suffering ones find respite from their pain,
Bless our friends who have so much to bear, May the homeless folk find shelter in your care.

Yai da dai . . . .

— Lyrics © Rabbi Shefa Gold (www.RabbiShefaGold.com)

A contemporary version of Birkat HaMazon by Hannah Tiferet Siegel.

וְאָכַלְתָּ וְשָׂבָעְתָּ וּבֵרַכְתָּ

V'a·chal·ta v'sa·va·ta u·vei·rach·ta And you shall eat, and be satisfied, and bless (DEUTERONOMY 8:10)

We ate when we were hungry and now we're satisfied.
We thank the Source of Blessing for all that S/He provides.

V'a·chal·ta v'sa·va·ta u·vei·rach·ta וְאָכַלְתָּ וְשָׂבָעְתָּ וּבֵרַכְתָּ

Hunger is a yearning in body and soul.
Earth, Air, Fire, Water, and spirit make us whole.

V'a·chal·ta v'sa·va·ta u·vei·rach·ta וְאָכַלְתָּ וְשָׂבָעְתָּ וּבֵרַכְתָּ

Giving and receiving we open up our hands,
From seedtime through harvest we're partners with the land.

V'a·chal·ta v'sa·va·ta u·vei·rach·ta וְאָכַלְתָּ וְשָׂבָעְתָּ וּבֵרַכְתָּ

We share in a vision of wholeness and release,
Where every child is nourished and we all live in peace.

V'a·chal·ta v'sa·va·ta u·vei·rach·ta וְאָכַלְתָּ וְשָׂבָעְתָּ וּבֵרַכְתָּ

— *RECORDED ON "OLAMAMA," AVAILABLE AS AN MP3 FROM CDFREEDOM.COM*

Blessings Before Eating Foods (other than bread)

For tree fruits:

Ba·ruch A·tah A·do·nai,
E·lo·hei·nu Me·lech ha·O·lam,
bo·rei p'ri ha·eitz.

בָּרוּךְ אַתָּה יְיָ,
אֱלֹהֵינוּ מֶלֶךְ הָעוֹלָם,
בּוֹרֵא פְּרִי הָעֵץ.

Blessed are You, Adonai,
our God, Ruler of the Universe,
Creator of the fruit of the tree.

For vegetables and fruits that grow in or on the ground:

Ba·ruch A·tah A·do·nai,
E·lo·hei·nu Me·lech ha·O·lam,
bo·rei p'ri ha·a·da·mah.

בָּרוּךְ אַתָּה יְיָ,
אֱלֹהֵינוּ מֶלֶךְ הָעוֹלָם,
בּוֹרֵא פְּרִי הָאֲדָמָה.

Blessed are You, Adonai,
our God, Ruler of the Universe,
Creator of the fruit of the earth.

For foods other than bread prepared from various grains (wheat, oats, rye, barley, spelt):

Ba·ruch A·tah A·do·nai,
E·lo·hei·nu Me·lech ha·O·lam,
bo·rei mi·nei m'zo·not.

בָּרוּךְ אַתָּה יְיָ,
אֱלֹהֵינוּ מֶלֶךְ הָעוֹלָם,
בּוֹרֵא מִינֵי מְזוֹנוֹת.

Blessed are You, Adonai,
our God, Ruler of the Universe,
Creator of all variety of grains.

For all other foods and drinks:

Ba·ruch A·tah A·do·nai,
E·lo·hei·nu Me·lech ha·O·lam,
she·ha·kol nih·yeh bid·va·ro.

בָּרוּךְ אַתָּה יְיָ,
אֱלֹהֵינוּ מֶלֶךְ הָעוֹלָם,
שֶׁהַכֹּל נִהְיֶה בִּדְבָרוֹ.

Blessed are You, Adonai,
our God, Ruler of the Universe,
through whose word all things exist.

Blessing After Foods Other than Bread　בְּרָכָה אַחֲרוֹנָה

This blessing is recited after eating any of the seven kinds of food for which the Torah praises the Land of Israel (Deuteronomy 8:8). These items include grain products made from wheat, barley, rye, oats, or spelt; grape wine or grape juice; and fruits including grapes, figs, pomegranates, olives, or dates.

Ba·ruch A·tah A·do·nai, *E·lo·hei·nu Me·lech ha·O·lam al*	בָּרוּךְ אַתָּה יְיָ, אֱלֹהֵינוּ מֶלֶךְ הָעוֹלָם עַל	Blessed are You, Adonai our God, Ruler of the Universe, for

After eating grain products:	After eating fruit:	After drinking wine:
הַמִּחְיָה וְעַל הַכַּלְכָּלָה,	הָעֵץ וְעַל פְּרִי הָעֵץ,	הַגֶּפֶן וְעַל פְּרִי הַגֶּפֶן,
nourishment and sustenance	the tree and the fruit of the tree	the vine and the fruit of the vine
ha·mich·yah v'al ha·kal·ka·lah	*ha·eitz v'al p'ri ha·eitz*	*ha·ge·fen v'al p'ri ha·ge·fen*

v'al t'nu·vat ha·sa·deh,	וְעַל תְּנוּבַת הַשָּׂדֶה,	and for the produce of the field,
v'al e·retz chem·dah to·vah u·r'cha·vah,	וְעַל אֶרֶץ חֶמְדָּה טוֹבָה וּרְחָבָה,	and for the land, beautiful, good, and expansive
she·ra·tzi·ta v'hin·chal·ta	שֶׁרָצִיתָ וְהִנְחַלְתָּ	that You have favored and bequeathed
la·a·vo·tei·nu [ul'i·mo·tei·nu],	לַאֲבוֹתֵינוּ [וּלְאִמּוֹתֵינוּ],	to our ancestors,
le·e·chol mi·pir·yah	לֶאֱכוֹל מִפִּרְיָהּ	to eat from its fruit
v'lis·bo·a mi·tu·vah.	וְלִשְׂבּוֹעַ מִטּוּבָהּ.	and be satisfied from its goodness.
Ra·cheim na, A·do·nai E·lo·hei·nu,	רַחֵם נָא יְיָ אֱלֹהֵינוּ,	Please have compassion, Adonai our God,
al Yis·ra·eil a·me·cha,	עַל יִשְׂרָאֵל עַמֶּךָ,	on Israel Your people,
v'al Y'ru·sha·la·yim i·re·cha,	וְעַל יְרוּשָׁלַיִם עִירֶךָ,	and on Jerusalem Your city,
v'al Tzi·yon mish·kan k'vo·de·cha,	וְעַל צִיּוֹן מִשְׁכַּן כְּבוֹדֶךָ,	and on Zion, the dwelling place of Your Glory,
v'al miz·b'che·cha v'al hei·cha·le·cha.	וְעַל מִזְבְּחֶךָ וְעַל הֵיכָלֶךָ.	and on Your altar and on Your sanctuary.

U·v'neih Y'ru·sha·la·yim ir ha·ko·desh bim·hei·rah v'ya·mei·nu, v'ha·a·lei·nu l'to·chah, v'sam·chei·nu b'vin·ya·nah, v'no·chal mi·pir·yah v'nis·ba mi·tu·vah, u·n'va·re·ch'cha a·le·ha bik·du·shah u·v'ta·ho·rah,

וּבְנֵה יְרוּשָׁלַיִם עִיר הַקֹּדֶשׁ בִּמְהֵרָה בְיָמֵינוּ, וְהַעֲלֵנוּ לְתוֹכָהּ, וְשַׂמְּחֵנוּ בְּבִנְיָנָהּ, וְנֹאכַל מִפִּרְיָהּ וְנִשְׂבַּע מִטּוּבָהּ, וּנְבָרֶכְךָ עָלֶיהָ בִּקְדֻשָּׁה וּבְטָהֳרָה,

And build Jerusalem, the Holy City, speedily in our days, and bring us up into it, and make us rejoice in its construction, so that we may eat of its fruit and be satisfied from its goodness and bless You for it in holiness and purity,

Shemini Atzeret:	Sukkot:	Shavuot:	Pesach:	Rosh Hodesh:	Shabbat:
וְשַׂמְּחֵנוּ בְּיוֹם הַשְּׁמִינִי חַג הָעֲצֶרֶת הַזֶּה	וְשַׂמְּחֵנוּ בְּיוֹם חַג הַסֻּכּוֹת הַזֶּה	וְשַׂמְּחֵנוּ בְּיוֹם חַג הַשָּׁבֻעוֹת הַזֶּה	וְשַׂמְּחֵנוּ בְּיוֹם חַג הַמַּצּוֹת הַזֶּה	וְזָכְרֵנוּ לְטוֹבָה, בְּיוֹם רֹאשׁ הַחֹדֶשׁ הַזֶּה.	וּרְצֵה וְהַחֲלִיצֵנוּ בְּיוֹם הַשַּׁבָּת הַזֶּה.
and make us happy on this festival of Shemini Atzeret,	and make us happy on this festival of Sukkot,	and make us happy on this festival of Shavuot,	and make us happy on this festival of Matzot,	and remember us for good on this day of Rosh Chodesh,	and favor and strengthen us on this day of Shabbat,
v'sam·chei·nu b'yom ha·sh'mi·ni, Chag ha·A·tze·ret ha·zeh,	v'sam·chei·nu b'yom Chag ha·Suk·kot ha·zeh,	v'sam·chei·nu b'yom Chag ha·Sha·vu·ot ha·zeh,	v'sam·chei·nu b'yom Chag ha·Ma·tzot ha·zeh,	v'zoch·rei·nu l'to·vah b'yom Rosh ha·Cho·desh ha·zeh,	u·r'tzeih v'ha·cha·li·tzei·nu b'yom ha·Shab·bat ha·zeh,

ki a·tah A·do·nai tov u·mei·tiv la·kol, v'no·deh l'cha al ha·a·retz v'al

כִּי אַתָּה יְיָ טוֹב וּמֵטִיב לַכֹּל, וְנוֹדֶה לְךָ עַל הָאָרֶץ וְעַל

for You, Adonai, are good and do good for all, and we thank You for the land and for

BLESSING AFTER OTHER FOODS

After eating grain products:

הַמִּחְיָה.

בָּרוּךְ אַתָּה יְיָ,

עַל הָאָרֶץ וְעַל הַמִּחְיָה.

the sustenance.

Blessed are You, Adonai,

for the land and for the sustenance.

ha·mich·yah.

Ba·ruch A·tah A·do·nai,

al ha·a·retz v'al ha·mich·yah.

After eating fruit:

הַפֵּרוֹת.

בָּרוּךְ אַתָּה יְיָ,

עַל הָאָרֶץ וְעַל הַפֵּרוֹת.

the fruit.

Blessed are You, Adonai,

for the land and for the fruit.

ha·pei·rot.

Ba·ruch A·tah A·do·nai,

al ha·a·retz v'al ha·pei·rot.

After drinking wine:

פְּרִי הַגָּפֶן.

בָּרוּךְ אַתָּה יְיָ,

עַל הָאָרֶץ וְעַל פְּרִי הַגָּפֶן.

the fruit of the vine.

Blessed are You, Adonai,

for the land and for the fruit of the vine.

p'ri ha·ga·fen.

Ba·ruch A·tah A·do·nai,

al ha·a·retz v'al p'ri ha·ga·fen.

After consuming grains, wine, and/or fruit:

הַמִּחְיָה/ וְעַל פְּרִי הַגָּפֶן/

וְעַל הַפֵּרוֹת. בָּרוּךְ אַתָּה יְיָ,

עַל הָאָרֶץ וְעַל הַמִּחְיָה/

וְעַל פְּרִי הַגָּפֶן/וְעַל הַפֵּרוֹת.

ha·mich·yah/ v'al p'ri ha·ge·fen/

v'al ha·pei·rot. Ba·ruch A·tah A·do·nai,

al ha·a·retz v'al ha·mich·yah/

v'al p'ri ha·ge·fen/v'al ha·pei·rot.

the sustenance/ and the fruit of the vine/

and the fruit. Blessed are You, Adonai,

for the land and for the sustenance/

and for the fruit of the vine/and for the fruit.

After eating or drinking other foods:

בָּרוּךְ אַתָּה יְיָ,

אֱלֹהֵינוּ מֶלֶךְ הָעוֹלָם,

בּוֹרֵא נְפָשׁוֹת רַבּוֹת וְחֶסְרוֹנָן,

עַל כָּל מַה שֶׁבָּרָא(תָ)

לְהַחֲיוֹת בָּהֶם נֶפֶשׁ כָּל חָי.

בָּרוּךְ חֵי הָעוֹלָמִים.

Ba·ruch A·tah A·do·nai,

E·lo·hei·nu Me·lech ha·O·lam,

Bo·rei n' fa·shot ra·bot v'ches·ro·nan,

al kol mah she·ba·ra(·ta)

l'ha·cha·yot ba·hem ne·fesh kol chai.

Ba·ruch Chei ha·O·la·mim.

Blessed are You, Adonai

our God, Ruler of the Universe,

Creator of many living things and their needs,

for everything that You have created

to sustain all living things.

Blessed is the Life of the Universe.

Candle Lighting ◆ Hadlakat Neirot ◆ הַדְלָקַת נֵרוֹת

Make circles to take in the light that brings us Shabbat joy.
Make circles to take in the light that brings us Shabbat rest.
Make circles to take in the light that brings us Shabbat holiness.
Make circles to take in the light that brings us Shabbat peace.

— MARK FRYDENBERG

We light candles at the onset of Shabbat or a festival to symbolize the light and the joy that these days bring into our lives.
Raise your hands as if to draw in the light, then cover your eyes as you say the blessing.
Many people precede candle lighting with a meditation, such as the one above.

Ba·ruch A·tah A·do·nai	בָּרוּךְ אַתָּה יְיָ,	Blessed are You, Adonai,
E·lo·hei·nu Me·lech ha·O·lam,	אֱלֹהֵינוּ מֶלֶךְ הָעוֹלָם,	Our God, Ruler of the Universe,
a·sher ki·d'sha·nu	אֲשֶׁר קִדְּשָׁנוּ	who made us holy
b'mitz·vo·tav,	בְּמִצְוֹתָיו,	with Your Commandments,
v'tzi·va·nu	וְצִוָּנוּ	and commanded us
l'had·lik neir shel . . .	לְהַדְלִיק נֵר שֶׁל . . .	to kindle the light of . . .

on Yom Kippur:	on Yom Tov:	on Shabbat:
(שַׁבָּת וְ)יוֹם הַכִּפּוּרִים.	(שַׁבָּת וְ)יוֹם טוֹב.	שַׁבָּת.
(Shabbat and) Yom Kippur.	(Shabbat and) Yom Tov.	Shabbat.
(Shab·bat v')Yom ha·Kip·pu·rim.	(Shab·bat v')Yom Tov.	Shab·bat.

Shehecheyanu שֶׁהֶחֱיָנוּ

Recite Shehecheyanu on the eve of Yom Kippur, on all festival nights except the last nights of Pesach, and to mark special occasions.

Ba·ruch A·tah A·do·nai	בָּרוּךְ אַתָּה יְיָ,	Blessed are You, Adonai,
E·lo·hei·nu Me·lech ha·O·lam,	אֱלֹהֵינוּ מֶלֶךְ הָעוֹלָם,	Our God, Ruler of the Universe,
she·he·che·ya·nu, v'ki·y'ma·nu,	שֶׁהֶחֱיָנוּ, וְקִיְּמָנוּ,	who has kept us alive, sustained us,
v'hi·gi·a·nu la·z'man ha·zeh.	וְהִגִּיעָנוּ לַזְּמַן הַזֶּה.	and enabled us to reach this season.

Shabbat HaMalkah שַׁבָּת הַמַּלְכָּה

This poem was written by Chaim Nachman Bialik (1873-1934).
It parallels the verses of Shalom Aleichem.
Some have the custom of saying the last verse right before Havdalah.

Ha·cha·mah mei·rosh	הַחַמָּה מֵרֹאשׁ	The sun from above
ha·i·la·not nis·ta·l'kah,	הָאִילָנוֹת נִסְתַּלְּקָה,	the treetops has faded,
bo·u v'nei·tzei	בֹּאוּ וְנֵצֵא	come, let us go out
lik·rat Shab·bat ha·mal·kah.	לִקְרַאת שַׁבָּת הַמַּלְכָּה.	to greet the Sabbath Queen.
Hi·neih hi yo·re·det,	הִנֵּה הִיא יוֹרֶדֶת,	Here she descends,
ha·k'do·shah, ha·b'ru·chah,	הַקְּדוֹשָׁה, הַבְּרוּכָה,	the holy one, the blessed one,
v'i·mah mal·a·chim,	וְעִמָּה מַלְאָכִים,	and with her the angels,
tz'va sha·lom u·m'nu·chah.	צְבָא שָׁלוֹם וּמְנוּחָה.	a force for peace and rest.
Bo·i bo·i ha·mal·kah!	בֹּאִי בֹּאִי הַמַּלְכָּה!	Come in, come in, [Sabbath] Queen!
Bo·i bo·i ha·ka·lah!	בֹּאִי בֹּאִי הַמַּלְכָּה!	Come in, come in, [Sabbath] Queen!
Sha·lom a·lei·chem,	שָׁלוֹם עֲלֵיכֶם,	Peace be with you,
mal·a·chei ha·sha·lom!	מַלְאֲכֵי הַשָּׁלוֹם!	angels of peace.

Ki·bal·nu p'nei Shab·bat	קִבַּלְנוּ פְּנֵי שַׁבָּת	We received the [face of] Sabbath
bir·na·nah u·t'fi·lah;	בְּרִנָּנָה וּתְפִלָּה;	with joyous song and prayer;
ha·bay·tah na·shu·vah	הַבַּיְתָה נָשׁוּבָה	now we return home
b'leiv ma·lei gi·lah.	בְּלֵב מָלֵא גִילָה.	with hearts full of gladness.
Sham a·ruch ha·shul·chan,	שָׁם עָרוּךְ הַשֻּׁלְחָן,	There the table is set,
ha·nei·rot ya·i·ru,	הַנֵּרוֹת יָאִירוּ,	the candles give off light,
kol pi·not ha·ba·yit	כָּל פִּנּוֹת הַבַּיִת	all corners of the house
yiz·ra·chu, yaz·hi·ru.	יִזְרְחוּ, יַזְהִירוּ.	shine and glow.
Shab·bat sha·lom u·m'vo·rach!	שַׁבַּת שָׁלוֹם וּמְבֹרָךְ!	A Sabbath of peace and blessing!
Shab·bat sha·lom u·m'vo·rach!	שַׁבַּת שָׁלוֹם וּמְבֹרָךְ!	A Sabbath of peace and blessing!
Bo·a·chem l'sha·lom,	בּוֹאֲכֶם לְשָׁלוֹם,	Come in peace,
mal·a·chei ha·sha·lom!	מַלְאֲכֵי הַשָּׁלוֹם!	angels of peace!
Sh'vi, za·kah, i·ma·nu	שְׁבִי, זַכָּה, עִמָּנוּ	Dwell, pure one, among us
u·v'zi·veich na o·ri	וּבְזִיוֵךְ נָא אוֹרִי	and with your radiance light up
lai·lah va·yom,	לַיְלָה וָיוֹם,	night and day,
a·char ta·a·vo·ri.	אַחַר תַּעֲבֹרִי.	then you will move on.
Va·a·nach·nu n'cha·b'deich	וַאֲנַחְנוּ נְכַבְּדֵךְ	We will honor you
b'vig·dei cha·mu·dot,	בְּבִגְדֵי חֲמוּדוֹת,	with fine clothes,
biz·mi·rot u·t'fi·lot	בִּזְמִירוֹת וּתְפִילוֹת	with songs, prayers,
u·v'sha·losh s'u·dot.	וּבְשָׁלֹשׁ סְעֻדוֹת.	and three feasts.

U·vim·nu·chah sh'lei·mah,	וּבִמְנוּחָה שְׁלֵמָה,	And with complete rest,
U·vim·nu·chah na·ei·mah.	וּבִמְנוּחָה נָעֵמָה.	And with pleasant rest.
Ba·r'chu·ni l'sha·lom,	בָּרְכוּנִי לְשָׁלוֹם,	Bless me with peace,
mal·a·chei ha·sha·lom!	מַלְאֲכֵי הַשָּׁלוֹם!	angels of peace!
Ha·cha·mah mei·rosh	הַחַמָּה מֵראשׁ	The sun from above
ha·i·la·not nis·ta·l'kah,	הָאִילָנוֹת נִסְתַּלְּקָה,	the treetops has faded,
bo·u u·n'la·veh	בֹּאוּ וּנְלַוֶּה	come, let us escort
et Shab·bat ha·mal·kah.	אֶת שַׁבָּת הַמַּלְכָּה.	the Sabbath Queen.
Tzei·teich l'sha·lom,	צֵאתֵךְ לְשָׁלוֹם,	Depart in peace,
ha·k'do·shah, ha·za·kah,	הַקְּדוֹשָׁה, הַזַּכָּה,	holy one, pure one,
d'i, shei·shet ya·mim	דְּעִי, שֵׁשֶׁת יָמִים	know that for six days
el shu·veich n'cha·keh . . .	אֶל שׁוּבֵךְ נְחַכֶּה . . .	we shall await your return . . .
Kein la·shab·bat ha·ba·ah!	כֵּן לַשַּׁבָּת הַבָּאָה!	So [may it be] for next Shabbat!
Kein la·shab·bat ha·ba·ah!	כֵּן לַשַּׁבָּת הַבָּאָה!	So [may it be] for next Shabbat!
Tzeit·chem l'sha·lom,	צֵאתְכֶם לְשָׁלוֹם,	Depart in peace,
mal·a·chei ha·sha·lom!	מַלְאֲכֵי הַשָּׁלוֹם!	angels of peace!

The practice of singing Shalom Aleichem at the dinner table was introduced by the mystics of Tz'fat (Safed) in the sixteenth century.

According to the Zohar Chadash: When coming home from the synagogue on Friday evening, a person is accompanied by angels on either side, and the Sh'chinah oversees them, as a mother does with her children. When the Sh'chinah sees the candles burning, the table set, and the family together in happiness and peace, the Sh'chinah says, "This is mine, Israel in whom I take pride."

This story, which has its origins in the Talmud (Shabbat 119b), has here been transformed.

A Chasidic interpretation suggests that just as Jacob had two camps of angels watching over him (one when he was inside, and another when he was outside the land of Israel), there are two groups of angels watching over us as well: those that watch over us during the week and those that watch over us on Shabbat.

We say *Shalom Aleichem* to welcome the Sabbath angels, and *Tzeitchem l'shalom* to bid farewell to the weekday angels, who can now celebrate Shabbat knowing that we are in good care.

Shalom Aleichem is traditionally recited before Kiddush.

Sha·lom a·lei·chem,	שָׁלוֹם עֲלֵיכֶם,	Peace to you,
mal·a·chei ha·sha·reit,	מַלְאֲכֵי הַשָּׁרֵת,	attending angels,
mal·a·chei El·yon,	מַלְאֲכֵי עֶלְיוֹן,	messengers of the Most High,
mi·Me·lech Mal·chei ha·M'la·chim,	מִמֶּלֶךְ[1] מַלְכֵי הַמְּלָכִים,	the Supreme Ruler,
ha·Ka·dosh Ba·ruch Hu.	הַקָּדוֹשׁ בָּרוּךְ הוּא.	the Blessed Holy One.

Bo·a·chem l'sha·lom,	בּוֹאֲכֶם לְשָׁלוֹם,	Come in peace,
mal·a·chei ha·sha·lom,	מַלְאֲכֵי הַשָּׁלוֹם,	angels of peace,
mal·a·chei El·yon,	מַלְאֲכֵי עֶלְיוֹן,	messengers of the Most High,
mi·Me·lech Mal·chei ha·M'la·chim,	מִמֶּלֶךְ מַלְכֵי הַמְּלָכִים,	the Supreme Ruler,
ha·Ka·dosh Ba·ruch Hu.	הַקָּדוֹשׁ בָּרוּךְ הוּא.	the Blessed Holy One.

Ba·r'chu·ni l'sha·lom,	בָּרְכוּנִי לְשָׁלוֹם,	Bless me with peace,
mal·a·chei ha·sha·lom,	מַלְאֲכֵי הַשָּׁלוֹם,	angels of peace,
mal·a·chei El·yon,	מַלְאֲכֵי עֶלְיוֹן,	messengers of the Most High,
mi·Me·lech Mal·chei ha·M'la·chim,	מִמֶּלֶךְ מַלְכֵי הַמְּלָכִים,	the Supreme Ruler,
ha·Ka·dosh Ba·ruch Hu.	הַקָּדוֹשׁ בָּרוּךְ הוּא.	the Blessed Holy One.

Tzeit·chem l'sha·lom,	צֵאתְכֶם לְשָׁלוֹם,	Go in peace,
mal·a·chei ha·sha·lom,	מַלְאֲכֵי הַשָּׁלוֹם,	angels of peace,
mal·a·chei El·yon,	מַלְאֲכֵי עֶלְיוֹן,	messengers of the Most High,
mi·Me·lech Mal·chei ha·M'la·chim,	מִמֶּלֶךְ מַלְכֵי הַמְּלָכִים,	the Supreme Ruler,
ha·Ka·dosh Ba·ruch Hu.	הַקָּדוֹשׁ בָּרוּךְ הוּא.	the Blessed Holy One.

1. The *mem* preceding *melech* seems to be redundant; it is left in the Hebrew text as a nod to tradition, but is not translated.
   The phrase Supreme Ruler translates literally as "the King of Kings of Kings."

AT THE TABLE

Family Blessings at the Table

Eishet Chayil is the last section of the book of Proverbs (31:10-31). It describes an ideal woman, successful in all her endeavors, caring for the needs of her family members, wisely managing her household, and operating a family business. She does all this with grace, aplomb, and seeming lack of effort, while her husband sits at the gate of the city, presumably conducting important business. In other words, she is a biblical version of a supermom. The poem is now generally seen as a hymn of praise to the ideal housewife, although some biblical scholars suggest that it may have been intended as an encomium to Lady Wisdom.

Many women in recent times have been put off by the tone and seeming intent of the poem, and reject the role model that it promotes. Therefore they resent having it sung at the Shabbat table. Nevertheless, it is important to bear in mind that it was introduced into the Friday night ritual by the kabbalists of Safed, who created most of the Friday night liturgy as we know it today. It was chosen because it was understood by them as a paean of praise to the Sh'chinah, the feminine aspect of God, which is welcomed on Friday evening and celebrated at the evening meal. (*Cf. L'cha dodi* in the Kabbalat shabbat service and *Azamer bi-sh'vachin*, the song by Isaac Luria in the *Z'mirot* section for Friday night.) It has been adorned by many lovely hasidic melodies.

Those seeking an alternative to the literal meaning of *Eishet Chayil* may follow the kabbalistic practice which encourages families to sing it together as a way of welcoming the Sabbath Queen. An alternative for those who wish to mutualize the sentiments expressed in *Eishet Chayil* is to add an appropriate psalm in praise of a worthy person, such as Psalm 15 (see page 56), or even use this psalm instead of *Eishet Chayil*. (Others may wish to use Psalm 1, 112, or 128, which mention men specifically.)

Another option is for partners to exchange blessings (p. 55). These blessings, taken and adapted from Song of Songs, were first used for this purpose by Marcia Falk, *The Book of Blessings* (San Francisco, 1996), 126-127. See her commentary, *ibid.* pp. 451-452. Our version is a variation on this theme.

Ei·shet cha·yil mi yim·tza?	אֵשֶׁת חַיִל מִי יִמְצָא?	A woman of strength who can find?
v'ra·chok mi·p'ni·nim mich·rah.	וְרָחֹק מִפְּנִינִים מִכְרָהּ.	Beyond pearls is her value.
Ba·tach bah leiv ba·lah,	בָּטַח בָּהּ לֵב בַּעְלָהּ,	Her husband's heart trusts in her,
v'sha·lal lo yech·sar.	וְשָׁלָל לֹא יֶחְסָר.	Gain shall not be lacking [for him].

G'ma·lat·hu tov v'lo ra	גְּמָלַתְהוּ טוֹב וְלֹא רָע	She does him only good, no harm
kol y'mei cha·ye·ha.	כֹּל יְמֵי חַיֶּיהָ.	all the days of her life.
Da·r'shah tze·mer u·fish·tim	דָּרְשָׁה צֶמֶר וּפִשְׁתִּים	She seeks out wool and flax
va·ta·as b'chei·fetz ka·pe·ha.	וַתַּעַשׂ בְּחֵפֶץ כַּפֶּיהָ.	and works willingly with her hands.

Ha·y'tah ka·o·ni·yot so·cheir,	הָיְתָה כָּאֳנִיּוֹת סוֹחֵר,	She is like the merchant ships,
mi·mer·chak ta·vi lach·mah.	מִמֶּרְחָק תָּבִיא לַחְמָהּ.	From afar she brings her food.
Va·ta·kom b'od lai·lah	וַתָּקָם בְּעוֹד לַיְלָה	She rises while it is yet night
va·ti·tein te·ref l'vei·tah	וַתִּתֵּן טֶרֶף לְבֵיתָהּ	and gives food to her household
v'chok l'na·a·ro·te·ha.	וְחֹק לְנַעֲרֹתֶיהָ.	and a portion to her maids.

Za·m'mah sa·deh va·ti·ka·chei·hu,	זָמְמָה שָׂדֶה וַתִּקָּחֵהוּ,	She considers a field and buys it,
mi·p'ri cha·pe·ha na·t'ah ka·rem.	מִפְּרִי כַפֶּיהָ נָטְעָה כָּרֶם.	with the fruit of her hands she plants a vineyard.
Cha·g'rah v'oz mot·ne·ha	חָגְרָה בְעֹז מָתְנֶיהָ	She girds with might her loins
va·t'a·meitz z'ro·o·te·ha.	וַתְּאַמֵּץ זְרוֹעֹתֶיהָ.	and strengthens her arms.

Ta·a·mah ki tov sach·rah,	טָעֲמָה כִּי טוֹב סַחְרָהּ,	She senses her wares are good,
Lo yich·beh ba·lai·lah nei·rah.	לֹא יִכְבֶּה בַלַּיְלָה נֵרָהּ.	Her lamp does not go out at night.
Ya·de·ha shi·l'chah va·ki·shor	יָדֶיהָ שִׁלְּחָה בַכִּישׁוֹר	Her hands she extends to the distaff
v'cha·pe·ha ta·m'chu fa·lech.	וְכַפֶּיהָ תָּמְכוּ פָלֶךְ.	and her palms grasp the spindle.
Ka·pah pa·r'sah le·a·ni	כַּפָּהּ פָּרְשָׂה לֶעָנִי	Her palm she opens to the poor;
v'ya·de·ha shi·l'chah la·ev·yon.	וְיָדֶיהָ שִׁלְּחָה לָאֶבְיוֹן.	Her hands she extends to the needy.
Lo ti·ra l'vei·tah mi·sha·leg	לֹא תִירָא לְבֵיתָהּ מִשָּׁלֶג	She has no fear for her household from the snow
Ki chol bei·tah la·vush sha·nim.	כִּי כָל בֵּיתָהּ לָבֻשׁ שָׁנִים.	For all her household are clothed in finery.
Mar·va·dim a·s'tah lah,	מַרְבַדִּים עָשְׂתָה לָּהּ	Coverings she makes herself,
Sheish v'ar·ga·man l'vu·shah.	שֵׁשׁ וְאַרְגָּמָן לְבוּשָׁהּ.	Fine linen and purple are her garb.
No·da ba·sh'a·rim ba·lah	נוֹדָע בַּשְּׁעָרִים בַּעְלָהּ	Her husband is known at the gates
B'shiv·to im zik·nei a·retz.	בְּשִׁבְתּוֹ עִם זִקְנֵי אָרֶץ.	Where he sits with the elders of the land.
Sa·din a·s'tah va·tim·kor	סָדִין עָשְׂתָה וַתִּמְכֹּר	A sheet she makes and sells
Va·cha·gor na·t'nah la·k'na·a·ni.	וַחֲגוֹר נָתְנָה לַכְּנַעֲנִי.	A sash she supplies the merchant.
Oz v'ha·dar l'vu·shah	עֹז וְהָדָר לְבוּשָׁהּ	Strength and dignity are her garb
va·tis·chak l'yom a·cha·ron.	וַתִּשְׂחַק לְיוֹם אַחֲרוֹן.	As she laughs at future days.[1]

---

1. According to the classical Jewish commentators (Rashi, Ibn Ezra, Ralbag): "She cheerfully awaits her final day."

Pi·ha pa·t'chah v'choch·mah, V'to·rat che·sed al l'sho·nah. Tzo·fi·yah ha·li·chot bei·tah, V'le·chem atz·lut lo to·cheil.	פִּיהָ פָּתְחָה בְחָכְמָה, וְתוֹרַת חֶסֶד עַל לְשׁוֹנָהּ. צוֹפִיָּה הֲלִיכוֹת בֵּיתָהּ, וְלֶחֶם עַצְלוּת לֹא תֹאכֵל.	Her mouth she opens in wisdom, A lesson in kindness is on her tongue. She watches the conduct of her household, The bread of sloth she never eats.
Ka·mu va·ne·ha va·y'a·sh'ru·ha, ba·lah va·y'ha·l'lah. Ra·bot ba·not a·su cha·yil, v'at a·lit al ku·la·nah.	קָמוּ בָנֶיהָ וַיְאַשְּׁרוּהָ, בַּעְלָהּ וַיְהַלְלָהּ. רַבּוֹת בָּנוֹת עָשׂוּ חָיִל, וְאַתְּ עָלִית עַל כֻּלָּנָה.	Her children rise up to make her happy, Her husband praises her. Many women have excelled, But you surpass them all.
She·ker ha·chein v'he·vel ha·yo·fi, i·shah yir·at A·do·nai hi tit·ha·lal. T'nu lah mi·p'ri ya·de·ha, viy·ha·l'lu·ha ba·sh'a·rim ma·a·se·ha.	שֶׁקֶר הַחֵן וְהֶבֶל הַיֹּפִי, אִשָּׁה יִרְאַת יְיָ הִיא תִתְהַלָּל. תְּנוּ לָהּ מִפְּרִי יָדֶיהָ, וִיהַלְלוּהָ בַשְּׁעָרִים מַעֲשֶׂיהָ.	Grace is deceitful, beauty illusory, A woman who fears God, she shall be praised. Give her credit for the fruit of her labors, May her deeds praise her at the gates.

Miz·mor l'Da·vid.	מִזְמוֹר לְדָוִד.	A psalm of David.
A·do·nai, mi ya·gur b'a·ho·le·cha?	יְיָ, מִי יָגוּר בְּאָהֳלֶךָ?	Adonai, who may abide in Your tent?
Mi yish·kon	מִי יִשְׁכֹּן	Who may dwell
b'har kod·she·cha?	בְּהַר קָדְשֶׁךָ?	on Your holy mountain?
Ho·leich ta·mim,	הוֹלֵךְ תָּמִים,	One who walks blameless,
u·fo·eil tze·dek,	וּפֹעֵל צֶדֶק,	and does justice,
v'do·veir e·met bi·l'va·vo.	וְדֹבֵר אֱמֶת בִּלְבָבוֹ.	and speaks the truth from the heart;
Lo ra·gal al l'sho·no,	לֹא רָגַל עַל לְשֹׁנוֹ,	whose tongue does not slander,
Lo a·sah l'rei·ei·hu ra·ah,	לֹא עָשָׂה לְרֵעֵהוּ רָעָה,	who has never harmed another,
v'cher·pah lo na·sa	וְחֶרְפָּה לֹא נָשָׂא	nor borne reproach for
al k'ro·vo.	עַל קְרֹבוֹ.	[acting against] a neighbor;
Niv·zeh b'ei·nav nim·as	נִבְזֶה בְּעֵינָיו נִמְאָס	who holds a vile person in contempt
v'et yir·ei A·do·nai y'cha·beid.	וְאֶת יִרְאֵי יְהֹוָה יְכַבֵּד.	but honors those who fear God;
Nish·ba	נִשְׁבַּע	who stands by an oath
l'ha·ra v'lo ya·mir,	לְהָרַע וְלֹא יָמִר,	even when it can cause harm;
Kas·po lo na·tan b'ne·shech	כַּסְפּוֹ לֹא נָתַן בְּנֶשֶׁךְ	who has never lent money at interest,
v'sho·chad al na·ki lo la·kach.	וְשֹׁחַד עַל נָקִי לֹא לָקָח.	or taken a bribe against the innocent.
o·seih ei·leh	עֹשֵׂה אֵלֶּה	One who does these things
lo yi·mot l'o·lam.	לֹא יִמּוֹט לְעוֹלָם.	shall never be shaken.

Couples can choose from the following verses as appropriate. One partner recites:

To a woman:

Hi·nach ya·fah, ra·ya·ti,
hi·nach ya·fah.

הִנָּךְ יָפָה, רַעְיָתִי,
הִנָּךְ יָפָה.

Indeed you are beautiful, my love,
beautiful indeed.[1]

To a man:

Hi·n'cha ya·feh, rei·i,
hi·n'cha ya·feh.

הִנְּךָ יָפֶה, רֵעִי,
הִנְּךָ יָפֶה.

Indeed you are handsome, my love,
handsome indeed.

The other partner responds:

To a man:

Hi·n'cha ya·feh, do·di,
af na·im.

הִנְּךָ יָפֶה, דּוֹדִי,
אַף נָעִים.

Indeed you are handsome, my beloved,
truly lovely.[2]

To a woman:

Hi·nach ya·fah, ra·ya·ti,
af ne·i·mah.

הִנָּךְ יָפָה, רַעְיָתִי,
אַף נְעִימָה.

Indeed you are beautiful, my love,
truly lovely.

Together:

Ma·yim ra·bim lo yuch·lu
l'cha·bot et ha·a·ha·vah,
u·n'ha·rot lo yish·t'fu·ha.

מַיִם רַבִּים לֹא יוּכְלוּ
לְכַבּוֹת אֶת הָאַהֲבָה,
וּנְהָרוֹת לֹא יִשְׁטְפוּהָ.

Vast floods cannot
quench love,
nor rivers drown it.[3]

---

1. Song of Songs 1:15   2. Ibid. 1:16   3. Ibid. 8:7

Blessing the Children בִּרְכַּת הַיְלָדִים

Parents bless their children at the start of Shabbat by placing their hands on their children's heads. This symbolizes the continued flow of God's blessings from one generation to another.

The blessing for sons is the same blessing that Jacob used to bless his grandchildren, Ephraim and Manasseh, who remained true to their Jewish heritage despite social pressures. The blessing for daughters recalls the merit of the Matriarchs, who, despite many obstacles, became the mothers of a great nation.

All children are then blessed with the blessing that Aaron and the Kohanim used to bless the Jewish people.

For Sons:

Y'sim·cha E·lo·him
k'Ef·ra·yim v·chiM·na·sheh.

יְשִׂמְךָ אֱלֹהִים
כְּאֶפְרַיִם וְכִמְנַשֶּׁה.

May God make you to be
like Ephraim and Menasseh.　　— GENESIS 48:20

For Daughters:

Y'si·meich E·lo·him
k'Sa·rah Riv·kah Ra·cheil v'Lei·ah.

יְשִׂמֵךְ אֱלֹהִים
כְּשָׂרָה רִבְקָה רָחֵל וְלֵאָה.

May God make you to be
like Sarah, Rebecca, Rachel, and Leah.

For All Children:

Y'va·re·ch'cha A·do·nai
v'yish·m're·cha.

יְבָרֶכְךָ יְיָ
וְיִשְׁמְרֶךָ.

May Adonai bless you
and watch over you.

Ya·eir A·do·nai pa·nav Ei·le·cha
vi·chu·ne·ka.

יָאֵר יְיָ פָּנָיו אֵלֶיךָ
וִיחֻנֶּךָּ.

May Adonai shine upon you
and be gracious to you.

Yi·sa A·do·nai pa·nav Ei·le·cha
v'ya·seim l'cha sha·lom.

יִשָּׂא יְיָ פָּנָיו אֵלֶיךָ
וְיָשֵׂם לְךָ שָׁלוֹם.

May Adonai look towards you,
and grant you peace.　　— NUMBERS 6:24-26

For girls, some may wish to use the feminine form of the blessing:

Y'va·r'cheich A·do·nai v'yish·m'reich.　　יְבָרֶכְךְ יְיָ וְיִשְׁמְרֵךְ.　　May Adonai bless you and watch over you.

Ya·eir A·do·nai pa·nav Ei·la·yich vi·chu·neich.　　יָאֵר יְיָ פָּנָיו אֵלַיִךְ וִיחֻנֵּךְ.　　May Adonai shine upon you and be gracious to you.

Yi·sa A·do·nai pa·nav Ei·la·yich　　יִשָּׂא יְיָ פָּנָיו אֵלַיִךְ　　May Adonai look towards you,
v'ya·seim lach sha·lom.　　וְיָשֵׂם לָךְ שָׁלוֹם.　　and grant you peace.

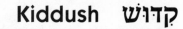
Kiddush for Friday Evening ◆ Kiddush L'Erev Shabbat   קִדּוּשׁ לְעֶרֶב שַׁבָּת

Following a Chasidic custom, some people begin:

Va·yar E·lo·him	וַיַּרְא אֱלֹהִים	And God saw
et kol a·sher a·sah	אֶת כָּל אֲשֶׁר עָשָׂה	all that God had made
v'hi·neih tov m'od.	וְהִנֵּה טוֹב מְאֹד.	and behold it was very good. — GENESIS 1:31

Many begin here (reciting the next line in an undertone):

Va·y'hi e·rev va·y'hi vo·ker	וַיְהִי עֶרֶב וַיְהִי בֹקֶר	And there was evening, and there was morning,
Yom Ha·shi·shi.	יוֹם הַשִּׁשִּׁי.	The sixth day.
Va·y'chu·lu Ha·sha·ma·yim v'ha·a·retz	וַיְכֻלּוּ הַשָּׁמַיִם וְהָאָרֶץ	Thus were completed the heavens and the earth
v'chol tz'va·am.	וְכָל צְבָאָם.	and all their array.
Va·y'chal E·lo·him ba·yom ha·sh'vi·i	וַיְכַל אֱלֹהִים בַּיּוֹם הַשְּׁבִיעִי	God completed on the seventh day
m'lach·to a·sher a·sah,	מְלַאכְתּוֹ אֲשֶׁר עָשָׂה,	the work that God had been doing,
va·yish·bot ba·yom ha·sh'vi·i	וַיִּשְׁבֹּת בַּיּוֹם הַשְּׁבִיעִי	and God ceased on the seventh day
mi·kol m'lach·to a·sher a·sah.	מִכָּל מְלַאכְתּוֹ אֲשֶׁר עָשָׂה.	from all the work that God had been doing.
Va·y'va·rech E·lo·him et yom ha·sh'vi·i	וַיְבָרֶךְ אֱלֹהִים אֶת יוֹם הַשְּׁבִיעִי	God blessed the seventh day
va·y'ka·deish o·to,	וַיְקַדֵּשׁ אֹתוֹ,	and made it holy,
ki vo sha·vat mi·kol m'lach·to	כִּי בוֹ שָׁבַת מִכָּל מְלַאכְתּוֹ	for on it God ceased from all the work
a·sher ba·ra E·lo·him la·a·sot.	אֲשֶׁר בָּרָא אֱלֹהִים לַעֲשׂוֹת.	that God had created to do. — GENESIS 1:31, 2:1-3

Sa·v'rei cha·vei·rai,	סָבְרֵי חֲבֵרַי,	With the approval of my friends,
Ba·ruch A·tah A·do·nai,	בָּרוּךְ אַתָּה יְיָ,	Blessed are You, Adonai,
E·lo·hei·nu Me·lech ha·O·lam,	אֱלֹהֵינוּ מֶלֶךְ הָעוֹלָם,	Our God, Ruler of the Universe,
bo·rei p'ri ha·ga·fen.	בּוֹרֵא פְּרִי הַגָּפֶן.	Creator of the fruit of the vine.
Ba·ruch A·tah A·do·nai,	בָּרוּךְ אַתָּה יְיָ,	Blessed are You, Adonai,
E·lo·hei·nu Me·lech ha·O·lam,	אֱלֹהֵינוּ מֶלֶךְ הָעוֹלָם,	Our God, Ruler of the Universe,
a·sher ki·d'sha·nu b'mitz·vo·tav	אֲשֶׁר קִדְּשָׁנוּ בְּמִצְוֹתָיו	who made us holy with Your Commandments
v'ra·tzah va·nu, v'Shab·bat kod·sho	וְרָצָה בָנוּ, וְשַׁבַּת קָדְשׁוֹ	and favored us. Your holy Sabbath
b'a·ha·vah u·v'ra·tzon hin·chi·la·nu,	בְּאַהֲבָה וּבְרָצוֹן הִנְחִילָנוּ,	in love and favor You gave us as our heritage,
zi·ka·ron l'ma·a·seih v'rei·shit.	זִכָּרוֹן לְמַעֲשֵׂה בְרֵאשִׁית.	a reminder of the work of Creation.
Ki hu yom t'chi·lah	כִּי הוּא יוֹם תְּחִלָּה	For it is first among the days
l'mik·ra·ei ko·desh,	לְמִקְרָאֵי קֹדֶשׁ,	called holy,
zei·cher li·tzi·at Mitz·ra·yim.	זֵכֶר לִיצִיאַת מִצְרָיִם.	a reminder of the Exodus from Egypt.
Ki va·nu va·char·ta v'o·ta·nu ki·dash·ta	כִּי בָנוּ בָחַרְתָּ וְאוֹתָנוּ קִדַּשְׁתָּ	For You have chosen us[1] and set us apart
[mi·kol ha·a·mim | la·a·vo·da·te·cha]	[מִכָּל הָעַמִּים | לַעֲבוֹדָתֶךָ]	[from all other peoples | to serve You]
v'Shab·bat kod·sh'cha	וְשַׁבַּת קָדְשְׁךָ	and Your holy Sabbath
b'a·ha·vah u·v'ra·tzon, hin·chal·ta·nu.	בְּאַהֲבָה וּבְרָצוֹן הִנְחַלְתָּנוּ.	with love and favor You have given us as a heritage.
Ba·ruch A·tah A·do·nai,	בָּרוּךְ אַתָּה יְיָ,	Blessed are You, Adonai,
m'ka·deish ha·Shab·bat.	מְקַדֵּשׁ הַשַּׁבָּת.	who makes the Sabbath holy.

---

1. Traditional Jews believe that God chose the Jewish people over all other nations and entered into an eternal covenant with it. A modern interpretation suggests that our distinction as a people reflects our task, to live our lives guided by God's teachings.

When the festival occurs on Friday evening, begin with Vay'hi erev, vay'hi voker וַיְהִי עֶרֶב וַיְהִי בֹקֶר on page 60 and continue until the end of the page. Then continue here, adding the words in parentheses for Shabbat.

Ba·ruch A·tah A·do·nai,	בָּרוּךְ אַתָּה יְיָ,	Blessed are You, Adonai,
E·lo·hei·nu Me·lech ha·O·lam,	אֱלֹהֵינוּ מֶלֶךְ הָעוֹלָם,	Our God, Ruler of the Universe,
bo·rei p'ri ha·ga·fen.	בּוֹרֵא פְּרִי הַגָּפֶן.	Creator of the fruit of the vine.
Ba·ruch A·tah A·do·nai,	בָּרוּךְ אַתָּה יְיָ,	Blessed are You, Adonai,
E·lo·hei·nu Me·lech ha·O·lam,	אֱלֹהֵינוּ מֶלֶךְ הָעוֹלָם,	Our God, Ruler of the Universe,
a·sher ba·char ba·nu	אֲשֶׁר בָּחַר בָּנוּ	who chose us
[mi·kol am	la·a·vo·da·to]	[מִכָּל עָם	לַעֲבוֹדָתוֹ]	[from all other nations	to serve You]
v'ro·m'ma·nu mi·kol la·shon,	וְרוֹמְמָנוּ מִכָּל לָשׁוֹן,	and raised us above every tongue,
v'ki·d'sha·nu	וְקִדְּשָׁנוּ	and made us holy
b'mitz·vo·tav.	בְּמִצְוֹתָיו.	with Your Commandments.
Va·ti·ten la·nu A·do·nai E·lo·hei·nu	וַתִּתֶּן לָנוּ יְיָ אֱלֹהֵינוּ	You gave us, Adonai our God,
b'a·ha·vah	בְּאַהֲבָה	with love
(Shab·ba·tot li·m'nu·chah u·)	(שַׁבָּתוֹת לִמְנוּחָה וּ)	(Sabbaths for rest and)
mo·a·dim l'sim·chah,	מוֹעֲדִים לְשִׂמְחָה,	festivals for joy,
cha·gim u·z'ma·nim l'sa·son,	חַגִּים וּזְמַנִּים לְשָׂשׂוֹן,	holidays and seasons for rejoicing,
et yom	אֶת יוֹם	this day of
(ha·Shab·bat ha·zeh v'et yom)	(הַשַּׁבָּת הַזֶּה וְאֶת יוֹם)	(the Sabbath, and this day of)

Sh'mini Atzeret/Simchat Torah:

הַשְּׁמִינִי חַג הָעֲצֶרֶת הַזֶּה,
זְמַן שִׂמְחָתֵנוּ,

the Eighth day Festival of Assembly,
the time of our Rejoicing,

ha-Sh'mi-ni chag ha-A-tze-ret ha-zeh,
z'man sim-cha-tei-nu,

Sukkot:

חַג הַסֻּכּוֹת הַזֶּה,
זְמַן שִׂמְחָתֵנוּ,

the Festival of Sukkot,
the time of our Rejoicing,

Chag ha-Suk-kot ha-zeh,
z'man sim-cha-tei-nu,

Shavuot:

חַג הַשָּׁבוּעוֹת הַזֶּה,
זְמַן מַתַּן תּוֹרָתֵנוּ,

the Festival of Weeks,
the time of the Giving of our Torah,

Chag ha-Sha-vu-ot ha-zeh,
z'man ma-tan to-ra-tei-nu,

Pesach:

חַג הַמַּצּוֹת הַזֶּה,
זְמַן חֵרוּתֵנוּ,

the Festival of Matzot,
the time of our freedom,

Chag ha-Ma-tzot ha-zeh,
z'man chei-ru-tei-nu,

(b'a-ha-vah) mik-ra ko-desh,	(בְּאַהֲבָה) מִקְרָא קֹדֶשׁ,	(in love) a sacred convocation,
zei-cher li-tzi-at Mitz-ra-yim.	זֵכֶר לִיצִיאַת מִצְרָיִם.	a reminder of the Exodus from Egypt.
Ki va-nu va-char-ta	כִּי בָנוּ בָחַרְתָּ	For You have chosen us
v'o-ta-nu ki-dash-ta	וְאוֹתָנוּ קִדַּשְׁתָּ	and set us apart
[mi-kol ha-a-mim | la-a-vo-da-te-cha]	[מִכָּל הָעַמִּים | לַעֲבוֹדָתֶךָ]	[from all other peoples | to serve You]
(v'Shab-bat) u-mo-a-dei kod-sh'cha	(וְשַׁבָּת) וּמוֹעֲדֵי קָדְשֶׁךָ	(and Your Sabbath) and sacred times
(b'a-ha-vah u-v'ra-tzon)	(בְּאַהֲבָה וּבְרָצוֹן)	(with love and favor)
b'sim-chah u-v'sa-son	בְּשִׂמְחָה וּבְשָׂשׂוֹן	with joy and gladness,
hin-chal-ta-nu.	הִנְחַלְתָּנוּ.	You have given us as a heritage.
Ba-ruch A-tah A-do-nai,	בָּרוּךְ אַתָּה יְיָ,	Blessed are You, Adonai,
m'ka-deish (ha-Shab-bat v')	מְקַדֵּשׁ (הַשַּׁבָּת וְ)	who sanctifies (the Sabbath and)
Yis-ra-eil v'ha-z'ma-nim.	יִשְׂרָאֵל וְהַזְּמַנִּים.	Israel and the seasons.

Ba·ruch A·tah A·do·nai,	בָּרוּךְ אַתָּה יְיָ,	Blessed are You, Adonai,
E·lo·hei·nu Me·lech ha·O·lam,	אֱלֹהֵינוּ מֶלֶךְ הָעוֹלָם,	our God Ruler of the Universe,
bo·rei m'o·rei ha·eish.	בּוֹרֵא מְאוֹרֵי הָאֵשׁ.	Creator of the fiery luminaries.
Ba·ruch A·tah A·do·nai,	בָּרוּךְ אַתָּה יְיָ,	Blessed are You, Adonai,
E·lo·hei·nu Me·lech ha·O·lam,	אֱלֹהֵינוּ מֶלֶךְ הָעוֹלָם,	our God Ruler of the Universe,
ha·mav·dil bein ko·desh l'chol,	הַמַּבְדִּיל בֵּין קֹדֶשׁ לְחוֹל,	who distinguishes between holy and ordinary,
bein or l'cho·shech,	בֵּין אוֹר לְחֹשֶׁךְ,	between light and darkness,
bein Yis·ra·eil la·a·mim,	בֵּין יִשְׂרָאֵל לָעַמִּים,	between Israel and other peoples,
bein yom ha·sh'vi·i	בֵּין יוֹם הַשְּׁבִיעִי	between the seventh day
l'shei·shet y'mei ha·ma·a·seh.	לְשֵׁשֶׁת יְמֵי הַמַּעֲשֶׂה.	and the six days of work.
Bein k'du·shat Shab·bat	בֵּין קְדֻשַּׁת שַׁבָּת	Between the holiness of Shabbat
lik·du·shat Yom Tov hiv·dal·ta,	לִקְדֻשַּׁת יוֹם טוֹב הִבְדַּלְתָּ,	and the holiness of the Festival You have distinguished,
v'et yom ha·sh'vi·i	וְאֶת יוֹם הַשְּׁבִיעִי	and the seventh day
mi·shei·shet y'mei ha·ma·a·seh	מִשֵּׁשֶׁת יְמֵי הַמַּעֲשֶׂה	[from] the six work days,
ki·dash·ta. Hiv·dal·ta v'ki·dash·ta	קִדַּשְׁתָּ. הִבְדַּלְתָּ וְקִדַּשְׁתָּ	You have set apart. You distinguished and sanctified
et a·m'cha Yis·ra·eil bik·du·sha·te·cha.	אֶת עַמְּךָ יִשְׂרָאֵל בִּקְדֻשָּׁתֶךָ.	Your people Israel with Your holiness.
Ba·ruch A·tah A·do·nai,	בָּרוּךְ אַתָּה יְיָ,	Blessed are You, Adonai,
Ha·mav·dil bein ko·desh l'ko·desh.	הַמַּבְדִּיל בֵּין קֹדֶשׁ לְקֹדֶשׁ.	who distinguishes between sacred time and sacred time.

On Sukkot add:

Ba·ruch A·tah A·do·nai,	בָּרוּךְ אַתָּה יְיָ,	Blessed are You, Adonai, Our God,
E·lo·hei·nu Me·lech ha·O·lam,	אֱלֹהֵינוּ מֶלֶךְ הָעוֹלָם,	Ruler of the Universe,
a·sher ki·d'sha·nu	אֲשֶׁר קִדְּשָׁנוּ	who made us holy
b'mitz·vo·tav	בְּמִצְוֹתָיו	with Your Commandments
v'tzi·va·nu	וְצִוָּנוּ	and commanded us
lei·sheiv ba·suk·kah.	לֵשֵׁב בַּסֻּכָּה.	to dwell in the Sukkah.

Conclude with Shehecheyanu on all festivals except for the last night(s) of Pesach.

Ba·ruch A·tah A·do·nai,	בָּרוּךְ אַתָּה יְיָ,	Blessed are You, Adonai, Our God,
E·lo·hei·nu Me·lech ha·O·lam,	אֱלֹהֵינוּ מֶלֶךְ הָעוֹלָם,	Ruler of the Universe,
she·he·che·ya·nu, v'ki·y'ma·nu,	שֶׁהֶחֱיָנוּ, וְקִיְּמָנוּ,	who has kept us alive, sustained us,
v'hi·gi·a·nu la·z'man ha·zeh.	וְהִגִּיעָנוּ לַזְּמַן הַזֶּה.	and enabled us to reach this season.

When Rosh Hashanah falls on Shabbat, begin with Vay'hi erev, vay'hi voker וַיְהִי עֶרֶב וַיְהִי בֹקֶר on page 60 and continue until the end of the page.

Then continue here, adding the words in parentheses for Shabbat.

Ba·ruch A·tah A·do·nai,	בָּרוּךְ אַתָּה יְיָ,	Blessed are You, Adonai,
E·lo·hei·nu Me·lech ha·O·lam,	אֱלֹהֵינוּ מֶלֶךְ הָעוֹלָם,	Our God, Ruler of the Universe,
bo·rei p'ri ha·ga·fen.	בּוֹרֵא פְּרִי הַגָּפֶן.	Creator of the fruit of the vine.
Ba·ruch A·tah A·do·nai,	בָּרוּךְ אַתָּה יְיָ	Blessed are You, Adonai
E·lo·hei·nu Me·lech ha·O·lam,	אֱלֹהֵינוּ מֶלֶךְ הָעוֹלָם,	Our God, Ruler of the Universe,
a·sher ba·char ba·nu	אֲשֶׁר בָּחַר בָּנוּ	who chose us
[mi·kol am | la·a·vo·da·to],	[מִכָּל עָם | לַעֲבוֹדָתוֹ],	[from all other nations | to serve You],
v'ro·m'ma·nu mi·kol la·shon,	וְרוֹמְמָנוּ מִכָּל לָשׁוֹן,	raised us above other languages,
v'ki·d'sha·nu b'mitz·vo·tav.	וְקִדְּשָׁנוּ בְּמִצְוֹתָיו.	and made us holy with Your Commandments.
Va·ti·ten la·nu A·do·nai E·lo·hei·nu	וַתִּתֶּן לָנוּ יְיָ אֱלֹהֵינוּ	You Gave us, Adonai our God,
b'a·ha·vah	בְּאַהֲבָה	with love
(et yom ha·Shab·bat ha·zeh v')	(אֶת יוֹם הַשַּׁבָּת הַזֶּה וְ)	(this Sabbath day for rest, and)
et Yom ha·Zi·ka·ron ha·zeh,	אֶת יוֹם הַזִּכָּרוֹן הַזֶּה,	this Day of Remembrance,
yom (zich·ron)	יוֹם (זִכְרוֹן)	a day for (recalling)
t'ru·ah (b'a·ha·vah)	תְּרוּעָה (בְּאַהֲבָה)	the Sounding of the Shofar (in love),
mik·ra ko·desh,	מִקְרָא קֹדֶשׁ,	a sacred convocation,
zei·cher li·tzi·at Mitz·ra·yim.	זֵכֶר לִיצִיאַת מִצְרָיִם.	a reminder of the Exodus from Egypt.

Ki va·nu va·char·ta	כִּי בָנוּ בָחַרְתָּ	For You have chosen us
v'o·ta·nu ki·dash·ta	וְאוֹתָנוּ קִדַּשְׁתָּ	and set us apart
[mi·kol ha·a·mim | la·a·vo·da·te·cha],	[מִכָּל הָעַמִּים | לַעֲבוֹדָתֶךָ],	[from all peoples | to serve You],
u'd·var·cha e·met v'ka·yam la·ad.	וּדְבָרְךָ אֱמֶת וְקַיָּם לָעַד.	and Your Word is true, enduring forever.

Ba·ruch A·tah A·do·nai,	בָּרוּךְ אַתָּה יְיָ,	Blessed are You, Adonai,
Me·lech al kol ha·a·retz,	מֶלֶךְ עַל כָּל הָאָרֶץ,	Ruler over all the earth,
m'ka·deish	מְקַדֵּשׁ	who makes holy
(ha·Shab·bat v') Yis·ra·eil	(הַשַּׁבָּת וְ) יִשְׂרָאֵל	(the Sabbath and) Israel
v'Yom ha·Zi·ka·ron.	וְיוֹם הַזִּכָּרוֹן.	and the Day of Remembrance.

When Rosh Hashanah occurs at the conclusion of Shabbat, turn back to page 64 and add the abbreviated Havdalah.

Conclude with Shehecheyanu.

Ba·ruch A·tah A·do·nai,	בָּרוּךְ אַתָּה יְיָ,	Blessed are You, Adonai, Our God,
E·lo·hei·nu Me·lech ha·O·lam,	אֱלֹהֵינוּ מֶלֶךְ הָעוֹלָם,	Ruler of the Universe,
she·he·che·ya·nu, v'ki·y'ma·nu,	שֶׁהֶחֱיָנוּ, וְקִיְּמָנוּ,	who has kept us alive, sustained us,
v'hi·gi·a·nu la·z'man ha·zeh.	וְהִגִּיעָנוּ לַזְּמַן הַזֶּה.	and enabled us to reach this season.

For Yom Tov that falls on a weekday, begin on page 70, second paragraph.

There is a custom to precede the Kiddush on Shabbat morning with the following passage:

Im ta·shiv mi·shab·bat rag·le·cha,	אִם תָּשִׁיב מִשַּׁבָּת רַגְלֶךָ,	If you turn away your foot because of the Sabbath,[1]
A·sot cha·fa·tze·cha	עֲשׂוֹת חֲפָצֶיךָ	[refrain] from pursuing your business
b'yom kod·shi,	בְּיוֹם קָדְשִׁי,	on My holy day,
V'ka·ra·ta la·shab·bat o·neg	וְקָרָאתָ לַשַּׁבָּת עֹנֶג	and call the Sabbath a delight,
Lik·dosh A·do·nai m'chu·bad,	לִקְדוֹשׁ יְיָ מְכֻבָּד,	the holy of Adonai honourable,
V'chi·bad·to	וְכִבַּדְתּוֹ	and honor it
mei·a·sot d'ra·che·cha,	מֵעֲשׂוֹת דְּרָכֶיךָ,	by not going your [usual] ways,
Mi·m'tzo chef·tz'cha,	מִמְּצוֹא חֶפְצְךָ,	nor pursuing your business,
V'da·beir da·var,	וְדַבֵּר דָּבָר,	nor speaking a word [thereof],
Az tit·a·nag al A·do·nai,	אָז תִּתְעַנַּג עַל יְיָ,	then shall you delight in Adonai,
V'hir·kav·ti·cha	וְהִרְכַּבְתִּיךָ	and I will set you astride
al ba·mo·tei a·retz,	עַל בָּמֳתֵי אָרֶץ,	the high places of the earth,
V'ha·a·chal·ti·cha na·cha·lat	וְהַאֲכַלְתִּיךָ נַחֲלַת	and I will let you enjoy the heritage
Ya·a·kov a·vi·cha,	יַעֲקֹב אָבִיךָ,	of Jacob your father,
Ki pi A·do·nai di·beir.	כִּי פִּי יְיָ דִּבֵּר.	for the mouth of Adonai has spoken.

— *ISAIAH 58:13-14*

---

1. i.e., you refrain from overstepping the Sabbath boundary (*t'chum Shabbat*).

V'sha·m'ru v'nei Yis·ra·eil	וְשָׁמְרוּ בְנֵי יִשְׂרָאֵל	And the Children of Israel shall keep
et ha·Shab·bat,	אֶת הַשַּׁבָּת,	the Sabbath,
la·a·sot et ha·Shab·bat	לַעֲשׂוֹת אֶת הַשַּׁבָּת	to make the Sabbath
l'do·ro·tam b'rit olam.	לְדֹרֹתָם בְּרִית עוֹלָם.	for generations as a lasting covenant.
Bei·ni u·vein b'nei Yis·ra·eil	בֵּינִי וּבֵין בְּנֵי יִשְׂרָאֵל	Between Me and the Children of Israel
ot hi l'o·lam,	אוֹת הִיא לְעוֹלָם,	it is a sign for all eternity,
ki shei·shet ya·mim a·sah A·do·nai	כִּי שֵׁשֶׁת יָמִים עָשָׂה יְיָ	since for six days Adonai made
et ha·sha·ma·yim v'et ha·a·retz,	אֶת הַשָּׁמַיִם וְאֶת הָאָרֶץ,	the heavens and the earth,
u·va·yom ha·sh'vi·i	וּבַיּוֹם הַשְּׁבִיעִי	and on the seventh day
sha·vat va·yi·na·fash.	שָׁבַת וַיִּנָּפַשׁ.	God rested and was refreshed. — EXODUS 31:16-17

Za·chor et yom ha·Shab·bat l'ka·d'sho.	זָכוֹר אֶת יוֹם הַשַּׁבָּת לְקַדְּשׁוֹ.	Remember the Sabbath day to keep it holy.
Shei·shet ya·mim ta·a·vod	שֵׁשֶׁת יָמִים תַּעֲבֹד	Six days shall you labor
v'a·si·ta kol m'lach·te·cha,	וְעָשִׂיתָ כָּל מְלַאכְתֶּךָ,	and do all of your work,
v'yom ha·sh'vi·i Shab·bat	וְיוֹם הַשְּׁבִיעִי שַׁבָּת	but the seventh day is a Sabbath
lA·do·nai E·lo·he·cha.	לַיְיָ אֱלֹהֶיךָ.	to Adonai your God.
Lo ta·a·seh chol m'la·chah	לֹא תַעֲשֶׂה כָל מְלָאכָה	Do not do any work:
A·tah u·vin·cha u·vi·te·cha	אַתָּה וּבִנְךָ וּבִתֶּךָ	not you, your son, or your daughter,
av·d'cha va·a·ma·t'cha	עַבְדְּךָ וַאֲמָתְךָ	nor your servingman or servingwoman,
u·v·hem·te·cha	וּבְהֶמְתֶּךָ	nor your cattle,
v'gei·r'cha a·sher bish·a·re·cha,	וְגֵרְךָ אֲשֶׁר בִּשְׁעָרֶיךָ,	nor the stranger within your gates,

Ki shei·shet ya·mim a·sah A·do·nai   כִּי שֵׁשֶׁת יָמִים עָשָׂה יְיָ   since for six days Adonai made

et ha·sha·ma·yim v'et ha·a·retz   אֶת הַשָּׁמַיִם וְאֶת הָאָרֶץ   the heavens and the earth,

et ha·yam v'et kol a·sher bam   אֶת הַיָּם וְאֶת כָּל אֲשֶׁר בָּם   the seas, and all they contain

va·ya·nach ba·yom ha·sh'vi·i.   וַיָּנַח בַּיּוֹם הַשְּׁבִיעִי.   and rested on the seventh day.

Al kein bei·rach A·do·nai   עַל כֵּן בֵּרַךְ יְיָ   Therefore Adonai blessed

et yom ha·Shab·bat va·y'ka·d'shei·hu.   אֶת יוֹם הַשַּׁבָּת וַיְקַדְּשֵׁהוּ.   the seventh day and made it holy. — EXODUS 20:8-11

On Sukkot, Sh'mini Atzeret/Simchat Torah, Pesach, and Shavuot, begin here. If it is also Shabbat, continue here.

Va·y'da·beir Mo·sheh et mo·a·dei A·do·nai   וַיְדַבֵּר מֹשֶׁה אֶת מֹעֲדֵי יְיָ   And Moses proclaimed the festivals of Adonai

el b'nei Yis·ra·eil.   אֶל בְּנֵי יִשְׂרָאֵל.   to the Children of Israel. — LEVITICUS 23:44

On Rosh Hashanah, begin here. If it is also Shabbat, continue here.

Tik·u va·cho·desh sho·far,   תִּקְעוּ בַחֹדֶשׁ שׁוֹפָר,   Sound the shofar on the new moon,

ba·ke·seh l'yom cha·gei·nu.   בַּכֶּסֶה לְיוֹם חַגֵּנוּ.   on the full moon for our festival day.

Ki chok l'Yis·ra·eil hu,   כִּי חֹק לְיִשְׂרָאֵל הוּא,   For this is a statute of Israel,

mish·pat lEi·lo·hei Ya·a·kov.   מִשְׁפָּט לֵאלֹהֵי יַעֲקֹב.   a law of the God of Jacob. — PSALMS 81: 4-5

On Shabbat, festivals, and Rosh Hashanah, continue here.
When making Kiddush over a beverage other than wine or grape juice, use the alternative blessing (shehakol nihyeh bidvaro).

Sav·rei cha·vei·rai,   סָבְרֵי חֲבֵרַי,   With the approval of my friends,

Ba·ruch A·tah A·do·nai,   בָּרוּךְ אַתָּה יְיָ,   Blessed are You, Adonai,

E·lo·hei·nu Me·lech ha·O·lam,   אֱלֹהֵינוּ מֶלֶךְ הָעוֹלָם,   Our God, Ruler of the Universe,

bo·rei p'ri ha·ga·fen.   בּוֹרֵא פְּרִי הַגָּפֶן.   Creator of the fruit of the vine.

When ritually washing hands before the meal, recite this blessing:

Ba·ruch A·tah A·do·nai,	בָּרוּךְ אַתָּה יְיָ,	Blessed are You, Adonai,
E·lo·hei·nu Me·lech ha·O·lam,	אֱלֹהֵינוּ מֶלֶךְ הָעוֹלָם,	Our God, Ruler of the Universe,
a·sher ki·d'sha·nu b'mitz·vo·tav,	אֲשֶׁר קִדְּשָׁנוּ בְּמִצְוֹתָיו,	who made us holy with Your Commandments,
v'tzi·va·nu	וְצִוָּנוּ	and commanded us
al n'ti·lat ya·da·yim.	עַל נְטִילַת יָדָיִם.	concerning washing the hands.

One of the connotations of the root *n-t-l* is "raising" or "lifting up." We wash our hands to spiritually prepare to eat the food God gave us, and raise our hands in thanksgiving. Some recite the verse at the right (Psalms 134:2) before saying the blessing.

S'u y'dei·chem ko·desh u·va·r'chu et A·do·nai.

שְׂאוּ יְדֵכֶם קֹדֶשׁ
וּבָרְכוּ אֶת־יְיָ.

Lift up your hands in holiness and bless Adonai.

It is customary not to speak between handwashing and reciting HaMotzi, making the preparation for the meal a single, complete act. For this reason, many hum a niggun (wordless melody) until all have gathered for HaMotzi.

Ba·ruch A·tah A·do·nai,	בָּרוּךְ אַתָּה יְיָ,	Blessed are You, Adonai,
E·lo·hei·nu Me·lech ha·O·lam,	אֱלֹהֵינוּ מֶלֶךְ הָעוֹלָם,	Our God, Ruler of the Universe,
ha·mo·tzi le·chem min ha·a·retz.	הַמּוֹצִיא לֶחֶם מִן הָאָרֶץ.	who brings forth bread from the earth.

After HaMotzi, the challah is dipped in honey instead of salt. It is the custom to then dip an apple in honey, recite the blessing borei p'ri ha'etz, followed by the y'hi ratzon prayer. Eating apples dipped in honey on Rosh Hashanah symbolizes our hope for a sweet new year.

Ba·ruch A·tah A·do·nai E·lo·hei·nu,	בָּרוּךְ אַתָּה יְיָ,	Blessed are You, Adonai, Our God,
Me·lech ha·O·lam,	אֱלֹהֵינוּ מֶלֶךְ הָעוֹלָם,	Ruler of the Universe,
bo·rei p'ri ha·eitz.	בּוֹרֵא פְּרִי הָעֵץ.	Creator of the fruit of the tree.

Y'hi ra·tzon mi·l' fa·ne·cha,	יְהִי רָצוֹן מִלְּפָנֶיךָ,	May it be Your Will,
A·do·nai E·lo·hei·nu	יְיָ אֱלֹהֵינוּ	Adonai our God
vEi·lo·hei a·vo·tei·nu [v'i·mo·tei·nu],	וֵאלֹהֵי אֲבוֹתֵינוּ [וְאִמּוֹתֵינוּ],	and God of our ancestors,
she·t'cha·deish a·leinu	שֶׁתְּחַדֵּשׁ עָלֵינוּ	to renew us
sha·nah to·vah u·m'tu·kah.	שָׁנָה טוֹבָה וּמְתוּקָה.	with a good, sweet year.

Some have the custom to make a blessing over various foods which have symbolic significance for the New Year. Here are a few suggestions.

Y'hi ra·tzon mi·l' fa·ne·cha	יְהִי רָצוֹן מִלְּפָנֶיךָ	May it be Your Will
A·do·nai E·lo·hei·nu	יְיָ אֱלֹהֵינוּ	Adonai our God
vEi·lo·hei a·vo·tei·nu [v'i·mo·tei·nu]	וֵאלֹהֵי אֲבוֹתֵינוּ [וְאִמּוֹתֵינוּ]	and God of our ancestors

On pomegranate (*rimon*):	On carrots (*gezer*):	On squash (*kara*):
שֶׁנִּהְיֶה מְלֵאִי מִצְוֹת כְּרִמּוֹן.	שֶׁיִּקָּרַע רוֹעַ גְּזַר דִּינֵנוּ.	שֶׁיִּקָּרְאוּ לְפָנֶיךָ זְכִיּוֹתֵינוּ.
that we should be filled with as many good deeds as there are seeds in a pomegranate.	that the evil decree against us will be torn up.	that our merits may be called out before you.
she·nih·yeh m'lei·ei mitz·vot k'ri·mon.	*she·yi·ka·ra ro·a g'zar di·nei·nu.*	*she·yi·ka·r'u l'fa·ne·cha z'chu·yo·tei·nu.*

The origin of the ceremony of Ushpizin (Aramaic for "guests") can be found in the Zohar (Emor 3:103b; cf. Pinchas 3:255b), which states that when a person sits in his sukkah, Abraham, five righteous ones, along with David, join him there. But the presence of the supernal guests was conditional upon the hosts inviting the poor to join them. From here evolved the custom of inviting many guests into our sukkot and inviting along with them distinguished biblical ancestors as guests of honor. The following text welcomes both male and female ancestors into the sukkah, that their virtues may inspire us. After inviting biblical guests, participants may also welcome other meaningful spiritual role models into the sukkah.

Ha·rei·ni [mu·chan u·m'zu·man (m)|	הֲרֵינִי [מוּכָן וּמְזוּמָּן		I am hereby
mu·cha·nah u·m'zu·me·net (f)]	מוּכָנָה וּמְזוּמֶּנֶת]	ready and prepared
l'ka·yeim mitz·vat su·kah,	לְקַיֵּם מִצְוַת סֻכָּה,	to fulfill the commandment of sukkah,
ka·a·sher tzi·va·ni ha·Bo·rei	כַּאֲשֶׁר צִוַּנִי הַבּוֹרֵא	as commanded by the Creator
yit·ba·rach sh'mo:	יִתְבָּרַךְ שְׁמוֹ:	Whose Name shall be blessed:
Ba·su·kot teish·vu shiv·at ya·mim,	בַּסֻּכֹּת תֵּשְׁבוּ שִׁבְעַת יָמִים,	"In sukkot shall you dwell for seven days,
kol ha·ez·rach b'Yis·ra·eil	כָּל הָאֶזְרָח בְּיִשְׂרָאֵל	all citizens of Israel
yeish·vu ba·su·kot.	יֵשְׁבוּ בַּסֻּכֹּת.	shall dwell in sukkot.
L'ma·an yei·d'u do·ro·tei·chem	לְמַעַן יֵדְעוּ דֹרֹתֵיכֶם	So that your [future] generations shall know
ki va·su·kot	כִּי בַסֻּכּוֹת	that it was in sukkot
ho·shav·ti et b'nei Yis·ra·eil	הוֹשַׁבְתִּי אֶת בְּנֵי יִשְׂרָאֵל	that I caused the Israelites to dwell
b'ho·tzi·i o·tam mei·e·retz Mitz·ra·yim.	בְּהוֹצִיאִי אוֹתָם מֵאֶרֶץ מִצְרָיִם.	when I took them out of the Land of Egypt."

— LEVITICUS 24:42-43

Y'hi ra·tzon mi·l'fa·ne·cha,	יְהִי רָצוֹן מִלְּפָנֶיךָ,	May it be Your will,
A·do·nai E·lo·hai	יְיָ אֱלֹהַי	Adonai my God
vEi·lo·hei a·vo·tai [v'i·mo·tai],	וֵאלֹהֵי אֲבוֹתַי [וְאִמּוֹתַי],	and God of my ancestors,
she·tash·reh sh'chi·nat·cha	שֶׁתַּשְׁרֶה שְׁכִינָתְךָ	to allow Your Divine Presence to dwell

bei·nei·nu v'tif·ros a·lei·nu	בֵּינֵינוּ וְתִפְרוֹשׂ עָלֵינוּ	in our midst; and spread over us
su·kat sh'lo·me·cha.	סֻכַּת שְׁלוֹמֶךָ.	the shelter of Your peace.
La·r'ei·vim gam tz'mei·im	לָרְעֵבִים גַּם צְמֵאִים	To all who are hungry and thirsty
tein lach·mam u·mei·mam ha·ne·e·ma·nim.	תֵּן לַחְמָם וּמֵימָם הַנֶּאֱמָנִים.	give sufficient bread and water.
U·t'za·kei·nu lei·sheiv ya·mim ra·bim	וּתְזַכֵּנוּ לֵישֵׁב יָמִים רַבִּים	Grant us many days to grow old
al ha·a·da·mah, ad·mat ko·desh,	עַל הָאֲדָמָה, אַדְמַת קֹדֶשׁ,	upon the earth, the holy land,
ba·a·vo·da·t'cha u·v'yir·a·te·cha.	בַּעֲבוֹדָתְךָ וּבְיִרְאָתֶךָ.	that we may serve and revere You.
Ba·ruch A·do·nai l'o·lam, a·mein v'a·mein.	בָּרוּךְ יְיָ לְעוֹלָם, אָמֵן וְאָמֵן.	Blessed be Adonai forever, amen, amen.

A·za·mein li·s'u·da·ti ush·pi·zin i·la·in:	אֲזַמֵּן לִסְעֻדָּתִי אֻשְׁפִּיזִין עִלָּאִין:	I invite to my meal the revered guests:
Av·ra·ham, Yitz·chak, Ya·a·kov,	אַבְרָהָם, יִצְחָק, יַעֲקֹב,	Abraham, Isaac, Jacob,
Yo·seif, Mo·sheh, A·ha·ron, v'Da·vid;	יוֹסֵף, מֹשֶׁה, אַהֲרֹן, וְדָוִד;	Joseph, Moses, Aaron, and David;
Sa·rah, Riv·kah, Ra·cheil, Lei·ah,	שָׂרָה, רִבְקָה, רָחֵל, לֵאָה,	Sarah, Rebecca, Leah, Rachel,
Mir·yam, D'vo·rah, v'Rut.	מִרְיָם, דְּבוֹרָה, וְרוּת.	Miriam, Deborah, and Ruth.

Insert the name of the night's special guests in the blank. Conclude the statement by reciting the names of the remaining pairs.

B'ma·tu mi·nach, _____,	_____ , בְּמָטוּ מִנָּךְ	May it please you, _____
ush·pi·zei i·la·ei, d'yeit·vu i·mi	אֻשְׁפִּיזֵי עִלָּאֵי, דְּיֵתְבוּ עִמִּי	exalted guests, that all the exalted guests
v'i·ma·chon kol ush·pi·zei i·la·ei:	וְעִמָּכוֹן כָּל אֻשְׁפִּיזֵי עִלָּאֵי:	may dwell with me and with you:

(Read the six remaining name pairs below.)

First Night:	Second Night:	Third Night:	Fourth Night:	Fifth Night:	Sixth Night:	Seventh Night:
אַבְרָהָם וְשָׂרָה	יִצְחָק וְרִבְקָה	יַעֲקֹב וְלֵאָה	יוֹסֵף וְרָחֵל	מֹשֶׁה וּמִרְיָם	אַהֲרֹן וּדְבוֹרָה	דָּוִד וְרוּת
Av·ra·ham v'Sa·rah	Yitz·chak v'Riv·kah	Ya·a·kov v'Lei·ah	Yo·seif v'Ra·cheil	Mo·sheh u·Mir·yam	A·ha·ron u·D'vo·rah	Da·vid v'Rut

Songs for the Sabbath Evening

Kol M'kadeish   כָּל מְקַדֵּשׁ

This song was probably composed by Moses ben Kalonimos of Mainz (end of tenth century) (see acrostic formed by words *mekadesh*, *shomer* and *harbeh*, which are the second words of the first three stichs). Every verse of this song ends with a biblical verse. Beginning with the second verse the song is arranged in an alphabetic acrostic.

Kol m'ka·deish sh'vi·i	כָּל **מְקַדֵּשׁ** שְׁבִיעִי	Whoever sanctifies the seventh [day]	1. Numbers 1:52
ka·ra·ui lo;	כָּרָאוּי לוֹ;	as one should;	2. The Temple.
kol sho·meir Shab·bat	כָּל **שׁוֹמֵר** שַׁבָּת	whoever keeps the Sabbath	3. i.e., the Torah.
ka·dat mei·cha·l'lo	כְּדָת מֵחַלְּלוֹ	properly, unprofaned	
s'cha·ro har·beih m'od	שְׂכָרוֹ **הַרְבֵּה** מְאֹד	will be greatly rewarded,	
al pi fa·o·lo,	עַל פִּי פָעֳלוֹ,	as deemed appropriate,	
ish al ma·cha·nei·hu	אִישׁ עַל מַחֲנֵהוּ	"whether in the camp	
v'ish al dig·lo.	וְאִישׁ עַל דִּגְלוֹ.	or under the banner." [1]	
O·ha·vei A·do·nai ha·m'cha·kim	**אוֹהֲבֵי** יְיָ הַמְחַכִּים	Lovers of God, those who wait	
b'vin·yan A·ri·eil,	בְּבִנְיַן אֲרִיאֵל,	for the building of Ariel,[2]	
b'yom ha·Shab·bat (ko·desh)	בְּיוֹם הַשַּׁבָּת (קֹדֶשׁ)	on the (holy) Sabbath	
si·su v'sim·chu	שִׂישׂוּ וְשִׂמְחוּ	rejoice and be happy	
kim·ka·b'lei ma·tan Na·cha·li·eil.	כִּמְקַבְּלֵי מַתַּן נַחֲלִיאֵל.	as if you received Nachaliel's gift.[3]	

Gam s'u y'dei·chem ko·desh	גַּם שְׂאוּ יְדֵיכֶם קֹדֶשׁ	Lift up your hands in holiness[4]
v'im·ru la·Eil:	וְאִמְרוּ לָאֵל:	and say to God:
Ba·ruch A·do·nai a·sher na·tan	בָּרוּךְ יְיָ אֲשֶׁר נָתַן	"Blessed is God who has given
m'nu·chah l'a·mo Yis·ra·eil.	מְנוּחָה לְעַמּוֹ יִשְׂרָאֵל.	rest to the People Israel."[5]

Do·r'shei A·do·nai,	דּוֹרְשֵׁי יְיָ,	God-seekers,
ze·ra Av·ra·ham o·ha·vo,	זֶרַע אַבְרָהָם אוֹהֲבוֹ,	seed of Abraham, lover of God,
ha·ma·cha·rim la·tzeit min ha·Shab·bat,	הַמְאַחֲרִים לָצֵאת מִן הַשַּׁבָּת,	who are late to leave the Sabbath,
u·m'ma·ha·rim la·vo,	וּמְמַהֲרִים לָבוֹא,	early to enter it,
u·s'mei·chim l'shom·ro,	וּשְׂמֵחִים לְשָׁמְרוֹ,	glad to keep it,
u·l'a·reiv ei·ru·vo.	וּלְעָרֵב עֵרוּבוֹ.	and prepare its eruv.[6]
Zeh ha·yom a·sah A·do·nai	זֶה הַיּוֹם עָשָׂה יְיָ	"This is the day God has made,
na·gi·lah v'nis·m'chah vo.	נָגִילָה וְנִשְׂמְחָה בוֹ.	let us rejoice and be happy in it."[7]

Zich·ru To·rat Mo·sheh	זִכְרוּ תּוֹרַת מֹשֶׁה	Remember the Torah of Moses,[8]
b'mitz·vat Shab·bat g'ru·sah.	בְּמִצְוַת שַׁבָּת גְּרוּסָה.	learnt through the Sabbath commandment.
Cha·ru·tah la·yom ha·sh'vi·i,	חֲרוּתָה לַיּוֹם הַשְּׁבִיעִי,	The seventh day is engraved,[9]
k'cha·lah bein rei·o·te·ha m'shu·ba·tzah.	כְּכַלָּה בֵּין רֵעוֹתֶיהָ מְשֻׁבָּצָה.	set [in stone] like a bride among her maids.
T'ho·rim yi·ra·shu·ha vi·ka·d'shu·ha	טְהוֹרִים יִירָשׁוּהָ וִיקַדְּשׁוּהָ	The pure inherit and sanctify it
b'ma·a·mar kol a·sher a·sah.	בְּמַאֲמַר כָּל אֲשֶׁר עָשָׂה.	with the words "all that [God] did."[10]
Va·y'chal E·lo·him ba·yom ha·sh'vi·i	וַיְכַל אֱלֹהִים בַּיּוֹם הַשְּׁבִיעִי	"And God ceased on the seventh day
m'lach·to a·sher a·sah.	מְלַאכְתּוֹ אֲשֶׁר עָשָׂה.	all the work God had done."[11]

---

4. Psalms 134:2   5. 1 Kings 8:56   6. Sabbath boundary within which carrying is permitted.

7. Psalms 118:24   8. Malachi 3:22   9. On the tablets.   10. Genesis 1:31   11. Genesis 2:2

Yom ka·dosh hu	יוֹם קָדוֹשׁ הוּא	It is a holy day
mi·bo·o v'ad tzei·to.	מִבּוֹאוֹ וְעַד צֵאתוֹ.	from beginning to end.
Kol ze·ra Ya·a·kov y'cha·b'du·hu	כָּל זֶרַע יַעֲקֹב יְכַבְּדוּהוּ	Let all of Jacob's seed honor it
kid·var ha·Me·lech v'da·to,	כִּדְבַר הַמֶּלֶךְ וְדָתוֹ,	as if it were the king's word and law,
la·nu·ach bo v'lis·mo·ach	לָנְוּחַ בּוֹ וְלִשְׂמְוֹחַ	by resting on it and enjoying
b'ta·a·nug a·chol v'sha·to.	בְּתַעֲנוּג אָכוֹל וְשָׁתוֹ.	food and drink.
Kol a·dat Yis·ra·eil	כָּל עֲדַת יִשְׂרָאֵל	"The entire community of Israel
ya·a·su o·to.	יַעֲשׂוּ אֹתוֹ.	shall keep it." [12]
M'shoch chas·d'cha l'yo·d'e·cha,	מְשׁוֹךְ חַסְדְּךָ לְיוֹדְעֶיךָ,	Extend your kindness to those who know you,[13]
Eil ka·no v'no·keim,	אֵל קַנּוֹא וְנוֹקֵם,	O jealous and vengeful God,[14]
no·t'rei la·yom ha·sh'vi·i	נוֹטְרֵי לַיּוֹם הַשְּׁבִיעִי	those who keep the seventh day
za·chor v'sha·mor l'ha·keim.	זָכוֹר וְשָׁמוֹר לְהָקֵם.	by upholding "remember and keep."[15]
Sa·m'cheim b'vin·yan sha·leim,	שַׂמְּחֵם בְּבִנְיַן שָׁלֵם,	Cause them to rejoice in the restoration of Jerusalem,
b'or pa·ne·cha tav·hi·keim.	בְּאוֹר פָּנֶיךָ תַּבְהִיקֵם.	let them bask in Your reflected glory.
Yir·v'yun mi·de·shen bei·te·cha,	יִרְוְיֻן מִדֶּשֶׁן בֵּיתֶךָ,	"Let them be sated from the abundance of your home
v'na·chal a·da·ne·cha tash·keim.	וְנַחַל עֲדָנֶיךָ תַשְׁקֵם.	and from the river of your delights give them to drink."[16]

---

12. Exodus 12:47

13. Psalms 36:11

14. Nahum 1:2. The poet is asking God to be merciful with those that know God even though they deserve to be punished for their sins.

15. These words begin the two versions of the Sabbath commmandment in the Ten Commandments in Exodus 19:7 and Deuteronomy 5:11.

16. Psalms 36:9

A·zor la·sho·v'tim ba·sh'vi·i,
be·cha·rish u·va·ka·tzir l'o·la·mim,
po·s'im bo p'si·ah k'ta·nah,
so·a·dim bo l'va·reich
sha·losh p'a·mim.
Tzid·ka·tam tatz·hir
k'or shiv·at ha·ya·mim.
A·do·nai E·lo·hei Yis·ra·eil,
ha·vah ta·mim.
A·do·nai E·lo·hei Yis·ra·eil,
t'shu·at o·la·mim.

עֲזוֹר לַשּׁוֹבְתִים בַּשְּׁבִיעִי,
בֶּחָרִישׁ וּבַקָּצִיר לְעוֹלָמִים,
פּוֹסְעִים בּוֹ פְּסִיעָה קְטַנָּה,
סוֹעֲדִים בּוֹ לְבָרֵךְ
שָׁלֹשׁ פְּעָמִים.
צִדְקָתָם תַּצְהִיר
כְּאוֹר שִׁבְעַת הַיָּמִים.
יְיָ אֱלֹהֵי יִשְׂרָאֵל,
הָבָה תָמִים.
יְיָ אֱלֹהֵי יִשְׂרָאֵל,
תְּשׁוּעַת עוֹלָמִים.

Help those who cease [working] on the seventh [day],
in plowtime and in harvest,[17] forever;
walking on it at a leisurely pace,[18]
dining on it, in order to bless [You]
three times.[19]
Let their righteousness shine forth
like the light of the seven days [of creation].
"Adonai, God of Israel,
declare the right."[20]
Adonai God of Israel,
source of everlasting salvation.[21]

---

17. After Exodus 34:21

18. According to the Talmud, your gait on the Sabbath should be different from that of the rest of the week (Shabbat 113b).

19. According to the Talmud, one is obligated to have three meals on the Sabbath.

20. 1 Samuel 14:41

21. This last line was substituted for the last stanza which was dropped from most siddurim. This last stanza, which completes the alphabetical acrostic, is found in *Machzor Vitry*, a twelfth-century siddur compiled by Simchah of Vitry, a student of Rashi.

M'nuchah v'Simchah מְנוּחָה וְשִׂמְחָה

The author's name, Mosheh, is indicated by the first letters of the first three verses. His identity is not known.

M'nu·chah v'sim·chah or la·y'hu·dim,
yom shab·ba·ton, yom ma·cha·ma·dim.
Sho·m'rav v'zo·ch'rav hei·mah m'i·dim
ki l'shi·shah kol b'ru·im v'o·m'dim.

מְנוּחָה וְשִׂמְחָה אוֹר לַיְּהוּדִים,
יוֹם שַׁבָּתוֹן, יוֹם מַחֲמַדִּים.
שׁוֹמְרָיו וְזוֹכְרָיו הֵמָּה מְעִידִים
כִּי לְשִׁשָּׁה כֹּל בְּרוּאִים וְעוֹמְדִים.

Rest and joy, light for the Jews,
a day of complete rest, a day of delights.
Those who keep and remember it[1] will attest
that in six days all creation was completed.[2]

Sh'mei sha·ma·yim, e·retz v'ya·mim,
kol tz'va ma·rom, g'vo·him v'ra·mim;
ta·nin va·dam, v'cha·yat r'ei·mim.
Ki b'yah A·do·nai tzur o·la·mim.

שְׁמֵי שָׁמַיִם, אֶרֶץ וְיַמִּים,
כָּל צְבָא מָרוֹם, גְּבוֹהִים וְרָמִים;
תַּנִּין וְאָדָם, וְחַיַּת רְאֵמִים.
כִּי בְּיָהּ יְיָ צוּר עוֹלָמִים.

The highest heavens, the land and seas,
all the heavenly forces, lofty and exalted;
sea-monsters, humans, and wild animals.
For in Yah Adonai there is strength everlasting.[3]

Hu a·sher di·ber l'am s'gu·la·to,
Sha·mor l'ka·d'sho mi·bo·o ad tzei·to,
Shab·bat ko·desh yom chem·da·to,
ki vo sha·vat mi·kol m'lach·to.

הוּא אֲשֶׁר דִּבֶּר לְעַם סְגֻלָּתוֹ,
שָׁמוֹר לְקַדְּשׁוֹ מִבּוֹאוֹ עַד צֵאתוֹ,
שַׁבַּת קֹדֶשׁ יוֹם חֶמְדָּתוֹ,
כִּי בוֹ שָׁבַת מִכָּל מְלַאכְתּוֹ.

It was God who spoke to the treasured people:
Keep it hallowed from its arrival till its departure,
the holy Sabbath, God's beloved day,
for on it God rested from all God's work.

---

1. An allusion to Exodus 20:8, "Remember the Sabbath day, to make it holy" and Deuteronomy 5:12 "Keep the Sabbath day to make it holy."

2. The next verse mentions the various parts of creation.

3. Isaiah 26.4

B'mitz·vat Shab·bat Eil ya·cha·li·tzach, / בְּמִצְוַת שַׁבָּת אֵל יַחֲלִיצָךְ,
kum k'ra ei·lav ya·chish l'a·m'tzach. / קוּם קְרָא אֵלָיו יָחִישׁ לְאַמְּצָךְ.
Nish·mat kol chai v'gam na·a·ri·tzach, / נִשְׁמַת כָּל חַי וְגַם נַעֲרִיצָךְ,
e·chol b'sim·chah ki ch'var ra·tzach. / אֱכוֹל בְּשִׂמְחָה כִּי כְבָר רָצָךְ.

With the mitzvah of Shabbat God makes you strong,
Arise, call out to God, who will hasten to fortify you.
[Pray] the *Nishmat*[4] and the *K'dushah*[5] prayers,
Eat with joy, God is already pleased with you.

B'mish·neh le·chem v'kid·dush ra·bah, / בְּמִשְׁנֶה לֶחֶם וְקִדּוּשׁ רַבָּה,
b'rov mat·a·mim v'ru·ach n'di·vah, / בְּרֹב מַטְעַמִּים וְרוּחַ נְדִיבָה,
yiz·ku l'rav tuv ha·mit·a·n'gim bah, / יִזְכּוּ לְרַב טוּב הַמִּתְעַנְּגִים בָּהּ,
b'vi·at go·eil l'o·lam ha·ba. / בְּבִיאַת גּוֹאֵל לְעוֹלָם הַבָּא.

With two loaves and the great [daytime] Kiddush,
with abundant delicacies and a generous spirit,
those who enjoy it shall merit much goodness,
the advent of the Redeemer, the world to come.[6]

---

4. The last prayer of the preliminary service before *Shacharit*.

5. The *K'dushah* prayer in the *Shacharit* service *(Nusach Sefarad)* begins with
   "*Nakdishach v'naaritzach.*"

6. The Sabbath is often compared to the World to Come.

Mah Y'didut מַה יְדִידוּת

The author's name, Menachem, is indicated by the first letters of verses 2, 3, 4, and 6. It is assumed that the author is Rabbi Menachem ben Machir of Ratisbon, who lived in the 11th century. This song mentions some of the pleasures encouraged and activities forbidden on Shabbat.

Mah Y'di·dut m'nu·cha·teich,	מַה יְדִידוּת מְנוּחָתֵךְ,	How beloved is your rest,[1]
at Shab·bat ha·Mal·kah.	אַתְּ שַׁבָּת הַמַּלְכָּה.	O Sabbath Queen.
b'chein na·rutz lik·ra·teich,	בְּכֵן נָרוּץ לִקְרָאתֵךְ,	Therefore we will run to receive you,
Bo·i, ka·lah n'su·chah.	בּוֹאִי, כַּלָּה נְסוּכָה.	"Come, anointed bride." [2]
La·vush big·dei cha·mu·dot,	לְבוּשׁ בִּגְדֵי חֲמוּדוֹת,	Dressed in fine clothing,
l'had·lik neir biv·ra·chah.	לְהַדְלִיק נֵר בִּבְרָכָה.	to kindle the light with a blessing.
Va·tei·chel kol ha·a·vo·dot,	וַתֵּכֶל כָּל הָעֲבוֹדוֹת,	All labors are completed,
lo ta·a·su m'la·chah.	לֹא תַעֲשׂוּ מְלָאכָה.	[as is written:] "Refrain from work." [3]

CHORUS:

CHORUS:

L'hit·a·neig b'ta·a·nu·gim,	לְהִתְעַנֵּג בְּתַעֲנוּגִים,	[It is a time] to enjoy delicacies,
bar·bu·rim u·s'lav v'da·gim.	בַּרְבּוּרִים וּשְׂלָו וְדָגִים.	[such as] geese, quail, and fish.

Mei·e·rev maz·mi·nim	מֵעֶרֶב מַזְמִינִים	Before evening are prepared
kol mi·nei mat·a·mim.	כָּל מִינֵי מַטְעַמִּים.	dainties galore.
Mi·b'od yom mu·cha·nim	מִבְּעוֹד יוֹם מוּכָנִים	While it is still daylight
tar·n'go·lim m'fu·ta·mim.	תַּרְנְגוֹלִים מְפֻטָּמִים.	fatted hens are readied.
V'la·a·roch ka·mah mi·nim,	וְלַעֲרֹךְ כַּמָּה מִינִים,	Many types of food are laid out,

1. After Psalms 84:2: *Mah y'didot mishk'notecha,* "how lovely are your habitations." Some versions have *y'didot* here instead of *y'didut,* but since neither form is without problems we have retained the more common "*y'didut.*"

2. Cf. Talmud Shabbat 119a, Bava Kamma 32a.

3. From Leviticus 23:3, "Six days shall work be done, but the seventh day is a Sabbath of solemn rest. You shall do no manner of work, it is a Sabbath to Adonai in all your dwellings."

4. i.e. meals

5. From Talmud Shabbat 118b, "Whoever enjoys him or herself on the Sabbath receives a boundless legacy."

6. According to tradition, if all of Israel observed just one Shabbat, the Messiah would come (Talmud Yerushalmi, Taanit 1:1).

7. From Exodus 19:5, "Now, therefore, if you will obey Me faithfully, and keep My covenant, then you shall be My treasured possession from among all the peoples . . . ."

8. From Exodus 20:9, "Six days shall you labor and do all of your work, but the seventh day is a Sabbath to Adonai your God."

9. For business purposes; see Talmud Shabbat 150a.

10. Ibid.

11. Arranging marriages was so important that it was even permitted to decide upon the amount of a dowry on the Sabbath.

sh'tot yei·not m'vu·sa·mim,	שְׁתוֹת יֵינוֹת מְבֻשָּׁמִים,	mulled wines for drinking,
v'taf·nu·kei ma·a·da·nim,	וְתַפְנוּקֵי מַעֲדַנִּים,	special treats to delight,
b'chol sha·losh p'a·mim.	בְּכָל שָׁלֹשׁ פְּעָמִים.	for all three times.[4]

CHORUS L'hit·a·neig b'ta·a·nu·gim . . .   . . . לְהִתְעַנֵּג בְּתַעֲנוּגִים CHORUS

Na·cha·lat Ya·a·kov yi·rash,	נַחֲלַת יַעֲקֹב יִירָשׁ,	Jacob's legacy shall they inherit,[5]
b'li m'tza·rim na·cha·lah.	בְּלִי מְצָרִים נַחֲלָה.	a boundless legacy.
Viy·chab·du·hu a·shir va·rash,	וִיכַבְּדוּהוּ עָשִׁיר וָרָשׁ,	Both wealthy and poor shall honor it,
v'tiz·ku lig·u·lah.	וְתִזְכּוּ לִגְאֻלָּה.	and will merit redemption.[6]
Yom Shab·bat im tish·mo·ru,	יוֹם שַׁבָּת אִם תִּשְׁמֹרוּ,	If you keep the Sabbath day,
vih·yi·tem li s'gu·lah,	וִהְיִיתֶם לִי סְגֻלָּה,	"you will be My treasured possession."[7]
Shei·shet ya·mim ta·a·vo·du,	שֵׁשֶׁת יָמִים תַּעֲבֹדוּ,	Six days shall you labor,[8]
u·va·sh'vi·i na·gi·lah.	וּבַשְּׁבִיעִי נָגִילָה.	and on the seventh, rejoice.

CHORUS L'hit·a·neig b'ta·a·nu·gim . . .   . . . לְהִתְעַנֵּג בְּתַעֲנוּגִים CHORUS

Cha·fa·tze·cha a·su·rim,	חֲפָצֶיךָ אֲסוּרִים,	Business is forbidden,
v'gam la·cha·shov chesh·bo·not.	וְגַם לַחֲשֹׁב חֶשְׁבּוֹנוֹת.	as is making calculations.[9]
Hir·hu·rim mu·ta·rim,	הִרְהוּרִים מֻתָּרִים,	Musings are permitted,[10]
u·l'sha·deich ha·ba·not,	וּלְשַׁדֵּךְ הַבָּנוֹת,	as is matchmaking,[11]
v'ti·nok l'la·m'do sei·fer,	וְתִינוֹק לְלַמְּדוֹ סֵפֶר,	teaching a child a text,
lam·na·tzei·ach bin·gi·not,	לַמְנַצֵּחַ בִּנְגִינוֹת,	singing melodies,
v'la·ha·got b'im·rei she·fer,	וְלַהֲגוֹת בְּאִמְרֵי שֶׁפֶר,	and contemplating the beautiful words
b'chol pi·not u·ma·cha·not.	בְּכָל פִּנּוֹת וּמַחֲנוֹת.	[of Torah], in all corners and places.

Chorus *L'hit·a·neig b'ta·a·nu·gim...*   ... לְהִתְעַנֵּג בְּתַעֲנוּגִים Chorus

Hi·lu·chach y'hei v'na·chat,   הִלּוּכָךְ יְהֵא בְנַחַת,   Your gait should be relaxed;[12]

o·neg k'ra la·Shab·bat.   עֹנֶג קְרָא לַשַּׁבָּת.   proclaim the Sabbath a pleasure.

V'ha·shei·nah m'shu·ba·chat,   וְהַשֵּׁנָה מְשֻׁבַּחַת,   Sleep is praiseworthy,

k'dat ne·fesh m'shi·vat.   כְּדָת נֶפֶשׁ מְשִׁיבַת.   it properly restores the soul.

B'chein naf·shi l'cha a·r'gah,   בְּכֵן נַפְשִׁי לְךָ עָרְגָה,   So my soul longs for You,[13]

v'la·nu·ach b'chi·bat.   וְלָנוּחַ בְּחִבַּת.   to rest [on it] in love.

Ka·sho·sha·nim su·gah,   כַּשׁוֹשַׁנִים סוּגָה,   It is hedged about with lilies,[14]

bo ya·nu·chu bein u·vat.   בּוֹ יָנוּחוּ בֵּן וּבַת.   on it [both] son and daughter rest.

Chorus *L'hit·a·neig b'ta·a·nu·gim...*   ... לְהִתְעַנֵּג בְּתַעֲנוּגִים Chorus

Mei·ein o·lam ha·ba   מֵעֵין עוֹלָם הַבָּא   A taste of the world to come

yom Shab·bat m'nu·chah.   יוֹם שַׁבָּת מְנוּחָה.   is the Sabbath day of rest.[15]

Kol ha·mit·a·n'gim bah   כָּל הַמִּתְעַנְּגִים בָּהּ   All who enjoy themselves on it

yiz·ku l'rov sim·chah.   יִזְכּוּ לְרֹב שִׂמְחָה.   will merit much happiness.

mei·chev·lei Ma·shi·ach   מֵחֶבְלֵי מָשִׁיחַ   From the pangs of the Messiah

yu·tza·lu lir·va·chah.   יֻצָּלוּ לִרְוָחָה.   they will be rescued to relief.[16]

P'du·tei·nu tatz·mi·ach,   פְּדוּתֵנוּ תַצְמִיחַ,   Our redemption will spring forth,

v'nas ya·gon va·a·na·chah.   וְנָס יָגוֹן וַאֲנָחָה.   and sorrow and sighing will flee.

Chorus *L'hit·a·neig b'ta·a·nu·gim...*   ... לְהִתְעַנֵּג בְּתַעֲנוּגִים Chorus

12. See Talmud Shabbat 113a: "Your Sabbath gait should be different from your weekday gait."

13. i.e., the Sabbath

14. From Song of Songs 7:3, "Your belly is like a heap of wheat hedged about with lilies." Just as being surrounded by lilies accentuates one's beauty, restrictions surrounding activities prohibited on Shabbat are intended to preserve and accentuate Shabbat's beauty. Cf. Shir Hashirim Rabbah 7:7: "'Hedged about with lilies,' these are the words of Torah which are tender like lilies." Here the point is that even though they are not physically enforced, the Torah's commands still carry great weight. The biblical verse and the context call for *bashoshanim* (with lilies), but all versions seem to have *kashoshanim*.

15. See Talmud B'rachot 57b

16. From Talmud Shabbat 118a, "One who partakes of three meals on the Sabbath is saved from the pangs of the Messiah."

Yom Zeh L'Yisraeil יוֹם זֶה לְיִשְׂרָאֵל

The author is Isaac Chandali, who lived in Feodosiya [Kaffa] in the Crimean peninsula during the latter half of the 15th century. Only the first four verses are original. The poem was later attributed to Isaac Luria, the renowned Kabbalist, and seven verses were added to the original to spell out the acrostic Yitzchak Luria Chazak! (Yitzchak Luria, be strong!)

This version, as printed in most siddurim, contains the four original verses (whose initial letters form an acrostic for "Yitzchak," whence the attribution to Yitzchak Luria) plus an additional two verses, one beginning with *lamed* (the first letter of *Luria*) and the second with *chet* (the first letter of *chazak*). The poem seems especially preoccupied with the troubles of Jewish existence in exile.

<table>
<tr>
<td>

1. See Jeremiah 40:5 *aruchah umaseit*, provisions and a present.

</td>
<td>

Yom zeh l'Yis·ra·eil
o·rah v'sim·chah,
Shab·bat m'nu·chah.

Tzi·vi·ta pi·ku·dim
b'ma·a·mad Si·nai,
Shab·bat u·mo·a·dim
lish·mor, b'chol sha·nai,
la·a·roch l'fa·nai
mas·eit va·a·ru·chah,
Shab·bat m'nu·chah.

<small>Chorus</small> *Yom zeh l'Yis·ra·eil . . .*

</td>
<td>

יוֹם זֶה לְיִשְׂרָאֵל
אוֹרָה וְשִׂמְחָה,
שַׁבָּת מְנוּחָה.

צִוִּיתָ פִּקּוּדִים
בְּמַעֲמַד סִינַי,
שַׁבָּת וּמוֹעֲדִים
לִשְׁמוֹר בְּכָל שָׁנַי,
לַעֲרֹךְ לְפָנַי
מַשְׂאֵת וַאֲרוּחָה,
שַׁבָּת מְנוּחָה.

יוֹם זֶה לְיִשְׂרָאֵל . . . <small>Chorus</small>

</td>
<td>

This day is for Israel [one of]
light and joy,
the Sabbath, day of rest.

You issued commands
at the Sinai event,
the Sabbath and the holidays
to keep for all time,
to arrange before Me
proper meals,[1]
on the Sabbath, day of rest.

</td>
</tr>
</table>

Chem·dat ha·l'va·vot	חֶמְדַּת הַלְּבָבוֹת	Hearts' desire
l'u·mah sh'vu·rah,	לְאֻמָּה שְׁבוּרָה,	for a broken nation,[2]
lin·fa·shot nich·a·vot	לִנְפָשׁוֹת נִכְאָבוֹת	for ailing spirits
n'sha·mah y'tei·rah.	נְשָׁמָה יְתֵרָה.	an extra soul.[3]
L'ne·fesh m'tzei·rah	לְנֶפֶשׁ מְצֵרָה	From the troubled spirit
ya·sir a·na·chah,	יָסִיר אֲנָחָה,	God will remove a sigh,
Shab·bat m'nu·chah.	שַׁבָּת מְנוּחָה.	on the Sabbath, day of rest.

Chorus *Yom zeh l'Yis·ra·eil . . .*　　יוֹם זֶה לְיִשְׂרָאֵל . . . Chorus

Ki·dash·ta bei·rach·ta	קִדַּשְׁתָּ בֵּרַכְתָּ	You sanctified and blessed
o·to mi·kol ya·mim;	אוֹתוֹ מִכָּל יָמִים;	it more than all days;
b'shei·shet ki·li·ta	בְּשֵׁשֶׁת כִּלִּיתָ	in six you completed
m'le·chet o·la·mim.	מְלֶאכֶת עוֹלָמִים.	the creation of the universe.
bo ma·tz'u a·gu·mim	בּוֹ מָצְאוּ עֲגוּמִים	On it the sad find
hash·keit u·vit·chah,	הַשְׁקֵט וּבִטְחָה,	quiet and security,
Shab·bat m'nu·chah.	שַׁבָּת מְנוּחָה.	on the Sabbath, day of rest.

Chorus *Yom zeh l'Yis·ra·eil . . .*　　יוֹם זֶה לְיִשְׂרָאֵל . . . Chorus

2. An allusion to the tribulations of the exile and perhaps even to the expulsion from Spain. The author was alive until the beginning of the 16th century.

3. According to tradition, we are granted an extra soul on the Sabbath, which departs at its conclusion (Talmud Beitzah 16a).

4. "Splendor of majesty" refers to the coming of the Messiah. According to tradition, if all Jews keep one Sabbath together, the Messiah will come.

5. God's "forlorn" refers to the People of Israel, who are in exile.

L'i·sur m'la·chah
tzi·vi·ta·nu, no·ra.
Ez·keh hod m'lu·chah
im Shab·bat esh·mo·rah.
Ak·riv shai la·mo·ra,
min·chah mer·ka·chah,
Shab·bat m'nu·chah.

לֶאֱסוֹר מְלָאכָה
צִוִּיתָנוּ, נוֹרָא.
אֶזְכֶּה הוֹד מְלוּכָה
אִם שַׁבָּת אֶשְׁמְרָה.
אַקְרִיב שַׁי לַמּוֹרָא,
מִנְחָה מֶרְקָחָה,
שַׁבָּת מְנוּחָה.

A ban on work
You commanded us, Awesome One.
I will merit the splendor of majesty[4]
if I keep Shabbat.
I will offer a gift to the Feared One,
a mixed offering,
on the Sabbath, day of rest.

CHORUS *Yom zeh l'Yis·ra·eil . . .*   . . . יוֹם זֶה לְיִשְׂרָאֵל CHORUS

Cha·deish mik·da·shei·nu,
zoch·rah ne·che·re·vet.
Tu·v'cha, mo·shi·ei·nu,
t'nah la·ne·e·tze·vet,
b'Shab·bat yo·she·vet
b'ze·mer u·sh'va·chah,
Shab·bat m'nu·chah.

חַדֵּשׁ מִקְדָּשֵׁנוּ,
זָכְרָה נֶחֱרֶבֶת.
טוּבְךָ, מוֹשִׁיעֵנוּ,
תְּנָה לַנֶּעֱצֶבֶת,
בְּשַׁבָּת יוֹשֶׁבֶת
בְּזֶמֶר וּשְׁבָחָה,
שַׁבָּת מְנוּחָה.

Renew our Temple,
remember Your ruined [city].
Of Your goodness, our Savior,
give to Your forlorn,[5]
who on the Sabbath sits
in song and praise,
on the Sabbath, day of rest.

CHORUS *Yom zeh l'Yis·ra·eil . . .*   . . . יוֹם זֶה לְיִשְׂרָאֵל CHORUS

Tzam'ah Nafshi צָמְאָה נַפְשִׁי

This song was written by Abraham Ibn Ezra (1092-1167), Spanish poet, philosopher, biblical exegete, and grammarian. The first letters of each verse spell his name in an acrostic.

Tza·m'ah naf·shi	צָמְאָה נַפְשִׁי	My soul thirsts
l'Ei·lo·him l'Eil Chai.	לֵאלֹהִים לְאֵל חָי.	for God, for the living God.[1]
Li·bi u·v'sa·ri	לִבִּי וּבְשָׂרִי	My soul and my body[2]
y'ra·n'nu el Eil Chai.	יְרַנְּנוּ אֶל אֵל חָי.	will joyfully sing to the living God.[3]
Eil e·chad b'ra·a·ni	אֵל אֶחָד בְּרָאַנִי	The One God created me
v'a·mar chai a·ni	וְאָמַר חַי אָנִי	and said, "I swear by my life
ki lo yir·a·ni	כִּי לֹא יִרְאַנִי	that no person shall see Me
ha·a·dam va·chai.	הָאָדָם וָחָי.	and live."[4]

CHORUS   CHORUS

Li·bi u·v'sa·ri	לִבִּי וּבְשָׂרִי	My soul and my body
y'ra·n'nu el Eil Chai.	יְרַנְּנוּ אֶל אֵל חָי.	will joyfully sing to the living God.
Ba·ra chol b'choch·mah,	בָּרָא כֹּל בְּחָכְמָה,	God created everything with wisdom,
b'ei·tzah u·vim·zi·mah	בְּעֵצָה וּבִמְזִמָּה	understanding and cunning
m'od ne·el·mah	מְאֹד נֶעְלָמָה	deeply is it hidden
mei·ei·nei chol Chai.	מֵעֵינֵי כָל חָי.	from the perception of all who live.[5]

CHORUS Li·bi u·v'sa·ri …   … לִבִּי וּבְשָׂרִי CHORUS

1. Psalms 42:3, "My soul thirsts for God, for the living God. When shall I come and behold the face of God?"

2. Lit. "my heart and my flesh." In his commentary on Psalms, Ibn Ezra views the heart as representative of the soul and flesh as representative of the body. The two are joined in the mouth, which, on behalf of both, sings to God.

3. Psalms 84:3, "My soul longs, indeed it faints for the courts of Adonai. My soul and my flesh sing for joy to the living God."

4. See Malachi 2:10, "Did not one God create us?" and Exodus 33:20, "God said, 'You cannot see my face; for no one shall see me and live.' "

5. Job 28:21, "It is hidden from the eyes of all living and concealed from the birds of the air." God's plan for creating the universe is beyond human understanding.

6. Job 12:10, "In God's hand is the life of every living thing and the breath of every human being."

7. A nickname for Jacob; see Genesis 25:27.

8. Leviticus 18:5, "You shall keep my statutes and my ordinances. By doing so one shall live: I am Adonai."

9. Psalms 143:2, "Do not enter into judgment with your servant, for no one living is righteous before you."

10. i.e., how can one cleanse oneself of the evil impulse? See Leviticus 13:10 and Exodus 4:7.

Ram al kol k'vo·do,	רָם עַל כָּל כְּבוֹדוֹ,	High above all is God's glory,
v'chol peh y'cha·veh ho·do.	וְכָל פֶּה יְחַוֶּה הוֹדוֹ.	Every mouth will pronounce God's majesty.
Ba·ruch a·sher b'ya·do	בָּרוּךְ אֲשֶׁר בְּיָדוֹ	Blessed is the One in whose hand
ne·fesh kol chai.	נֶפֶשׁ כָּל חָי.	is the soul of each living creature.[6]

CHORUS *Li·bi u·v'sa·ri* . . .   . . . לִבִּי וּבְשָׂרִי CHORUS

Hiv·dil ni·nei	הִבְדִּיל נִינֵי	God distinguished the descendants of
tam	תָם	"the Simple One"[7]
chu·kim l'ho·ro·tam	חֻקִּים לְהוֹרוֹתָם	to teach them laws
a·sher ya·a·seh o·tam	אֲשֶׁר יַעֲשֶׂה אוֹתָם	that a person may follow
ha·a·dam va·chai.	הָאָדָם וָחָי.	and live.[8]

CHORUS *Li·bi u·v'sa·ri* . . .   . . . לִבִּי וּבְשָׂרִי CHORUS

Mi zeh yitz·ta·dak	מִי זֶה יִצְטַדָּק	Can someone who is compared
nim·shal l'a·vak dak?	נִמְשַׁל לְאָבָק דָּק?	to fine dust be justified?
E·met ki lo yitz·dak	אֱמֶת כִּי לֹא יִצְדָּק	Indeed, no living creature
l'fa·ne·cha kol chai.	לְפָנֶיךָ כָּל חָי.	can be justified before You.[9]

CHORUS *Li·bi u·v'sa·ri* . . .   . . . לִבִּי וּבְשָׂרִי CHORUS

B'leiv yei·tzer cha·shuv	בְּלֵב יֵצֶר חָשׁוּב	In the heart the inclination is thought
kid·mut cha·mat ach·shuv,	כִּדְמוּת חֲמַת עַכְשׁוּב,	to be like viper's venom,
v'ei·cha·chah ya·shuv	וְאֵיכָכָה יָשׁוּב	so how can there return
ha·ba·sar he·chai.	הַבָּשָׂר הֶחָי.	healthy flesh?[10]

CHORUS *Li·bi u·v'sa·ri* . . .   . . . לִבִּי וּבְשָׂרִי CHORUS

N'so·gim im a·vu mi·dar·kam sha·vu te·rem yish·ka·vu beit mo·eid l'chol chai.	נְסוֹגִים אִם אָבוּ מִדַּרְכָּם שָׁבוּ טֶרֶם יִשְׁכָּבוּ בֵּית מוֹעֵד לְכָל חָי.	Those gone astray — if they so desire — can return from their wayward path before they lie down to rest in the house appointed for all the living.[11]
CHORUS *Li·bi u·v'sa·ri* …	… לִבִּי וּבְשָׂרִי CHORUS	
Al kol a·ho·de·cha, kol peh t'ya·cha·de·cha. Po·tei·ach et ya·de·cha u·mas·bi·a l'chol chai.	עַל כָּל אֲהוֹדֶךָ, כָּל פֶּה תְּיַחֲדֶךָ. פּוֹתֵחַ אֶת יָדֶךְ וּמַשְׂבִּיעַ לְכָל חָי.	For everything I will thank You, every mouth will declare You are One. You open Your hands and satisfy all living things.[12]
CHORUS *Li·bi u·v'sa·ri* …	… לִבִּי וּבְשָׂרִי CHORUS	
Z'chor a·ha·vat k'du·mim v'ha·cha·yeih nir·da·mim. V'ka·reiv ha·ya·mim a·sher ben Yi·shai chai.	זְכוֹר אַהֲבַת קְדוּמִים וְהַחֲיֵה נִרְדָּמִים. וְקָרֵב הַיָּמִים אֲשֶׁר בֶּן יִשַׁי חָי.	Remember the love of the ancient ones[13] and revive those deep in slumber.[14] Bring near the days when the son of Jesse will live.[15]
CHORUS *Li·bi u·v'sa·ri* …	… לִבִּי וּבְשָׂרִי CHORUS	
R'eih lig·ve·ret e·met, shif·chah no·e·met lo ki v'neich ha·meit u·v'ni he·chai.	רְאֵה לִגְבֶרֶת אֱמֶת, שִׁפְחָה נוֹאֶמֶת לֹא כִּי בְנֵךְ הַמֵּת וּבְנִי הֶחָי.	Recognize the true mistress, when the maidservant declares: "No, rather your son is dead and my son is alive."[16]
CHORUS *Li·bi u·v'sa·ri* …	… לִבִּי וּבְשָׂרִי CHORUS	

11. Job 30:23. "I know that You will bring me to death, and to the house appointed for all living."

12. Psalms 145:16. "You open your hands, satisfying the desire of every living thing."

13. The forefathers and fore-mothers.

14. A reference to the resurrection.

15. 1 Samuel 20:31. A wish for the redemption and coming of the Messiah.

16. 1 Kings 3:22. A reference to the story of King Solomon resolving the conflict between the two mothers. Here, the two mothers are Sarah the mistress, mother of Isaac, and Hagar the maidservant, mother of Ishmael. This may be a response to Islam's claim of having superseded Judaism.

Ha·lo chel·k'cha mei·rosh
cha·lak da·mo d'rosh.
Sh'foch af al rosh
ha·sa·ir he·chai.

הֲלֹא חֶלְקְךָ מֵרֹאשׁ
חָלָק דָּמוֹ דְרוֹשׁ.
שְׁפוֹךְ אַף עַל רֹאשׁ
הַשָּׂעִיר הֶחָי.

Wasn't Your portion from the beginning[17]
The "smoothed-skin one?"[18] Avenge his blood!
Pour out wrath upon the head
of the living goat.[19]

CHORUS *Li·bi u·v'sa·ri …*   לִבִּי וּבְשָׂרִי … CHORUS

E·kod al a·pi
v'ef·ros l'cha ka·pi
eit ki ef·tach pi
b'nish·mat kol chai.

אֶקֹּד עַל אַפִּי
וְאֶפְרוֹשׁ לְךָ כַּפִּי
עֵת כִּי אֶפְתַּח פִּי
בְּנִשְׁמַת כָּל חָי.

I will prostrate myself upon my face
and open my palm to You
at the time that I open my mouth
with "The Soul of All Living."[20]

CHORUS *Li·bi u·v'sa·ri …*   לִבִּי וּבְשָׂרִי … CHORUS

17. This verse is omitted from many editions. The first letter does not fit the acrostic. But it is included in Israel Levin's critical edition. Just as the previous verse expressed the hope that God would recognize the truth of Judaism over the claims of Islam, this verse prays for revenge against the Jews' Christian oppressors. These verses reflect the reality in which the Jewish people lived in the Middle Ages, often facing pressures from their host societies to convert, having the foundations of their faith challenged, or being persecuted for stubbornly clinging to it.

18. A nickname for Jacob. Genesis 27:11. " … 'Look, my brother Esau is a hairy man, and I am a man of smooth skin.' "

19. The word for goat is a homonym of Seir, Esau's inheritance. Rabbinic literature linked Esau with Rome and later with Christianity. It also alludes to the scapegoat sent to the wilderness as part of the biblical Yom Kippur ritual. (Leviticus 16:21-22).

20. "The Soul of All Living" נִשְׁמַת כָּל חַי is the prayer that immediately precedes the morning (*Shacharit*) service on the Sabbath and holidays. This poem was written by Ibn Ezra to serve as an introduction to the *Nishmat* prayer. Only later was it incorporated into the Shabbat *z'mirot*.

Yah Ribon Alam　יָהּ רִבּוֹן עָלַם

This Aramaic song was written by Rabbi Israel Najara, who lived in Palestine in the sixteenth century. The first letters of each verse spell his first name, Yisraeil. This song has no connection with the Sabbath, yet has become one of the most popular Sabbath table songs.

Yah Ri·bon a·lam v'al·ma·ya,	יָהּ רִבּוֹן עָלַם וְעָלְמַיָּא,	God, Sovereign of all the Worlds,
ant hu mal·ka me·lech mal·cha·ya.	אַנְתְּ הוּא מַלְכָּא מֶלֶךְ מַלְכַיָּא.	You are the Ruler, above all rulers.
O·vad g'vur·tach v'tim·ha·ya	עוֹבַד גְּבוּרְתָּךְ וְתִמְהַיָּא	Your mighty deeds and wonders
sh'far ko·da·mai l'ha·cha·va·ya.	שְׁפַר קֳדָמַי לְהַחֲוָיָה.	I am pleased to relate.[1]

CHORUS

Yah Ri·bon a·lam v'al·ma·ya,	יָהּ רִבּוֹן עָלַם וְעָלְמַיָּא,	God, Sovereign of all the Worlds,
Ant hu mal·ka me·lech mal·cha·ya.	אַנְתְּ הוּא מַלְכָּא מֶלֶךְ מַלְכַיָּא.	You are the Ruler, above all rulers.

Sh'va·chin a·sa·deir tzaf·ra v'ram·sha,	שְׁבָחִין אֲסַדֵּר צַפְרָא וְרַמְשָׁא,	Praises I arrange morning and evening,
lach E·la·ha Ka·di·sha di v'ra	לָךְ אֱלָהָא קַדִּישָׁא דִּי בְרָא	to You, Holy God, Creator of
chol naf·sha,	כָּל נַפְשָׁא,	all Life,
i·rin ka·di·shin, u·v'nei e·na·sha,	עִירִין קַדִּישִׁין וּבְנֵי אֱנָשָׁא,	Sacred spirits, human beings,
chei·vat ba·ra, v'o·fei sh'ma·ya.	חֵיוַת בָּרָא וְעוֹפֵי שְׁמַיָּא.	Beasts of the field, birds of the sky.

CHORUS Yah Ri·bon . . . 　יָהּ רִבּוֹן . . . CHORUS

1. From Daniel 3:32: "The Signs and Wonders that the Most High God has worked for me,
   I am pleased to relate." Many later versions have *kodamakh* which may have been the work
   of a later copyist who found the language of the original too daring.

Rav·r'vin o·va·dach v'ta·ki·fin,
ma·cheich ra·ma·ya, za·keif k'fi·fin.
Lu y'chei g'var sh'nin al·fin,
la yei·ol g'vur·tach b'chush·b'na·ya.

Chorus *Yah Ri·bon …*

רַבְרְבִין עוֹבָדָיךְ וְתַקִּיפִין,
מָכֵךְ רָמַיָּא, זָקֵף כְּפִיפִין.
לוּ יְחֵא גְבַר שְׁנִין אַלְפִין,
לָא יֵעֹל גְּבוּרְתָּךְ בְּחֻשְׁבְּנַיָּא.

יָהּ רִבּוֹן … Chorus

Great are your deeds and mighty,
humbling the proud, raising the humble.
Even if one lived a thousand years,
one could not fathom Your mighty deeds.

E·la·ha di leih y'kar u·r'vu·ta,
p'ruk yat a·nach mi·pum ar·ya·va·ta.
V'a·peik yat a·mach mi·go ga·lu·ta,
a·ma di v'chart mi·kol u·ma·ya.

Chorus *Yah Ri·bon …*

אֱלָהָא דִּי לֵהּ יְקַר וּרְבוּתָא,
פְּרֻק יָת עָנָךְ מִפֻּם אַרְיָוָתָא.
וְאַפֵּק יָת עַמָּךְ מִגּוֹ גָלוּתָא,
עַמָּא דִּי בְחַרְתְּ מִכָּל אֻמַּיָּא.

יָהּ רִבּוֹן … Chorus

O God of glory and greatness,
save Your flock from the lions' jaws.[2]
Take Your people out of exile,
The people You chose from all nations.

L'mik·d'shach tuv u·l'ko·desh ku·d'shin,
a·tar di veih ye·che·don ru·chin v'naf·shin.
Viy·za·m'run lach shi·rin v'ra·cha·shin
BiY·ru·sh'leim kar·ta d'shuf·ra·ya.

Chorus *Yah Ri·bon …*

לְמִקְדָּשָׁךְ תּוּב וּלְקֹדֶשׁ קֻדְשִׁין,
אֲתַר דִּי בֵהּ יֶחֱדוֹן רוּחִין וְנַפְשִׁין.
וִיזַמְּרוּן לָךְ שִׁירִין וְרַחֲשִׁין
בִּירוּשְׁלֵם קַרְתָּא דְשֻׁפְרַיָּא.

יָהּ רִבּוֹן … Chorus

Return to Your Temple and to the Holy of Holi
the place where spirits and souls will rejoice.
They will sing to You songs and melodies
In Jerusalem, city of beauty.

2. See Daniel 6:23; the lions probably allude to the nations
   persecuting Israel.

Tzur Mishelo Achalnu צוּר מִשֶּׁלּוֹ אָכַלְנוּ

This song whose verses are based on the blessings of *Birkat HaMazon*, is traditionally recited immediately before it. It has no connection with the Sabbath; some say it should be sung on holidays as well. The author is unknown.

Tzur mi·she·lo a·chal·nu	צוּר מִשֶּׁלּוֹ אָכַלְנוּ	The Rock, whose food we have eaten
ba·r'chu e·mu·nai.	בָּרְכוּ אֱמוּנַי.	let us bless, my faithful [friends].
Sa·va·nu v'ho·tar·nu,	שָׂבַעְנוּ וְהוֹתַרְנוּ,	We are sated and have left over,
kid·var A·do·nai.	כִּדְבַר יְיָ.	as God has said.[1]
Ha·zan et o·la·mo,	הַזָּן אֶת עוֹלָמוֹ,	You feed the world,
ro·ei·nu A·vi·nu.	רוֹעֵנוּ אָבִינוּ.	our Shepherd and Parent.
A·chal·nu et lach·mo	אָכַלְנוּ אֶת לַחְמוֹ	We have eaten Your bread
v'yei·no sha·ti·nu.	וְיֵינוֹ שָׁתִינוּ.	and drunk Your wine.
Al kein no·deh lish·mo	עַל כֵּן נוֹדֶה לִשְׁמוֹ	Therefore let us praise Your Name
u·n'ha·l'lo b'fi·nu.	וּנְהַלְּלוֹ בְּפִינוּ.	and extol you with our mouths.
A·mar·nu va·a·ni·nu:	אָמַרְנוּ וְעָנִינוּ:	Loudly we proclaim:
Ein ka·dosh kA·do·nai.	אֵין קָדוֹשׁ כַּיְיָ.	"There is none as holy as God."
CHORUS *Tzur mi·she·lo …*	צוּר מִשֶּׁלּוֹ … CHORUS	
B'shir v'kol to·dah	בְּשִׁיר וְקוֹל תּוֹדָה	With song and voice of thanks,
n'va·reich E·lo·hei·nu	נְבָרֵךְ אֱלֹהֵינוּ	let us bless our God
al e·retz chem·dah to·vah	עַל אֶרֶץ חֶמְדָּה טוֹבָה	for the desirable goodly land
she·hin·chil la·a·vo·tei·nu.	שֶׁהִנְחִיל לַאֲבוֹתֵינוּ.	You bestowed upon our ancestors.
Ma·zon v'tzei·dah	מָזוֹן וְצֵדָה	Food and provision

1. From 2 Kings 4:43-44, [Elisha] said: "Give it to the people and let them eat. For thus said God: 'They shall eat and have some left over.' So he set it before them, and when they had eaten, they had some left over, as God had said."

his·bi·a l'naf·shei·nu,
Chas·do ga·var a·lei·nu,
ve·e·met A·do·nai.

CHORUS *Tzur mi·she·lo . . .*

הִשְׂבִּיעַ לְנַפְשֵׁנוּ,
חַסְדּוֹ גָּבַר עָלֵינוּ,
וֶאֱמֶת יְיָ.

CHORUS ‏. . . ‏צוּר מִשֶּׁלוֹ

You grant us in abundance,
Your kindness overwhelms us,
God is true.

Ra·cheim b'chas·de·cha
al a·m'cha tzu·rei·nu,
al Tzi·yon mish·kan k'vo·de·cha
z'vul beit tif·ar·tei·nu.
Ben Da·vid av·de·cha
ya·vo v'yig·a·lei·nu,
ru·ach a·pei·nu,
m'shi·ach A·do·nai.

CHORUS *Tzur mi·she·lo . . .*

רַחֵם בְּחַסְדֶּךָ
עַל עַמְּךָ צוּרֵנוּ,
עַל צִיּוֹן מִשְׁכַּן כְּבוֹדֶךָ
זְבוּל בֵּית תִּפְאַרְתֵּנוּ.
בֶּן דָּוִד עַבְדֶּךָ
יָבוֹא וְיִגְאָלֵנוּ,
רוּחַ אַפֵּינוּ,
מְשִׁיחַ יְיָ.

CHORUS ‏. . . ‏צוּר מִשֶּׁלוֹ

Have mercy in Your kindness
on Your people, our Rock,
on Zion, home of Your Glory,
our splendid Temple shrine.
May Your servant, David's scion,
come to redeem us,
breath of our nostrils,
anointed of God.

Yi·ba·neh ha·mik·dash,
ir Tzi·yon ti·ma·lei.
V'sham na·shir shir cha·dash
u·vir·na·nah na·a·leh.
Ha·ra·cha·man ha·nik·dash
yit·ba·rach v'yit·a·leh
al kos ya·yin ma·lei
k'vir·kat A·do·nai.

CHORUS *Tzur mi·she·lo . . .*

יִבָּנֶה הַמִּקְדָּשׁ,
עִיר צִיּוֹן תִּמָּלֵא.
וְשָׁם נָשִׁיר שִׁיר חָדָשׁ
וּבִרְנָנָה נַעֲלֶה.
הָרַחֲמָן הַנִּקְדָּשׁ
יִתְבָּרַךְ וְיִתְעַלֶּה
עַל כּוֹס יַיִן מָלֵא
כְּבִרְכַּת יְיָ.

CHORUS ‏. . . ‏צוּר מִשֶּׁלוֹ

May the Temple be rebuilt,
the city of Zion filled up.[2]
There may we sing a new song,
and in joy go up.
May the merciful sanctified One
be blessed and exalted
over a full cup of wine,
a sign of God's blessing.

Baruch Eil Elyon   בָּרוּךְ אֵל עֶלְיוֹן

The author is Baruch ben Samuel, of Mainz, who lived in the 11th century. The verses spell out the acrostic Baruch, Chazak (blessed one, be strong)! This poem is full of biblical allusions, as indicated in the notes.

Ba·ruch Eil el·yon,	בָּרוּךְ אֵל עֶלְיוֹן,	Blessed is the exalted God,[1]
a·sher na·tan m'nu·chah,	אֲשֶׁר נָתַן מְנוּחָה,	who gave rest,[2]
l'naf·shei·nu fid·yon,	לְנַפְשֵׁנוּ פִדְיוֹן,	respite for our souls,
mi·sheit va·a·na·chah.	מִשֵּׁאת וַאֲנָחָה.	from calamity[3] and woe.
V'hu yid·rosh l'Tzi·yon,	וְהוּא יִדְרֹשׁ לְצִיוֹן,	God will seek out Zion,
ir ha·ni·da·chah.	עִיר הַנִּדָּחָה.	the rejected city.[4]
Ad a·na to·g'yun	עַד אָנָה תוֹגְיוּן	How long will you torment
ne·fesh ne·e·na·chah.	נֶפֶשׁ נֶאֱנָחָה.	a sighing soul.[5]

CHORUS   CHORUS

Ha·sho·meir Shab·bat,	הַשּׁוֹמֵר שַׁבָּת,	The keepers of the Sabbath,
ha·bein im ha·bat,	הַבֵּן עִם הַבַּת,	both male and female,[6]
la·Eil yei·ra·tzu	לָאֵל יֵרָצוּ	are as pleasing to God
k'min·chah al ma·cha·vat.	כְּמִנְחָה עַל מַחֲבַת.	as a meal-offering on a fire pan.

1. From Genesis 14:20, "Blessed be God the Most High."

2. From 1 Kings 8:56, "Blessed be Adonai, who has given rest to The People Israel."

3. From Lamentations 3:47, "Fear and the pit have come upon us, calamity and destruction." The word הַשֵּׁאת (calamity) appears only here in the Bible.

4. From Jeremiah 30:17, "Though they called you 'outcast,' that Zion, whom no one seeks out."

5. From Job 19:2, "How long will you torment my soul, and crush me with words?"

6. Lit., the son with the daughter

7. From Psalms 68:5, "Sing to God, sing praises to God's name; extol the One who rides on the clouds."

8. Lit., made them hear.

9. From 1 Samuel 20:29, [David said to Jonathan] "Please let me go, for we are going to have a family feast in our town."

10. From Isaiah 30:18, "Happy are those who wait for God."

11. Those who spend generously for the Sabbath will be amply rewarded.

12. From 1 Kings 8:12, and 2 Chronicles 6:1, "God has chosen to dwell in a dense cloud."

13. i.e., Jacob, from Genesis 32:32, "The sun rose upon him as he passed Penuel."

Ro·cheiv ba·a·ra·vot,	רוֹכֵב בָּעֲרָבוֹת,	The cloud-rider,[7]
Me·lech O·la·mim,	מֶלֶךְ עוֹלָמִים,	Ruler of Worlds,
et a·mo lish·bot	אֶת עַמּוֹ לִשְׁבֹּת	instructed[8] the people to enjoy
i·zein ba·n'i·mim,	אָזֵן בַּנְעִימִים,	pleasant rest,
b'ma·a·cha·lot a·rei·vot,	בְּמַאֲכָלוֹת עֲרֵבוֹת,	with tasty foods
b'mi·nei mat·a·mim,	בְּמִינֵי מַטְעַמִּים,	and assorted dainties,
b'mal·bu·shei cha·vod,	בְּמַלְבּוּשֵׁי כָבוֹד,	with elegant clothing,
ze·vach mish·pa·chah.	זֶבַח מִשְׁפָּחָה.	a family feast.[9]

CHORUS *Ha·sho·meir Shab·bat . . .*   . . . הַשּׁוֹמֵר שַׁבָּת   CHORUS

V'ash·rei chol cho·cheh	וְאַשְׁרֵי כָּל חוֹכֶה	Happy is anyone who waits[10]
l'tash·lu·mei chei·fel	לְתַשְׁלוּמֵי כֵפֶל	for the double reward[11]
mei·eit kol so·cheh,	מֵאֵת כָּל סוֹכֶה,	from the All-Seeing One,
sho·chein ba·a·ra·fel.	שׁוֹכֵן בָּעֲרָפֶל.	who dwells in a dense cloud.[12]
Na·cha·lah lo yiz·keh,	נַחֲלָה לוֹ יִזְכֶּה,	An inheritance shall one merit
ba·har u·va·sha·fel,	בָּהָר וּבַשָּׁפֶל,	on mountain or in valley,
na·cha·lah u·m'nu·chah	נַחֲלָה וּמְנוּחָה	an inheritance and resting place
k'she·mesh lo zar·chah.	כְּשֶׁמֶשׁ לוֹ זָרְחָה.	like [that of the one] upon whom

CHORUS *Ha·sho·meir Shab·bat . . .*   . . . הַשּׁוֹמֵר שַׁבָּת   CHORUS   the sun rose.[13]

Kol sho·meir Shab·bat	כָּל שׁוֹמֵר שַׁבָּת	Whoever keeps the Sabbath
ka·dat mei·cha·l'lo,	כַּדָּת מֵחַלְּלוֹ,	properly, unprofaned,[14]
hein hach·sheir	הֵן הַכְשֵׁר	fitness for
chi·bat ko·desh go·ra·lo.	חִבַּת קֹדֶשׁ גּוֹרָלוֹ.	holy love is their lot.[15]
V'im yei·tzei cho·vat	וְאִם יֵצֵא חוֹבַת	Whoever fulfills the obligation
ha·yom ash·rei lo.	הַיּוֹם אַשְׁרֵי לוֹ.	of the day is praiseworthy.
L'Eil A·don m'cho·l'lo,	לְאֵל אָדוֹן מְחוֹלְלוֹ,	To God, the Master, the Creator,
min·chah hi sh'lu·chah.	מִנְחָה הִיא שְׁלוּחָה.	it is sent as an offering.[16]

CHORUS *Ha·sho·meir Shab·bat . . .*   . . . הַשּׁוֹמֵר שַׁבָּת CHORUS

Chem·dat ha·ya·mim	חֶמְדַּת הַיָּמִים	"Most coveted of days"[17] was it
k'ra·o Ei·li Tzur,	קְרָאוֹ אֵלִי צוּר,	called by my God, the Rock,[18]
v'ash·rei li·t'mi·mim	וְאַשְׁרֵי לִתְמִימִים	fortunate are the blameless[19]
im yi·h'yeh na·tzur.	אִם יִהְיֶה נָצוּר.	if it is kept.
Ke·ter hi·lu·mim	כֶּתֶר הִלּוּמִים	A fitting crown
al ro·sham ya·tzur,	עַל רֹאשָׁם יָצוּר,	will be placed on their heads,
tzur ha·o·la·mim	צוּר הָעוֹלָמִים	the spirit of the Eternal Rock[20]
ru·cho bam na·chah.	רוּחוֹ בָּם נָחָה.	rests among them.[21]

CHORUS *Ha·sho·meir Shab·bat . . .*   . . . הַשּׁוֹמֵר שַׁבָּת CHORUS

14. From Isaiah 56:6, "everyone who keeps the Sabbath and does not profane it . . . I will bring to My holy mountain."

15. Based on Talmud Chullin 33a: *chibat hakodesh machshartan* "the honor of the sacred makes them fit [for ritual impurity]," but taken out of its original context to refer to the Sabbath observer's greater ability to achieve holiness. Alternatively, in a sacrificial context, it could refer to the individual's fitness to enjoy the sacrifices in the rebuilt temple.

16. The Sabbath observer offers his observance as a sacrifice to God.

17. This phrase describing Shabbat, attributed to God, is also found in the Amidah of the Shabbat *Shacharit* service: *chemdat yamim oto karata.* It does not appear in the sources, which is puzzling. The closest source that has been found is Targum Yerushalmi at Gen 2:2, where the word *vay'chal* (he completed) is rendered *vachamid* (he coveted), thus implying that God coveted the Sabbath, something not said about any other day of the week. Perhaps this was also a way of avoiding the disturbing thought that God actually completed his work of creation on the seventh day.

20. From Isaiah 26:4, "Trust in Adonai forever, for God is an Eternal Rock."

21. From Isaiah 11:2, "And the spirit of God shall rest upon him."

18. From Psalms 89:27, "You are my Parent, my God, and the Rock of my salvation."

19. From Psalms 119:1, "Fortunate are those whose way is blameless, who follow the teaching of God."

22. From Exodus 20:8, "Remember the Sabbath day, to keep it holy."

23. Of the Sabbath observer. From Numbers 6:7, "the crown of God is upon his head" [referring to the hair of the Nazirite].

24. From Exodus 29:29, "And the holy garments of Aaron shall be his sons' after him, to be anointed and ordained in them." On "anointed," Rashi comments, "To be exalted through them."

25. From Talmud Shabbat 119a, "Come and let us go forth to welcome the Sabbath Queen."

26. From Ezekiel 44:30, "You shall also give to the priest the first of your dough, that he may place a blessing in your home."

27. From Exodus 20:10, "The seventh day is the Sabbath to Adonai your God. Do not do any work: not you, nor your son, nor your daughter, nor your servingman, nor your servingwoman, nor your cattle, nor the stranger that is within your gates."

Za·chor et yom ha·Shab·bat l'ka·d'sho.	זָכוֹר אֶת יוֹם הַשַּׁבָּת לְקַדְּשׁוֹ.	Remember the Sabbath day to keep it holy.[22]
Kar·no ki ga·v'hah, nei·zer al ro·sho.	קַרְנוֹ כִּי גָבְהָה, נֵזֶר עַל רֹאשׁוֹ.	Its glory is great, it is a crown on the head.[23]
Al kein yi·tein ha·a·dam l'naf·sho o·neg v'gam sim·chah, ba·hem lo l'mosh·chah.	עַל כֵּן יִתֵּן הָאָדָם לְנַפְשׁוֹ עוֹנֶג וְגַם שִׂמְחָה, בָּהֶם לוֹ לְמָשְׁחָה.	So let everyone give themselves delight and joy, through which to be exalted.[24]

CHORUS *Ha·sho·meir Shab·bat . . .*   . . . הַשּׁוֹמֵר שַׁבָּת CHORUS

Ko·desh hi la·chem, Shab·bat ha·Mal·kah, el toch ba·tei·chem l'ha·ni·ach b'ra·chah.	קֹדֶשׁ הִיא לָכֶם, שַׁבָּת הַמַּלְכָּה, אֶל תּוֹךְ בָּתֵּיכֶם לְהָנִיחַ בְּרָכָה.	Holy is she to you, the Sabbath Queen,[25] within your homes to place a blessing.[26]
B'chol mosh·vo·tei·chem lo ta·a·su m'la·chah, b'nei·chem u·v'no·tei·chem, e·ved v'gam shif·chah.	בְּכָל מוֹשְׁבוֹתֵיכֶם לֹא תַעֲשׂוּ מְלָאכָה, בְּנֵיכֶם וּבְנוֹתֵיכֶם, עֶבֶד וְגַם שִׁפְחָה.	In all your dwellings do no work, [neither] your sons nor your daughters, [neither] servant nor maid.[27]

CHORUS *Ha·sho·meir Shab·bat . . .*   . . . הַשּׁוֹמֵר שַׁבָּת CHORUS

The author's name, Yisraeil, is spelled out by the acrostic formed by the first letters of the first five verses.

Yom zeh m'chu·bad mi·kol ya·mim,
ki vo sha·vat Tzur O·la·mim.

יוֹם זֶה מְכֻבָּד מִכָּל יָמִים,
כִּי בוֹ שָׁבַת צוּר עוֹלָמִים.

This day is most honored of all days,[1]
because on it, the Eternal Rock ceased from work.[2]

Shei·shet ya·mim a·seih m'lach·te·cha,
v'yom ha·sh'vi·i lEi·lo·he·cha.
Shab·bat lo ta·a·seh vo m'la·chah,
ki chol a·sah shei·shet ya·mim.

שֵׁשֶׁת יָמִים עֲשֵׂה מְלַאכְתֶּךָ,
וְיוֹם הַשְּׁבִיעִי לֵאלֹהֶיךָ.
שַׁבָּת לֹא תַעֲשֶׂה בוֹ מְלָאכָה,
כִּי כֹל עָשָׂה שֵׁשֶׁת יָמִים.

Six days perform your work,
but the seventh day is for Your God.
On the Sabbath day you shall not perform work,
for God created all in six days.[3]

Chorus *Yom zeh m'chu·bad . . .*

. . . יוֹם זֶה מְכֻבָּד Chorus

Ri·shon hu l'mik·ra·ei ko·desh,
yom shab·ba·ton, yom Shab·bat ko·desh.
Al kein kol ish b'yei·no y'ka·deish,
al sh'tei le·chem yiv·tz'u t'mi·mim.

רִאשׁוֹן הוּא לְמִקְרָאֵי קֹדֶשׁ,
יוֹם שַׁבָּתוֹן, יוֹם שַׁבָּת קֹדֶשׁ.
עַל כֵּן כָּל אִישׁ בְּיֵינוֹ יְקַדֵּשׁ,
עַל שְׁתֵּי לֶחֶם יִבְצְעוּ תְּמִימִים.

It is foremost among the days proclaimed holy,[4]
a day of rest, the holy Sabbath.[5]
Hence let each recite Kiddush over wine,
with two loaves[6] let the blameless break bread.

Chorus *Yom zeh m'chu·bad . . .*

. . . יוֹם זֶה מְכֻבָּד Chorus

1. From Isaiah 58:13, " . . . call God's holy day 'honored' . . . ."

2. From Genesis 2:3, "And God blessed the seventh day, because on it, God ceased from all the work . . . ."

3. From Exodus 31:17, 20:9-11, "For in six days Adonai made heaven and earth;" "Six days shall you labor . . . but the seventh day is the Sabbath of Adonai your God . . . ."

4. From Leviticus 23:2-3, "The feasts of Adonai, which you shall proclaim to be holy gatherings . . . the seventh day is the Sabbath of rest, a holy gathering . . . ."

5. From Exodus 16:23, "Tomorrow is . . . Adonai's holy Sabbath"

6. A reminder of the double portion of manna which was provided for Shabbat.

E·chol mash·ma·nim sh'teih mam·ta·kim,	אֱכֹל מַשְׁמַנִּים שְׁתֵה מַמְתַּקִּים,	Eat dainties, drink sweet drinks,[7]
ki Eil yi·tein l'chol bo d'vei·kim	כִּי אֵל יִתֵּן לְכָל בּוֹ דְבֵקִים	for God provides for all who cleave to the One[8]
be·ged lil·bosh, le·chem chu·kim,	בֶּגֶד לִלְבּוֹשׁ, לֶחֶם חֻקִּים,	clothes to wear, fixed portions of food,[9]
ba·sar v'da·gim v'chol mat·a·mim.	בָּשָׂר וְדָגִים וְכָל מַטְעַמִּים.	meat, fish, and all sorts of delicacies.[10]

CHORUS *Yom zeh m'chu·bad...*   יוֹם זֶה מְכֻבָּד... CHORUS   The heavens declare God's glory,

Lo tech·sar kol bo,	לֹא תֶחְסַר כֹּל בּוֹ,	You should lack nothing on this day,
v'a·chal·ta v'sa·va·ta u'vei·rach·ta,	וְאָכַלְתָּ וְשָׂבַעְתָּ וּבֵרַכְתָּ,	eat and be satisfied, then bless[11]
et A·do·nai E·lo·he·cha a·sher a·hav·ta,	אֶת יְיָ אֱלֹהֶיךָ אֲשֶׁר אָהַבְתָּ,	Adonai your God, whom you love,
ki vei·ra·ch'cha mi·kol ha·a·mim.	כִּי בֵרֶכְךָ מִכָּל הָעַמִּים.	for having blessed you above all peoples.[12]

CHORUS *Yom zeh m'chu·bad...*   יוֹם זֶה מְכֻבָּד... CHORUS

Ha·sha·ma·yim m'sa·p'rim k'vo·do,	הַשָּׁמַיִם מְסַפְּרִים כְּבוֹדוֹ,	The heavens declare God's glory,[13]
v'gam ha·a·retz ma·l'ah chas·do.	וְגַם הָאָרֶץ מָלְאָה חַסְדּוֹ.	the earth too is full of God's kindness.[14]
R'u ki chol ei·leh a·s'tah ya·do,	רְאוּ כִּי כָל אֵלֶה עָשְׂתָה יָדוֹ,	See, all these God's hand has made,[15]
ki hu ha·Tzur, pa·o·lo ta·mim.	כִּי הוּא הַצּוּר, פָּעֳלוֹ תָמִים.	for You are our Rock, Your work is perfect.[16]

CHORUS *Yom zeh m'chu·bad...*   יוֹם זֶה מְכֻבָּד... CHORUS

---

7. From Nehemiah 8:10, "Drink sweet drinks for this day is holy to God."

8. From Deuteronomy 4:4, "You who cleave to Adonai your God are alive . . . this day."

9. From Proverbs 30:8, "Remove from me falsehood and lies; feed me with a fixed portion."

10. According to Talmud Shabbat 118a-b, the best food should be prepared for the Sabbath, for "one who delights in Shabbat is granted one's heart's desire."

11. From Deuteronomy 8:9-10, ". . . a land . . . where you will lack nothing . . . . When you have eaten and are full, then you shall bless Adonai."

12. From Deuteronomy 7:14, 15:6, "You shall be blessed above all peoples;" "You shall reign over nations, but they shall not reign over you."

13. From Psalms 19:2, "The heavens declare the Glory of God."

14. From Psalms 33:5, "The earth is full of God's kindness."

15. From Isaiah 66:2, "For all those things has My hand made."

16. From Deuteronomy 32:4, "The Rock whose Work is perfect."

Yom Shabbaton   יוֹם שַׁבָּתוֹן

This song was written by Judah Halevi in twelfth-century Spain. His first name is spelled out by the initial letters of each verse.

Yom Shab·ba·ton ein lish·ko·ach,	יוֹם שַׁבָּתוֹן אֵין לִשְׁכּוֹחַ,	One should not forget the Sabbath day,
zich·ro k'rei·ach ha·ni·cho·ach.	זִכְרוֹ כְּרֵיחַ הַנִּיחֹחַ.	its mention is like sacrificial incense.[1]
Yo·nah ma·tz'ah vo ma·no·ach,	יוֹנָה מָצְאָה בוֹ מָנוֹחַ,	The dove found a resting place on this day,[2]
v'sham ya·nu·chu y'gi·ei cho·ach.	וְשָׁם יָנוּחוּ יְגִיעֵי כֹחַ.	on it the weary will be at rest.[3]
Yo·nah ma·tz'ah vo ma·no·ach,	יוֹנָה מָצְאָה בוֹ מָנוֹחַ,	The dove found a resting place on this day,
v'sham ya·nu·chu y'gi·ei cho·ach.	וְשָׁם יָנוּחוּ יְגִיעֵי כֹחַ.	on it the weary will be at rest.
Ha·yom nich·bad liv·nei e·mu·nim,	הַיּוֹם נִכְבָּד לִבְנֵי אֱמוּנִים,	The day is important for the faithful,
z'hi·rim l'shom·ro a·vot u·va·nim.	זְהִירִים לְשָׁמְרוֹ אָבוֹת וּבָנִים.	parents and children guard it with care.
Cha·kuk bish·nei lu·chot a·va·nim	חָקוּק בִּשְׁנֵי לֻחוֹת אֲבָנִים	It is carved on two tablets of stone[4]
mei·rov o·nim v'a·mitz ko·ach.	מֵרֹב אוֹנִים וְאַמִּיץ כֹּחַ.	from the mighty, powerful One.[5]
CHORUS *Yo·nah ma·tz'ah . . .*	יוֹנָה מָצְאָה . . . CHORUS	

---

1. i.e., it is very pleasing to God.

2. After Genesis 8:9, "[Noah] put forth his hand and took [the dove] . . .;" here the dove symbolizes the Jewish people.

3. From Job 3:17, "On it will rest those of spent strength."

4. Keeping Shabbat is one of the Ten Commandments.

5. From Isaiah 40:26, "who created these? . . . Because of God's great might and vast power, not one fails to appear."

U·va·u chu·lam biv·rit ya·chad,
Na·a·seh v'nish·ma, a·m'ru k'e·chad.
U·fa·t'chu va·nu A·do·nai e·chad,
ba·ruch ha·no·tein la·ya·eif ko·ach.

CHORUS *Yo·nah ma·tz'ah . . .*

Di·ber b'kod·sho b'har ha·mor:
Yom ha·sh'vi·i za·chor v'sha·mor,
v'chol pi·ku·dav ya·chad lig·mor,
cha·zeik mot·na·yim a·meitz ko·ach.

CHORUS *Yo·nah ma·tz'ah . . .*

Ha·am a·sher na ka·tzon ta·ah
yiz·kor l'fok·do b'rit u·sh'vu·ah,
l'val ya·a·vor bam mik·reih ra·ah,
ka·a·sher nish·ba al mei No·ach.

CHORUS *Yo·nah ma·tz'ah . . .*

וּבָאוּ כֻלָּם בִּבְרִית יַחַד,
נַעֲשֶׂה וְנִשְׁמַע, אָמְרוּ כְּאֶחָד.
וּפָתְחוּ וְעָנוּ יְיָ אֶחָד,
בָּרוּךְ הַנֹּתֵן לַיָּעֵף כֹּחַ.

CHORUS ... יוֹנָה מָצְאָה

דִּבֶּר בְּקָדְשׁוֹ בְּהַר הַמּוֹר:
יוֹם הַשְּׁבִיעִי זָכוֹר וְשָׁמוֹר,
וְכָל פִּקֻּדָיו יַחַד לִגְמוֹר,
חַזֵּק מָתְנַיִם אַמֵּץ כֹּחַ.

CHORUS ... יוֹנָה מָצְאָה

הָעָם אֲשֶׁר נָע כַּצֹאן תָּעָה
יִזְכֹּר לְפָקְדוֹ בְּרִית וּשְׁבוּעָה,
לְבַל יַעֲבָר בָּם מִקְרֶה רָעָה,
כַּאֲשֶׁר נִשְׁבַּע עַל מֵי נֹחַ.

CHORUS ... יוֹנָה מָצְאָה

All entered the covenant together,[6]
"We will do and we will obey," they said as one.[7]
They further declared: "God is One,
blessed is the Giver of strength to the weary."[8]

[God] in holiness, spoke at the Mount of Myrrh:[9]
"The seventh day — remember and keep [it],"[10]
study all God's commandments,
"gird your loins, gather strength."[11]

The people who wandered and strayed like sheep
God will, by covenant and vow, remember to notice,
so that no evil befall them,
as God swore over the waters of Noah.[12]

---

6. At Sinai.

7. From Exodus 24:7, "All that Adonai has said, we will do, and we will obey."

8. From Isaiah 40:29, "God gives strength to the weary and fresh vigor to the spent."

9. In Hebrew, *Har haMor*, mountain of myrrh, probably an allusion to the root *yarah*, which means "to teach." Sinai is the mountain from which the Teaching went out to Israel.

10. An allusion to Exodus 20:8, "Remember the Sabbath day, to make it holy" and Deuteronomy 5:12, "Keep the Sabbath day to make it holy."

11. From Nachum 2:2, "The shatterer has come against you; guard the ramparts, watch the road, gird your loins, gather strength."

12. From Isaiah 54:9, "For this is like the waters of Noah to Me; for just as I have sworn that the waters of Noah should no more flood the earth, so I swear that I will not be angry with you, and I will not rebuke you."

Shimru Shabtotai   שִׁמְרוּ שַׁבְּתוֹתַי

The author's name is Sh'lomoh, as indicated by the first letters of the first four verses.

Shim·ru Sha·b'to·tai	שִׁמְרוּ שַׁבְּתוֹתַי	Keep My Sabbaths
l'ma·an tin·ku u·s'va·tem	לְמַעַן תִּינְקוּ וּשְׂבַעְתֶּם	so you may absorb and be sated[1]
mi·ziz bir·cho·tai,	מִזִּיז בִּרְכוֹתַי,	with the abundance of My blessings,[2]
el ha·m'nu·chah ki va·tem.	אֶל הַמְּנוּחָה כִּי בָאתֶם.	when you come to rest.[3]
U·l'vu a·lai ba·nai,	וּלְווּ עָלַי בָּנַי,	Borrow at My expense, My children,[4]
v'id·nu ma·a·da·nai.	וְעִדְנוּ מַעֲדָנָי.	treat yourself to delicacies.
Shab·bat ha·yom lA·do·nai.	שַׁבָּת הַיּוֹם לַייָ.	"Today is a Sabbath of Adonai."[5]
Le·a·meil kir·u d'ror,	לֶעָמֵל קִרְאוּ דְרוֹר,	Proclaim freedom for the laborer,
v'na·ta·ti et bir·cha·ti.	וְנָתַתִּי אֶת בִּרְכָתִי.	I will give my blessing.
I·shah el a·cho·tah litz·ror	אִשָּׁה אֶל אֲחוֹתָהּ לִצְרֹר	Women will compete with each other
l'ga·lot al yom sim·cha·ti	לְגַלּוֹת עַל יוֹם שִׂמְחָתִי	to display on my day of joy
big·dei sheish im sha·nai.	בִּגְדֵי שֵׁשׁ עִם שָׁנָי.	garments of velvet and silk.
V'hit·bo·n'nu mi·z'kei·nai,	וְהִתְבּוֹנְנוּ מִזְּקֵנַי,	Regard what our sages have said,[6]
Shab·bat ha·yom lA·do·nai.	שַׁבָּת הַיּוֹם לַייָ.	"Today is a Sabbath of Adonai."

1. From Isaiah 66:11, "That you may suck and be satisfied with the breast of her consolations." "Her" refers to Jerusalem.

2. The verse continues: "that you may draw from her bosom glory to your delight (lemaan tamotzu v'hitanagtem miziz k'vodah). The meaning of ziz is uncertain. Some commentators derive it from the word to move; Even-Shoshan's dictionary gives "flow" and by derivation, "abundance." This seems to be what the context calls for.

3. From Deuteronomy 12:9, "For you are not as yet come to the rest and to the inheritance which Adonai your God gives you."

4. One should not be hesitant to buy the best for the Sabbath, but should have the faith that God will provide recompense.

5. From Exodus 16:25, "And Moses said, 'Today is a Sabbath of Adonai.'"

6. The reference to women rivals comes from Leviticus 18:18. Shanai is unusual but is required for the rhyme. It come from the plural form shanim (Isaiah 1:18, Proverbs 31:21). The sages said, "Dress on the Sabbath should differ from that of the rest of the week." (Talmud Shabbat 113a)

7. The Sabbath meal should be fit for a king, as was the banquet Esther prepared for Ahasuerus.

8. "The owner" refers to God.

9. From 2 Kings 4:43, "Give the people, that they may eat; for God said, 'They shall eat, and have some left over.'"

10. From Exodus 19:5, "Now, then, if you will obey Me faithfully and keep My covenant, then you shall be My treasured possession . . . .'"

11. The exile is symbolized by the night. If you keep the Sabbath properly, the exile will be a temporary stopover for you on your way to the Land of Israel.

12. In the Land of Israel.

13. Jerusalem.

14. The Temple.

15. From Isaiah 58:14, "Then you will enjoy the Presence of Adonai, and I will cause you to ride upon the high places of the earth . . . ."

16. This line is superfluous as each verse has seven stichs. It seems to be a later addition.

Ma·ha·ru et ha·ma·neh	מַהֲרוּ אֶת הַמָּנֶה	Quickly bring the portion
la·a·sot et d'var Es·teir.	לַעֲשׂוֹת אֶת דְּבַר אֶסְתֵּר.	to fulfill Esther's command.[7]
V'chish·vu im ha·ko·neh	וְחִשְׁבוּ עִם הַקּוֹנֶה	Settle the account with the owner[8]
l'sha·leim a·chol v'ho·teir.	לְשַׁלֵּם אָכֹל וְהוֹתֵר.	to provide more than is required.[9]
Bit·chu vi, e·mu·nai,	בִּטְחוּ בִי, אֱמוּנַי,	Trust in Me, My faithful,
u·sh'tu yein mash·ma·nai.	וּשְׁתוּ יֵין מַשְׁמַנַּי.	drink My best wine.
Shab·bat ha·yom lA·do·nai.	שַׁבָּת הַיּוֹם לַיָי.	"Today is a Sabbath of Adonai."

Hi·neih yom g'u·lah,	הִנֵּה יוֹם גְּאֻלָּה,	It is a day of redemption,
Yom Shab·bat im tish·mo·ru.	יוֹם שַׁבָּת אִם תִּשְׁמֹרוּ.	if you keep the Sabbath day.
vih·yi·tem li s'gu·lah,	וִהְיִיתֶם לִי סְגֻלָּה,	You will be My treasure,[10]
li·nu va·char ta·a·vo·ru.	לִינוּ וְאַחַר תַּעֲבֹרוּ.	spend the night then move on.[11]
V'az tich·yu l'fa·nai,	וְאָז תִּחְיוּ לְפָנַי,	Then you will live before Me,[12]
l'ti·ma·l'u tz'fu·nai.	וְתִמָּלְאוּ צְפוּנַי.	filled with My hidden treasures.
Shab·bat ha·yom lA·do·nai.	שַׁבָּת הַיּוֹם לַיָי.	"Today is a Sabbath of Adonai."

Cha·zeik kir·ya·ti,	חַזֵּק קִרְיָתִי,	Strengthen My city,[13]
Eil E·lo·him el·yon,	אֵל אֱלֹהִים עֶלְיוֹן,	God, exalted God,
v'ha·sheiv et n'va·ti	וְהָשֵׁב אֶת נְוָתִי	restore My dwelling[14]
b'sim·chah u·v'hi·ga·yon.	בְּשִׂמְחָה וּבְהִגָּיוֹן.	with joy and music.
Y'sho·r'ru sham r'na·nai,	יְשׁוֹרְרוּ שָׁם רְנָנַי,	There let them sing my songs —
L'vi·yai v'cho·ha·nai,	לְוִיַּי וְכֹהֲנַי,	my Levites and Priests —
v'az tit·a·nag al A·do·nai.	וְאָז תִּתְעַנַּג עַל יְיָ.	then you will enjoy Adonai's Presence.[15]
Shab·bat ha·yom lA·do·nai.	שַׁבָּת הַיּוֹם לַיָי.	["Today is a Sabbath of Adonai."][16]

D'ror Yikra　דְּרוֹר יִקְרָא

The author's name, Dunash (apparently Dunash ben Labrat, 10th century), is spelled by the first letters of each line in verses 1, 2, 3, and 6.

D'ror yik·ra l'vein im bat,	דְּרוֹר יִקְרָא לְבֵן עִם בַּת,	God will proclaim liberty for son and daughter,[1]
v'yin·tzor·chem k'mo va·vat,	וְיִנְצָרְכֶם כְּמוֹ בָבַת,	God will guard you like the apple of an eye,
n'im shim·chem, v'lo yush·bat,	נָעִים שִׁמְכֶם, וְלֹא יֻשְׁבַּת,	your name is good, it will not be destroyed,
sh'vu nu·chu b'yom Shab·bat.	שְׁבוּ נוּחוּ בְּיוֹם שַׁבָּת.	Sit and rest on the Sabbath day.
D'rosh na·vi v'u·la·mi,	דְּרוֹשׁ נָוִי וְאוּלַמִּי,	Seek out my Temple and its chamber,
v'ot ye·sha a·seih i·mi.	וְאוֹת יֶשַׁע עֲשֵׂה עִמִּי.	perform for me a sign of salvation.[2]
N'ta so·reik b'toch kar·mi,	נְטַע שׂוֹרֵק בְּתוֹךְ כַּרְמִי,	Plant a choice vine in my vineyard,[3]
sh'eih shav·at b'nei a·mi.	שְׁעֵה שַׁוְעַת בְּנֵי עַמִּי.	take heed of the cry of my people.[4]
D'roch pu·rah b'toch Botz·rah	דְּרוֹךְ פּוּרָה בְּתוֹךְ בָּצְרָה	Trample the vintage in Bozrah[5]
v'gam Ba·vel a·sher ga·v'rah.	וְגַם בָּבֶל, אֲשֶׁר גָּבְרָה.	and Babylon, too, which has gained supremacy.[6]
N'totz tza·rai b'af ev·rah,	נְתוֹץ צָרַי בְּאַף עֶבְרָה,	Smash my enemies with a mighty rage,
sh'ma ko·li b'yom ek·ra.	שְׁמַע קוֹלִי בְּיוֹם אֶקְרָא.	hear my voice on the day I call.[7]

1. For male and female alike. The coming of the Sabbath is likened to being freed from slavery, i.e., the toils of the work week. From Jeremiah 34:8, 15, 17, "Proclaim liberty to them . . . ."
2. A prayer of redemption.
3. Restore the Jewish people to its glory.
4. In their exile.

5. Bozrah, the ancient capital of Edom, here symbolizes the Christian nations. From Isaiah 63:1, "Who is this who comes from Edom, in crimsoned garments from Bozrah?"
6. The Arabs, or nations of Islam, who have also gained supremacy over Israel.
7. From Psalms 27:7, "Hear, Adonai, when I cry with my voice; be gracious to me, and answer me."

E·lo·him tein b'mid·bar har
ha·das, shi·tah, b'rosh tid·har.
V'la·maz·hir v'la·niz·har,
sh'lo·mim tein k'mei na·har.

Ha·doch ka·mai Eil ka·na,
b'mug lei·vav u·vim·gi·nah.
V'nar·chiv peh u·n'ma·le·nah,
l'sho·nei·nu l'cha ri·nah.

D'eh choch·mah l'naf·she·cha,
v'hi che·ter l'ro·she·cha.
N'tzor mitz·vat k'do·she·cha,
sh'mor Shab·bat kod·she·cha.

אֱלֹהִים תֵּן בְּמִדְבָּר הַר
הֲדַס, שִׁטָּה, בְּרוֹשׁ תִּדְהָר.
וְלַמַּזְהִיר וְלַנִּזְהָר,
שְׁלוֹמִים תֵּן כְּמֵי נָהָר.

הֲדוֹךְ קָמַי אֵל קַנָּא,
בְּמוּג לֵבָב וּבִמְגִנָּה.
וְנַרְחִיב פֶּה וּנְמַלְאֶנָּה,
לְשׁוֹנֵנוּ לְךָ רִנָּה.

דְּעֵה חָכְמָה לְנַפְשֶׁךָ,
וְהִיא כֶתֶר לְרֹאשֶׁךָ.
נְצוֹר מִצְוַת קְדוֹשֶׁךָ,
שְׁמוֹר שַׁבַּת קָדְשֶׁךָ.

God, plant in the mountain wasteland[8]
the myrtle, acacia, cypress, and elm.[9]
To the admonisher[10] and the careful one,[11]
grant abundant peace[12] like the waters of a river.

Bring down my enemies, jealous God,
[so they flee] in cowardice[13] and anguish.
We open wide and fill our mouths,[14]
[on] our tongues joyous song to You.[15]

Know wisdom[16] for your soul's sake,
it shall be a crown upon your head.
Keep the command of your Holy One,
guard your holy Sabbath.

---

8. Mount Zion.

9. From Isaiah 41:19, "I will plant cedars in the wilderness, acacias and myrtles and oil trees; I will set cypresses in the desert, box trees and elms as well."

10. About keeping the Sabbath.

11. The one careful to observe it.

12. The use of the term *shalom* in the plural is unusual, and signifies abundance.

13. After Ezekiel 21:20 "Thus hearts shall lose courage."

14. From Psalms 81:11, "Open your mouth wide, and I will fill it."

15. From Psalms 126:2, "Then our mouths will fill with laughter and on our tongues, joyous song."

16. From Proverbs 24:14, "Such is wisdom for your soul." Wisdom refers to the Torah.

SONGS FOR THE SABBATH DAY

Shabbat Hayom שַׁבָּת הַיּוֹם

The author's name is Sh'mueil, as indicated by the first letter of each verse.

Shab·bat ha·yom lA·do·nai,
m'od tza·ha·lu b'ri·nu·nai,
v'gam har·bu ma·a·da·nai,
o·to lish·mor k'mitz·vat A·do·nai.

שַׁבָּת הַיּוֹם לַיְיָ,
מְאֹד צַהֲלוּ בְּרִנּוּנַי,
וְגַם הַרְבּוּ מַעֲדַנַי,
אוֹתוֹ לִשְׁמוֹר כְּמִצְוַת יְיָ.

Today is a Sabbath of Adonai,
rejoice greatly with songs,
be generous with delicacies,
keep it, as Adonai has commanded.

שַׁבָּת הַיּוֹם לַיְיָ . . . Chorus

Mei·a·vor de·rech u·g'vu·lim,
mei·a·sot ha·yom p'a·lim.
Le·e·chol v'lish·tot b'hi·lu·lim,
zeh ha·yom a·sah A·do·nai.

מֵעֲבוֹר דֶּרֶךְ וּגְבוּלִים,
מֵעֲשׂוֹת הַיּוֹם פְּעָלִים.
לֶאֱכוֹל וְלִשְׁתּוֹת בְּהִלּוּלִים,
זֶה הַיּוֹם עָשָׂה יְיָ.

Travelling and passing boundaries [are forbidden],[1]
as is doing work on this day.
Eating and drinking in praise [of God is permitted],
"this is the day Adonai has made!"[2]

שַׁבָּת הַיּוֹם לַיְיָ . . . Chorus

---

1. The boundary for walking on the Sabbath was 2000 *amot* (just over a kilometer) beyond the town or city.

2. From Psalms 118:24, "This is the day that God has made, on it we will be glad and rejoice."

V'im tish·m're·nu, Yah yin·tzor·cha k'va·vat,	וְאִם תִּשְׁמְרֶנּוּ, יָהּ יִנְצָרְךָ כְּבָבַת,	If you keep it, God will guard you like a treasure,
a·tah u·vin·cha v'gam ha·bat.	אַתָּה וּבִנְךָ וְגַם הַבַּת.	you, your son, and daughter.
V'ka·ra·ta o·neg la·Shab·bat,	וְקָרֵאתָ עֹנֶג לַשַּׁבָּת,	Call the Sabbath "delight,"[3]
az tit·a·nag al A·do·nai.	אָז תִּתְעַנַּג עַל יְיָ.	"then you can seek the favor of Adonai."[4]

שַׁבָּת הַיּוֹם לַייָ ... CHORUS

E·chol mash·ma·nim u·ma·a·da·nim,	אֱכֹל מַשְׁמַנִּים וּמַעֲדַנִּים,	Eat dainties and delicacies,
u·mat·a·mim har·beih mi·nim —	וּמַטְעַמִּים הַרְבֵּה מִינִים –	and a variety of delights —
e·go·zei fe·rech v'ri·mo·nim,	אֱגוֹזֵי פֶרֶךְ וְרִמּוֹנִים,	soft-shelled nuts and pomegranates,
va·chal·ta v'sa·va·ta u·vei·rach·ta et A·do·nai.	וְאָכַלְתָּ וְשָׂבָעְתָּ וּבֵרַכְתָּ אֶת יְיָ.	"eat and be satisfied, and bless Adonai."[5]

שַׁבָּת הַיּוֹם לַייָ ... CHORUS

La·a·roch ba·shul·chan le·chem cha·mu·dot,	לַעֲרֹךְ בַּשֻּׁלְחָן לֶחֶם חֲמוּדוֹת,	Arrange on the table fancy bread,
la·a·sot ha·yom sha·losh s'u·dot,	לַעֲשׂוֹת הַיּוֹם שָׁלֹשׁ סְעוּדוֹת,	make today three meals,[6]
et ha·Sheim ha·nich·bad l'va·reich u·l'ho·dot,	אֶת הַשֵּׁם הַנִּכְבָּד לְבָרֵךְ וּלְהוֹדוֹת,	bless and thank the Glorious Name,
shik·du v'shim·ru va·a·su va·nai.	שִׁקְדוּ וְשִׁמְרוּ וַעֲשׂוּ בָנַי.	be diligent, My children,
		to keep and observe [it].[7]

שַׁבָּת הַיּוֹם לַייָ ... CHORUS

---

3. From Isaiah 58:13, "If you . . . shall honor . . . [the Sabbath], then you shall delight yourself in Adonai."

4. From Isaiah 58:14, "Then you can seek the favor of Adonai, and I will set you astride the high places of the earth . . . ."

5. From Deuteronomy 8:9-10, "When you have eaten and are full, then you shall bless Adonai."

6. Talmud Shabbat 118a teaches that "Food may be saved for three meals on Shabbat."

7. Cf. Ezra 8:29 "Guard them diligently . . . ." Keeping and observing the Sabbath are mentioned in Exodus 31:16.

Ki Eshm'rah Shabbat   כִּי אֶשְׁמְרָה שַׁבָּת

This poem was written by Abraham Ibn Ezra (1092-1167), a famous Spanish poet and grammarian, whose first name is spelled out by the initial letters of each verse.

Ki esh·m'rah Shab·bat,	כִּי אֶשְׁמְרָה שַׁבָּת,	If I keep the Sabbath,
Eil yish·m'rei·ni.	אֵל יִשְׁמְרֵנִי.	God will watch over me.
Ot hi l'ol·mei ad,	אוֹת הִיא לְעוֹלְמֵי עַד,	It is a sign forever,
bei·no u·vei·ni.	בֵּינוֹ וּבֵינִי.	between God and me.[1]
A·sur m'tzo chei·fetz,	אָסוּר מְצֹא חֵפֶץ,	Forbidden are business
a·sot d'ra·chim,	עֲשׂוֹת דְּרָכִים,	and travel,
gam mi·l'da·beir bo	גַּם מִלְדַבֵּר בּוֹ	also talk of[2]
div·rei tz'ra·chim,	דִּבְרֵי צְרָכִים,	weekday affairs,[3]
div·rei s'cho·rah,	דִּבְרֵי סְחוֹרָה,	matters of commerce,
af div·rei m'la·chim.	אַף דִּבְרֵי מְלָכִים.	or politics.[4]
Eh·geh b'To·rat Eil	אֶהְגֶּה בְּתוֹרַת אֵל	I will ponder God's Torah,
u·t'cha·k'mei·ni.	וּתְחַכְּמֵנִי.	it will enlighten me.[5]

אוֹת הִיא לְעוֹלְמֵי עַד . . . Chorus

1. From Exodus 31:17, "It is a sign between me and the people of Israel forever."

2. The form *asur mi* . . . as in *asur mil'daber* is not very common, but is attested in some rabbinic sources.

3. From Isaiah 58:13, "If you . . . shall honor . . . [the Sabbath], then you shall delight yourself in Adonai."

4. Literally, "royal affairs."

5. The Sabbath is an ideal time for Torah study.

6. The generation of the Exodus.

7. From Exodus 16:22, "On the sixth day they gathered twice as much bread, two omers for each one."

8. lit., law.

9. From Leviticus 24:5-8, "And you shall . . . bake twelve cakes . . . Every Sabbath you shall set it in order before Adonai."

10. An allusion to early Karaite practice.

11. Yom Kippur is the only fast day which may occur on Shabbat.

Bo em·tz'ah ta·mid	בּוֹ אֶמְצְאָה תָמִיד	On it I will always find
no·fesh l'naf·shi.	נֶפֶשׁ לְנַפְשִׁי.	rest for my soul.
Hi·neih l'dor ri·shon	הִנֵּה לְדוֹר רִאשׁוֹן	To the first generation[6]
na·tan k'do·shi	נָתַן קְדוֹשִׁי	the Holy One gave
mo·feit, b'teit	מוֹפֵת, בְּתֵת	a sign, by giving
le·chem mish·neh ba·shi·shi.	לֶחֶם מִשְׁנֶה בַּשִּׁשִּׁי.	a double portion on the sixth day.[7]
Ka·chah b'chol shi·shi	כָּכָה בְּכָל שִׁשִּׁי	So every Sabbath eve
yach·pil m'zo·ni.	יַכְפִּיל מְזוֹנִי.	may [God] double my portion.

אוֹת הִיא לְעוֹלְמֵי עַד . . . CHORUS

Ra·sham b'dat ha·Eil	רָשַׁם בְּדַת הָאֵל	God wrote in the Torah[8]
chok el s'ga·nav	חוֹק אֶל סְגָנָיו	a law for the priests
bo la·a·roch	בּוֹ לַעֲרוֹךְ	on it [the Sabbath] to array
le·chem pa·nim l' fa·nav.	לֶחֶם פָּנִים לְפָנָיו.	the shewbread before God.[9]
Gam bo l'hit·a·not	גַּם בּוֹ לְהִתְעַנּוֹת	Fasting on it,[10]
al pi n'vo·nav	עַל פִּי נְבוֹנָיו	according to the Sages,
a·sur, l'vad mi·Yom	אָסוּר, לְבַד מִיוֹם	is forbidden, except for the Day
Kip·pur a·vo·ni.	כִּפּוּר עֲוֹנִי.	of Atonement for one's sins.[11]

אוֹת הִיא לְעוֹלְמֵי עַד . . . CHORUS

Hu yom m'chu·bad,	הוּא יוֹם מְכֻבָּד,	It is an honored day,
hu yom ta·a·nu·gim,	הוּא יוֹם תַּעֲנוּגִים,	a day of pleasures,
le·chem v'ya·yin tov,	לֶחֶם וְיַיִן טוֹב,	bread, good wine,
ba·sar v'da·gim.	בָּשָׂר וְדָגִים.	meat, and fish.
Ha·mit·a·b'lim bo	הַמִּתְאַבְּלִים בּוֹ	Those that mourn on it
a·chor n'so·gim,	אָחוֹר נְסוֹגִים,	are backsliders,
ki yom s'ma·chot hu	כִּי יוֹם שְׂמָחוֹת הוּא	for it is a day to rejoice
viy·sam·chei·ni.	וִישַׂמְּחֵנִי.	and it shall make me happy.[12]

אוֹת הִיא לְעוֹלְמֵי עַד ... Chorus

Mei·cheil m'la·chah bo	מְחַל מְלָאכָה בּוֹ	Anyone who works on it
so·fo l'hach·rit.	סוֹפוֹ לְהַכְרִית.	shall be cut off.[13]
Al kein a·cha·bes bo	עַל כֵּן אֲכַבֵּס בּוֹ	With it I shall cleanse
li·bi k'vo·rit.	לִבִּי כְּבֹרִית.	my heart, as with soap.[14]
Et·pa·l'lah el Eil	אֶתְפַּלְּלָה אֶל אֵל	I shall pray to God
ar·vit v'shach·rit,	עַרְבִית וְשַׁחְרִית,	the evening and morning prayers,
mu·saf v'gam min·chah,	מוּסָף וְגַם מִנְחָה,	the additional[15] and afternoon prayers,
Hu ya·a·nei·ni.	הוּא יַעֲנֵנִי.	God will answer me.

אוֹת הִיא לְעוֹלְמֵי עַד ... Chorus

12. This is possibly a polemic against the Karaites, who fasted and abstained from pleasures on the Sabbath.

13. The penalty for desecration of the Sabbath in post-Temple times is *karet*, excision, the definition of which is unclear. In any case, it is a punishment meted out by heaven, not an earthly court.

14. The Sabbath has a purifying effect on the soul. *K'vorit*: context requires *kiv'vorit*, but meter does not allow it.

15. Musaf, which commemorates the additional offering sacrificed at the Temple on the Sabbath and holidays.

Mizmor L'David   מִזְמוֹר לְדָוִד

Singing Psalm 23 at the Third Meal gives us comfort and confidence as we are about to make the transition from the serenity of Shabbat into the challenges of the new week.

Miz·mor L'Da·vid.	מִזְמוֹר לְדָוִד.	A Psalm of David.
A·do·nai ro·i,	יְיָ רֹעִי,	Adonai is my shepherd,
lo ech·sar.	לֹא אֶחְסָר.	I shall not want.
Bin·ot de·she yar·bi·tzei·ni,	בִּנְאוֹת דֶּשֶׁא יַרְבִּיצֵנִי,	You make me lie down in grassy meadows,
al mei m'nu·chot y'na·ha·lei·ni.	עַל מֵי מְנֻחוֹת יְנַהֲלֵנִי.	You lead me to still waters.
Naf·shi y'sho·veiv,	נַפְשִׁי יְשׁוֹבֵב,	You renew my soul,
Yan·chei·ni v'ma·g'lei tze·dek	יַנְחֵנִי בְמַעְגְּלֵי צֶדֶק	You guide me on pathways of justice
l'ma·an sh'mo.	לְמַעַן שְׁמוֹ.	for the sake of Your name.
Gam ki ei·leich	גַּם כִּי אֵלֵךְ	Though I walk
b'gei tzal·ma·vet,	בְּגֵיא צַלְמָוֶת,	through a valley of deepest darkness,
lo i·ra ra,	לֹא אִירָא רָע,	I fear no harm,
ki A·tah i·ma·di.	כִּי אַתָּה עִמָּדִי.	for You are with me.

Shiv·t'cha u·mish·an·te·cha
hei·mah y'na·cha·mu·ni.
Ta·a·roch l' fa·nai shul·chan
Ne·ged tzo·r'rai.
Di·shan·ta va·she·men ro·shi,
ko·si r'va·yah.

Ach tov va·che·sed
yir·d' fu·ni kol y'mei cha·yai,
v'shav·ti b'veit A·do·nai
l'o·rech ya·mim.

שִׁבְטְךָ וּמִשְׁעַנְתֶּךָ
הֵמָּה יְנַחֲמֻנִי.
תַּעֲרֹךְ לְפָנַי שֻׁלְחָן
נֶגֶד צֹרְרָי.
דִּשַּׁנְתָּ בַשֶּׁמֶן רֹאשִׁי,
כּוֹסִי רְוָיָה.

אַךְ טוֹב וָחֶסֶד
יִרְדְּפוּנִי כָּל יְמֵי חַיָּי,
וְשַׁבְתִּי בְּבֵית יְיָ
לְאֹרֶךְ יָמִים.

Your rod and your staff —
they comfort me.
You spread out before me a table
in full view of my enemies.
You anoint my head with oil,
my cup overflows.

May only goodness and steadfast love
pursue me all the days of my life,
and I shall dwell in the house of Adonai
for many long years.

Many communities follow the Chasidic custom of beginning Kabbalat Shabbat and ending *S'udah Sh'lishit* with *Y'did Nefesh*, a love poem to God, written by Rabbi Eleazar Azikri, a sixteenth-century Kabbalist of Safed (Tz'fat). The poet speaks of God as parent, master, and especially lover, expressing a profound desire for union with the Divine Presence and asking for healing, mercy, and protection. The fourth verse expresses the poet's desire to be sheltered under God's canopy of peace, a theme that resonates with the *Hashkiveinu* prayer in the *Maariv* service. The first letters of each verse of this song form an acrostic, spelling out the four-letter name of God.

Y'did ne·fesh, av ha·ra·cha·man,	יְדִיד נֶפֶשׁ, אָב הָרַחֲמָן,	Soul-mate, Merciful Parent,
m'shoch av·dach el r'tzo·nach.	מְשׁוֹךְ עַבְדָּךְ אֶל רְצוֹנָךְ.	draw Your servant to do Your will.
Ya·rutz av·dach k'mo a·yal,	יָרוּץ עַבְדָּךְ כְּמוֹ אַיָּל,	Your servant will run like a ram,
yish·ta·cha·veh el mul ha·da·rach.	יִשְׁתַּחֲוֶה אֶל מוּל הֲדָרָךְ.	will bow down before Your splendor.
Ki ye·rav lo y'di·du·tach	כִּי יֶעֱרַב לוֹ יְדִידוּתָךְ	For Your love is tastier
mi·no·fet tzuf v'chol ta·am.	מִנּוֹפֶת צוּף וְכָל טָעַם.	than nectar or any imaginable delight.
Ha·dur na·eh, ziv ha·o·lam,	הָדוּר נָאֶה, זִיו הָעוֹלָם,	Pleasing in splendor, light of the world,
naf·shi cho·lat a·ha·va·tach.	נַפְשִׁי חוֹלַת אַהֲבָתָךְ.	my soul is love-sick for You.
A·na, Eil na, r'fa na lah,	אָנָא, אֵל נָא, רְפָא נָא לָהּ,	Please, God, heal her,[1]
b'har·ot lah no·am zi·vach.	בְּהַרְאוֹת לָהּ נוֹעַם זִיוָךְ.	shine on her Your soothing light.
Az tit·cha·zeik v'tit·ra·pei	אָז תִּתְחַזֵּק וְתִתְרַפֵּא	Then she will be strengthened and healed
v'ha·y'tah lach shif·chat o·lam.	וְהָיְתָה לָךְ שִׁפְחַת עוֹלָם.	and will be Your hand-maiden forever.

1. Numbers 12:13

Va·tik, ye·he·mu ra·cha·me·cha
v'chus na al bein o·ha·vach,
ki zeh ka·mah nich·sof nich·saf
lir·ot b'tif·e·ret u·zach.
A·na, Ei·li, mach·mad li·bi,
chu·shah na, v'al tit·a·lam.

Hi·ga·leh na, u·f'ros, cha·viv, a·lai
et suk·kat sh'lo·mach.
Ta·ir e·retz mi·k'vo·dach,
na·gi·lah v'nis·m'chah bach.
Ma·heir, a·huv, ki va mo·eid,
v'cho·nei·ni kiy·mei o·lam.

וָתִיק, יֶהֱמוּ רַחֲמֶיךָ
וְחוּס נָא עַל בֵּן אוֹהֲבָךְ,
כִּי זֶה כַּמָּה נִכְסוֹף נִכְסַף
לִרְאוֹת בְּתִפְאֶרֶת עֻזָּךְ.
אָנָּא, אֵלִי, מַחְמַד לִבִּי,
חוּשָׁה נָא וְאַל תִּתְעַלָּם.

הִגָּלֶה נָא, וּפְרוֹס, חָבִיב, עָלַי
אֶת סֻכַּת שְׁלוֹמָךְ.
תָּאִיר אֶרֶץ מִכְּבוֹדָךְ,
נָגִילָה וְנִשְׂמְחָה בָּךְ.
מַהֵר, אָהוּב, כִּי בָא מוֹעֵד,
וְחָנֵּנִי כִּימֵי עוֹלָם.

Ancient One, let Your mercies be aroused
and take pity on Your beloved child,
who has so longed to see
the beauty of Your power.
Pray, my God, my heart's desire,
hurry, please, and do not hide.

Reveal Yourself, Beloved, and spread over me
Your canopy of peace.
Let the land be lit up with Your glory,
let us rejoice and revel in You.
Come quickly, my Love, the time has come,
show me Your grace as of old.

הַבְדָּלָה

Separation ◆ Havdalah

Havdalah הַבְדָּלָה

Recite Havdalah at the end of Shabbat when there are three stars in the sky. One should have a cup of wine, grape juice, or other beverage, a special candle with at least two wicks and sweet-smelling spices.
Light the Havdalah candle. Dim the lights. Hold the wine cup in your right hand.

1. Others "song."
2. Isaiah 12:2.
3. Isaiah 12:3.
4. Psalms 3:9.
5. Psalms 46:12.
6. Psalms 84:13
7. Psalms 20:10.

Hi·neih Eil y'shu·a·ti,	הִנֵּה אֵל יְשׁוּעָתִי,	Behold the God of my salvation!
ev·tach v'lo ef·chad,	אֶבְטַח וְלֹא אֶפְחָד,	I have trust and do not fear,
ki o·zi v'zim·rat Yah A·do·nai	כִּי עָזִּי וְזִמְרָת יָהּ יְיָ	for Yah/Adonai is my strength and my might[1]
va·y'hi li liy·shu·ah.	וַיְהִי לִי לִישׁוּעָה.	and has been my salvation.[2]
U·sh'av·tem ma·yim b'sa·son	וּשְׁאַבְתֶּם מַיִם בְּשָׂשׂוֹן	And you shall draw water with joy
mi·ma·ai·nei ha·y'shu·ah.	מִמַּעַיְנֵי הַיְשׁוּעָה.	from the wells of salvation.[3]
lA·do·nai ha·y'shu·ah,	לַיְיָ הַיְשׁוּעָה,	Salvation belongs to Adonai,
al a·m'cha bir·cha·te·cha, se·lah.	עַל עַמְּךָ בִרְכָתֶךָ, סֶּלָה.	Upon your people be Your blessing, Selah.[4]
A·do·nai Tz'va·ot i·ma·nu,	יְיָ צְבָאוֹת עִמָּנוּ,	Adonai of all Forces is with us,
mis·gav la·nu E·lo·hei Ya·a·kov,	מִשְׂגָּב לָנוּ אֱלֹהֵי יַעֲקֹב,	the God of Jacob is a fortress for us,
se·lah.	סֶּלָה.	Selah.[5]
A·do·nai Tz'va·ot,	יְיָ צְבָאוֹת,	Adonai of all Forces,
ash·rei a·dam bo·tei·ach bach.	אַשְׁרֵי אָדָם בֹּטֵחַ בָּךְ.	fortunate is the one who trusts in You.[6]
A·do·nai, ho·shi·ah, ha·Me·lech	יְיָ, הוֹשִׁיעָה, הַמֶּלֶךְ	Adonai, save [us], may the Sovereign
ya·a·nei·nu v'yom ko·rei·nu.	יַעֲנֵנוּ בְיוֹם קָרְאֵנוּ.	answer us on the day we call.[7]

8. Esther 8:16.

9. Psalms 116:13.

Light and wine are used to end Shabbat, just as they marked its beginning. Blessing the wine marks the end of sacred time, the Shabbat that is ending.

Lighting the Havdalah candle is our first creative act of the new week. Examining our fingernails is the first use of light in the new week.

The spices refresh and restore us, compensating for the extra soul which tradition teaches we are given on the Sabbath.

The final blessing acknowledges our ability as human beings to make distinctions in our lives.

Raise the candle.

La·Y'hu·dim ha·y'tah	לַיְּהוּדִים הָיְתָה	For the Jews there was
o·rah v'sim·chah,	אוֹרָה וְשִׂמְחָה,	light and happiness,
v'sa·son viy·kar.	וְשָׂשׂוֹן וִיקָר.	joy and honor.[8]
Kein tih·yeh la·nu.	כֵּן תִּהְיֶה לָּנוּ.	So may it be it for us.

Raise the cup of wine.

Kos y'shu·ot e·sa	כּוֹס יְשׁוּעוֹת אֶשָּׂא	I will raise the cup of deliverance
u·v'sheim A·do·nai ek·ra.	וּבְשֵׁם יְיָ אֶקְרָא.	and in the Name of Adonai, I will call.[9]

Recite the blessing on the wine, but do not drink yet.
If using another beverage the blessing is "shehakol nihyeh bidvaro."

Ba·ruch A·tah A·do·nai,	בָּרוּךְ אַתָּה יְיָ,	Blessed are You, Adonai,
E·lo·hei·nu Me·lech ha·O·lam,	אֱלֹהֵינוּ מֶלֶךְ הָעוֹלָם,	Our God, Ruler of the Universe,
bo·rei p'ri ha·ga·fen.	בּוֹרֵא פְּרִי הַגָּפֶן.	Creator of the fruit of the vine.

Set down the cup; lift the spice box.

Ba·ruch A·tah A·do·nai,	בָּרוּךְ אַתָּה יְיָ,	Blessed are You, Adonai,
E·lo·hei·nu Me·lech ha·O·lam,	אֱלֹהֵינוּ מֶלֶךְ הָעוֹלָם,	Our God, Ruler of the Universe,
bo·rei mi·nei v'sa·mim.	בּוֹרֵא מִינֵי בְשָׂמִים.	Creator of various kinds of spices.

Smell the spices, then set them down or, if others are present, pass them around. Turn to the candle.

Ba·ruch A·tah A·do·nai,	בָּרוּךְ אַתָּה יְיָ,	Blessed are You, Adonai,
E·lo·hei·nu Me·lech ha·O·lam,	אֱלֹהֵינוּ מֶלֶךְ הָעוֹלָם,	Our God, Ruler of the Universe,
bo·rei m'o·rei ha·eish.	בּוֹרֵא מְאוֹרֵי הָאֵשׁ.	Creator of the lights of fire.

Look at the reflection of the light in your fingernails.

Raise the wine glass again. Continue with the blessing marking separation.

Ba·ruch A·tah A·do·nai,	בָּרוּךְ אַתָּה יְיָ,	Blessed are You, Adonai
E·lo·hei·nu Me·lech ha·O·lam,	אֱלֹהֵינוּ מֶלֶךְ הָעוֹלָם,	our God, Ruler of the Universe,
ha·mav·dil	הַמַּבְדִּיל	who distinguishes
bein ko·desh l'chol,	בֵּין קֹדֶשׁ לְחֹל,	between holy and ordinary,
bein or l'cho·shech,	בֵּין אוֹר לְחשֶׁךְ,	between light and darkness,
bein Yis·ra·eil la·a·mim,	בֵּין יִשְׂרָאֵל לָעַמִּים,	between Israel and other peoples,
bein yom ha·sh'vi·i	בֵּין יוֹם הַשְּׁבִיעִי	between the seventh day
l'shei·shet y'mei ha·ma·a·seh.	לְשֵׁשֶׁת יְמֵי הַמַּעֲשֶׂה.	and the six days of work.
Ba·ruch A·tah A·do·nai,	בָּרוּךְ אַתָּה יְיָ,	Blessed are You Adonai,
ha·mav·dil	הַמַּבְדִּיל	who distinguishes
bein ko·desh l'chol.	בֵּין קֹדֶשׁ לְחֹל.	between holy and ordinary.

After havdalah: Drink some of the wine. Douse the candle. Turn lights back on.

Ha·mav·dil	הַמַּבְדִּיל	May the One who distinguishes
bein ko·desh l'chol	בֵּין קֹדֶשׁ לְחֹל	between holy and ordinary
cha·to·tei·nu hu yim·chol,	חַטֹּאתֵינוּ הוּא יִמְחֹל,	forgive our sins, [and]
Zar·ei·nu v'chas·pei·nu	זַרְעֵנוּ וְכַסְפֵּנוּ	cause our offspring and our wealth
yar·beh ka·chol	יַרְבֶּה כַּחוֹל	to increase like the sand
v'cha·ko·cha·vim ba·lai·lah.	וְכַכּוֹכָבִים בַּלָּיְלָה.	and like the stars in the night.[1]

1. This is the first stanza of a longer piyyut by the unknown Yitzchak Hakatan. For all the verses, see pp. 122-124.

Sha·vu·a tov!	שָׁבוּעַ טוֹב!	A good week!
A gu·te voch!	אַ גוטע וואָך!	A good week!
A ma·zl·di·ke voch!	אַ מזלדיקע וואָך!	A successful week!

A good week, a week of peace, may gladness reign and joy increase!

Ei·li·ya·hu ha·Na·vi,	אֵלִיָּהוּ הַנָּבִיא,	Elijah the Prophet,
Ei·li·ya·hu ha·Tish·bi,	אֵלִיָּהוּ הַתִּשְׁבִּי,	Elijah the Tishbite,
Ei·li·ya·hu ha·Gil·a·di.	אֵלִיָּהוּ הַגִּלְעָדִי.	Elijah the Gileadite.
Bim·hei·rah v'ya·mei·nu	בִּמְהֵרָה בְיָמֵינוּ	Speedily in our days
ya·vo ei·lei·nu	יָבוֹא אֵלֵינוּ	may he come to us
im Ma·shi·ach ben Da·vid.	עִם מָשִׁיחַ בֶּן דָּוִד.	with the Messiah, a descendant of David.

SOME ADD:

Mir·yam ha·N'vi·ah	מִרְיָם הַנְּבִיאָה	Miriam the Prophet
oz v'zim·rah b'ya·dah.	עֹז וְזִמְרָה בְּיָדָהּ.	strength and song are in her hands.
Mir·yam tir·kod i·ta·nu	מִרְיָם תִּרְקוֹד אִתָּנוּ	Miriam will dance with us
l'hag·dil zim·rat o·lam.	לְהַגְדִּיל זִמְרַת עוֹלָם.	to increase the world's song.
Mir·yam tir·kod i·ta·nu	מִרְיָם תִּרְקוֹד אִתָּנוּ	Miriam will dance with us
l'ta·kein et ha·o·lam.	לְתַקֵּן אֶת הָעוֹלָם.	to repair the world.
Bim·hei·rah v'ya·mei·nu	בִּמְהֵרָה בְיָמֵינוּ	Speedily in our days,
hi t'vi·ei·nu	הִיא תְּבִיאֵנוּ	she will bring us
el mei ha·y'shu·ah.	אֶל מֵי הַיְשׁוּעָה.	to the waters of redemption.

— *Rabbi Leila Gal Berner*

HaMavdil הַמַּבְדִּיל

The name of the author, Yitzchak HaKatan, appears as an acrostic formed by the first letters of the second to ninth verses. The last three verses are probably a later addition; their first letters spell out אמת (truth). Each verse ends with the word "night." Some think that the poem was written to be said at the conclusion of Yom Kippur, which explains its many references to forgiveness. In the first verse, some substitute *ush'lomeinu*, our peace, for *v'chaspeinu*, following the suggestion of R. Elijah of Vilna.

Ha·mav·dil	הַמַּבְדִּיל	May the One who distinguishes
bein ko·desh l'chol	בֵּין קֹדֶשׁ לְחֹל	between holy and ordinary
cha·to·tei·nu hu yim·chol,	חַטֹּאתֵינוּ הוּא יִמְחוֹל,	forgive our sins, [and]
zar·ei·nu v'chas·pei·nu	זַרְעֵנוּ וְכַסְפֵּנוּ	cause our offspring and our wealth
yar·beh ka·chol	יַרְבֶּה כַּחוֹל	to increase like the sand
v'cha·ko·cha·vim ba·lai·lah.	וְכַכּוֹכָבִים בַּלָּיְלָה.	and like the stars in the night.[1]
Yom pa·nah	יוֹם פָּנָה	The day has moved on
k'tzeil to·mer,	כְּצֵל תֹּמֶר,	like the shadow of a date-palm,
ek·ra la·Eil a·lai go·mer	אֶקְרָא לָאֵל עָלַי גּוֹמֵר	I will call to God to fulfill for me
a·mar sho·mer:	אָמַר שׁוֹמֵר:	[what] the guard said:
a·ta vo·ker v'gam lai·lah.	אָתָא בֹקֶר וְגַם לָיְלָה.	"morning comes and also night."[2]
Tzid·ka·t'cha k'har ta·vor,	צִדְקָתְךָ כְּהַר תָּבוֹר,	Your righteousness is as Mt. Tabor,[3]
al cha·ta·ai a·vor ta·a·vor	עַל חֲטָאַי עָבוֹר תַּעֲבוֹר	forgive my sins absolutely
k'yom et·mol ki ya·a·vor	כְּיוֹם אֶתְמוֹל כִּי יַעֲבוֹר	like yesterday when it is past
v'ash·mu·rah va·lai·lah.	וְאַשְׁמוּרָה בַּלָּיְלָה.	like a watch in the night.[4]

1. Reminiscent of God's promise to the ancestors of Israel, e.g., Genesis 15:5 "…and God said, 'Look at the sky and count the stars, if you are able to count them … thus will your descendants be.'"

2. Isaiah 21:12. "The sentinel said, 'Morning comes and also night …'" The morning may refer to Israel's redemption while night may refer to the retribution of Israel's enemies.

3. The mountain that Deborah and Barak's troops climbed in Judges 4. In other words, God's righteousness is as great as the tallest mountain.

4. Psalms 90:4. "For a thousand years in Your sight are like yesterday when it is past, or like a watch in the night."

5. *Minchah* refers to the afternoon offering or prayer, a time associated on Shabbat with God's mercy.

6. Psalms 6:7

7. Similar to a line in the piyyut *Anim Z'mirot*. Based on Song of Songs 5:2. "... Listen, my beloved is knocking, 'Open to me, my sister, my love, my dove, my perfect one; for my head is wet with dew, my locks with the drops of night.'"

8. cf. Proverbs 7:9. Darkness and night are metaphors for the exile.

9. i.e., how to live the good life that will lead to the ultimate reward.

10. Based on Isaiah 38:12, "My life is rolled up like a web and cut from the thrum. Only from daybreak to nightfall was I kept whole." The author gives a new meaning to elements of the verse, *dalah* (thrum, edge of a garment) becoming poverty, *t'vatseni* meaning "save me," and *miyom ad lailah* meaning as quickly as possible, from the time it takes for day to turn to night.

11. Job 35:10. Because of the multitude of oppressions people cry out; they call for help because of the arm of the mighty, but no one says, 'Where is God my Maker, who gives strength in the night?'"

Cha·l' fah o·nat min·cha·ti	חָלְפָה עוֹנַת מִנְחָתִי	The time of my Minchah[5] has passed —
mi yi·tein m'nu·cha·ti?	מִי יִתֵּן מְנוּחָתִי?	who will grant me rest?
Ya·ga·ti v'an·cha·ti,	יָגַעְתִּי בְּאַנְחָתִי,	I grow weary in my sighing,[6]
as·cheh v'chol lai·lah.	אַשְׂחֶה בְכָל לָיְלָה.	I am soaked with tears every night.
Ko·li bal yun·tal,	קוֹלִי בַּל יֻנְטָל,	May my voice not be taken away,
p'tach li sha·ar ha·m'nu·tal,	פְּתַח לִי שַׁעַר הַמְּנֻטָּל,	Open for me the lofty gate,
she·ro·shi nim·la tal,	שֶׁרֹאשִׁי נִמְלָא טָל,	for my head is filled with dew,
k'vu·tzo·tai r'si·sei lai·lah.	קְוֻצּוֹתַי רְסִיסֵי לָיְלָה.	my locks with slivers of night.[7]
Hei·a·teir no·ra v'a·yom,	הַעֲתֵר נוֹרָא וְאָיוֹם,	Answer me, Awesome, Feared One,
a·sha·vei·a t'nah fid·yom	אֲשַׁוֵּעַ תְּנָה פִּדְיוֹם	I cry out — grant redemption
b'ne·shef b'e·rev yom	בְּנֶשֶׁף בְּעֶרֶב יוֹם	in the evening, at twilight,
b'i·shon lai·lah.	בְּאִישׁוֹן לָיְלָה.	in the dead of night.[8]
K'ra·ti·cha Yah ho·shi·ei·ni	קְרָאתִיךָ יָהּ הוֹשִׁיעֵנִי	I called to You, God, save me!
o·rach cha·yim to·di·ei·ni	אֹרַח חַיִּים תּוֹדִיעֵנִי	Make known to me the way of life,[9]
mi·da·lah t'vatz·ei·ni	מִדַּלָּה תְּבַצְעֵנִי	from poverty save me
mi·yom ad lai·lah.	מִיּוֹם עַד לָיְלָה.	from day to night.[10]
Ta·heir ti·nuf ma·a·sai	טַהֵר טִנּוּף מַעֲשַׂי	Purify the filth of my deeds
pen yo·m'ru mach·i·sai:	פֶּן יֹאמְרוּ מַכְעִסַי:	lest my tormentors say:
a·yeih na E·lo·ah o·sai,	אַיֵּה נָא אֱלוֹהַּ עֹשָׂי,	"Where is God my maker,
ha·no·tein z'mi·rot ba·lai·lah.	הַנּוֹתֵן זְמִירוֹת בַּלָּיְלָה.	Who gives strength in the night."[11]

Nach·nu v'yad·cha ka·cho·mer, s'lach na al kal va·cho·mer, yom l'yom ya·bi·a o·mer v'lai·lah l'lai·lah.	נַחְנוּ בְיָדְךָ כַּחוֹמֶר, סְלַח נָא עַל קַל וָחוֹמֶר, יוֹם לְיוֹם יַבִּיעַ אֹמֶר וְלַיְלָה לְלַיְלָה.	We are like clay in your hands, please forgive both trivial and grave,[12] day to day makes utterance and night to night.[13]
Eil po·deh mi·kol tzar k'ra·nu·cha min ha·mei·tzar. Ya·d'cha lo tik·tzar lo yom v'lo lai·lah.	אֵל פּוֹדֶה מִכָּל צָר קְרָאנוּךָ מִן הַמֵּצָר. יָדְךָ לֹא תִקְצָר לֹא יוֹם וְלֹא לָיְלָה.	God who saves from every trouble, we call from the straits.[14] Your hand will not fall short[15] neither by day nor by night.
Mi·cha·eil sar Yis·ra·eil Eli·ya·hu v'Gav·ri·eil ya·vo·u na im ha-go·eil, Ku·mu [ro·nu] ba·cha·tzi ha·lai·lah.	מִיכָאֵל שַׂר יִשְׂרָאֵל אֵלִיָּהוּ וְגַבְרִיאֵל יָבֹאוּ נָא עִם הַגּוֹאֵל, קוּמוּ [רְנּוּ] בַּחֲצִי הַלָּיְלָה.	Michael, Guardian of Israel, Elijah and Gabriel — come, please, with the redeemer, arise, [cry out] in the middle of the night.[16]
T'nah la·nu sha·vu·a tov ra·a·nan k'gan ra·tov. Gam A·do·nai yi·ten ha·tov kol ha·yom v'chol ha·lai·lah.	תְּנָה לָנוּ שָׁבוּעַ טוֹב רַעֲנָן כְּגַן רָטוֹב. גַּם יְיָ יִתֵּן הַטּוֹב כָּל הַיּוֹם וְכָל הַלָּיְלָה.	Give us a good week fresh as a moist garden. May God also give goodness all day and all night.

12. i.e. transgressions. An allusion to *a fortiori*, one of the thirteen hermeneutical priniciples.

13. Taken from Psalms 19:3: "Day to day makes utterance and night to night declares knowledge." An allusion to the wonders of creation.

14. Cf. Psalms 118:5.

15. See Numbers 11:23.

16. See Lamentations 2:19, Exodus 12:29. Some versions omit word in brackets.

This piyyut of unknown authorship is one of the most popular songs sung at the *hakkafot* on Simchat Torah. It is in the form of an alphabetic acrostic with *kof* and *reish* repeated to fill out the last verse. It praises God, Moses, the Torah, and Israel in superlatives.

CHORUS (2X):

Mi·pi Eil, mi·pi Eil,
y'vo·rach kol Yis·ra·eil.

מִפִּי אֵל, מִפִּי אֵל,
יְבוֹרַךְ כָּל יִשְׂרָאֵל.

CHORUS (2X):

From the mouth of God, from the mouth of God,
will all of Israel be blessed.

Ein a·dir kA·do·nai,
v'ein ba·ruch k'ven Am·ram,
ein g'du·lah ka·To·rah,
V'ein do·r'she·ha k'Yis·ra·eil.

אֵין אַדִּיר כַּייָ,
וְאֵין בָּרוּךְ כְּבֶן עַמְרָם,
אֵין גְּדֻלָּה כַּתּוֹרָה,
וְאֵין דּוֹרְשֶׁיהָ כְּיִשְׂרָאֵל.

There is no one as exalted as Adonai,
no one as blessed as Amram's son,
nothing as great as the Torah,
no better exegetes than Israel.

CHORUS Mi·pi Eil, mi·pi Eil...

CHORUS מִפִּי אֵל, מִפִּי אֵל...

Ein ha·dur kA·do·nai,
v'ein va·tik k'ven Am·ram,
ein z'chi·yah ka·To·rah,
v'ein cha·cha·me·ha k'Yis·ra·eil.

אֵין הָדוּר כַּייָ,
וְאֵין וָתִיק כְּבֶן עַמְרָם,
אֵין זְכִיָּה כַּתּוֹרָה,
וְאֵין חֲכָמֶיהָ כְּיִשְׂרָאֵל.

There is no one as glorious as Adonai,
no one as venerable as Amram's son,
no prize as great as the Torah,
no better scholars than Israel.

CHORUS Mi·pi Eil, mi·pi Eil...

CHORUS מִפִּי אֵל, מִפִּי אֵל...

Ein ta·hor kA·do·nai,
v'ein ya·chid k'ven Am·ram,
ein k'vu·dah ka·To·rah,
v'ein lo·m'de·ha k'Yis·ra·eil.

Chorus *Mi·pi Eil, mi·pi Eil . . .*

אֵין טָהוֹר כַּיְיָ,
וְאֵין יָחִיד כְּבֶן עַמְרָם,
אֵין כְּבֻדָּה כַּתּוֹרָה,
וְאֵין לוֹמְדֶיהָ כְּיִשְׂרָאֵל.

Chorus מִפִּי אֵל, מִפִּי אֵל . . .

There is no one as pure as Adonai,
no one as singular as Amram's son,
no possession like the Torah,
no better students than Israel.

Ein me·lech kA·do·nai,
v'ein na·or k'ven Am·ram,
ein s'gu·lah ka·To·rah,
v'ein o·s'ke·ha k'Yis·ra·eil.

Chorus *Mi·pi Eil, mi·pi Eil . . .*

אֵין מֶלֶךְ כַּיְיָ,
וְאֵין נָאוֹר כְּבֶן עַמְרָם,
אֵין סְגֻלָּה כַּתּוֹרָה,
וְאֵין עוֹסְקֶיהָ כְּיִשְׂרָאֵל.

Chorus מִפִּי אֵל, מִפִּי אֵל . . .

There is no king like Adonai,
no one as enlightened as Amram's son,
no treasure like the Torah,
none that study it better than Israel.

Ein po·deh kA·do·nai,
v'ein tza·dik k'ven Am·ram,
ein k'du·shah ka·To·rah,
v'ein ro·m'me·ha k'Yis·ra·eil.

Chorus *Mi·pi Eil, mi·pi Eil . . .*

אֵין פּוֹדֶה כַּיְיָ,
וְאֵין צַדִּיק כְּבֶן עַמְרָם,
אֵין קְדֻשָּׁה כַּתּוֹרָה,
וְאֵין רוֹמְמֶיהָ כְּיִשְׂרָאֵל.

Chorus מִפִּי אֵל, מִפִּי אֵל . . .

There is no redeemer like Adonai,
no one as righteous as Amram's son,
nothing as holy as the Torah,
none that exalt it better than Israel.

Ein ka·dosh kA·do·nai,
v'ein ra·chum k'ven Am·ram,
ein sh'mi·rah ka·To·rah,
v'ein to·m'che·ha k'Yis·ra·eil.

Chorus *Mi·pi Eil, mi·pi Eil . . .*

אֵין קָדוֹשׁ כַּיְיָ,
וְאֵין רַחוּם כְּבֶן עַמְרָם,
אֵין שְׁמִירָה כַּתּוֹרָה,
וְאֵין תּוֹמְכֶיהָ כְּיִשְׂרָאֵל.

Chorus מִפִּי אֵל, מִפִּי אֵל . . .

There is no one as holy as Adonai,
no one as merciful as Amram's son,
no talisman like the Torah,
none that support it better than Israel.

Or za·ru·a la·tza·dik,	אוֹר זָרֻעַ לַצַּדִּיק,	Light is sown for the righteous,
u·l'yish·rei leiv sim·chah.	וּלְיִשְׁרֵי לֵב שִׂמְחָה.	joy for the upright in heart.

— PSALMS 97:11

SOME CONTINUE:

Gits a·rayn a ne·cho·me·le	גיטס אַריַין אַ נחמהלע	Put in a bit of comfort
in a yi·di·she ne·sho·me·le.	אין אַ ייִדישע נשמהלע.	into a Jewish soul.

Or cha·dash	אוֹר חָדָשׁ	Cause a new light
al Tzi·yon ta·ir	עַל צִיּוֹן תָּאִיר	to shine on Zion
v'niz·keh chu·la·nu	וְנִזְכֶּה כֻלָּנוּ	and may we all be worthy
[bi]m·hei·rah l'o·ro.	[בִּ]מְהֵרָה לְאוֹרוֹ.	soon to share its light.

— MORNING SERVICE LITURGY

A·chat sha·al·ti mei·eit Adonai	אַחַת שָׁאַלְתִּי מֵאֵת יְיָ	One thing I ask of Adonai
o·tah a·va·keish,	אוֹתָהּ אֲבַקֵּשׁ,	this is what I seek —
shiv·ti b'veit Adonai	שִׁבְתִּי בְּבֵית יְיָ	to reside in the house of Adonai
kol y'mei cha·yai,	כָּל יְמֵי חַיַּי,	all the days of my life,
la·cha·zot b'no·am Adonai	לַחֲזוֹת בְּנֹעַם יְיָ	to behold the pleasantness of Adonai
u·l'va·keir b'hei·cha·lo.	וּלְבַקֵּר בְּהֵיכָלוֹ.	and to visit the divine sanctuary.

— PSALMS 27:4

Al ti·ra mi·pa·chad pit·om
u·mi·sho·at r'sha·im ki ta·vo.
U·tzu ei·tzah v'tu·far,
da·b'ru da·var v'lo ya·kum,
ki i·ma·nu Eil.

אַל תִּירָא מִפַּחַד פִּתְאֹם
וּמִשֹּׁאַת רְשָׁעִים כִּי תָבֹא.
עֻצוּ עֵצָה וְתֻפָר,
דַּבְּרוּ דָבָר וְלֹא יָקוּם,
כִּי עִמָּנוּ אֵל.

Do not fear sudden terror
or the disaster befalling the wicked.
Hatch a plot — it shall be foiled,
make a plan — it will not succeed
for God is with us.

— Proverbs 3:25; Isaiah 8:10

Ei·leh cham·dah li·bi,
[v']chu·sah na
v'al na tit·a·leim.

אֵלֶּה חָמְדָה לִבִּי,
[וְ]חוּסָה נָא
וְאַל נָא תִּתְעַלֵּם.

These things my heart desires,
have mercy, please
and do not hide yourself.

— Yedid Nefesh, Chasidic Version

E·lo·hai, n'sha·mah
she·na·ta·ta bi t'ho·rah hi.

אֱלֹהַי, נְשָׁמָה
שֶׁנָּתַתָּ בִּי טְהוֹרָה הִיא.

My God, the soul
You placed in me is pure.

— Morning blessings

I·lu fi·nu
ma·lei shi·rah ka·yam . . .

אִלּוּ פִינוּ
מָלֵא שִׁירָה כַּיָּם . . .

Were our mouths
full of song as the sea . . .

— Nishmat, Shabbat Morning Service

Ei·li A·tah v'o·de·ka,
E·lo·hai a·ro·m'me·ka.
Ho·du lA·do·nai ki tov,
ki l'o·lam chas·do.

אֵלִי אַתָּה וְאוֹדֶךָּ,
אֱלֹהַי אֲרוֹמְמֶךָּ.
הוֹדוּ לַיְיָ כִּי טוֹב,
כִּי לְעוֹלָם חַסְדּוֹ.

You are my God and I thank You,
my God, I exalt You.
Give thanks to Adonai for being good,
for the One's kindness is eternal.

— PSALMS 118: 28-29

Ei·li, Ei·li,
she·lo yi·ga·meir l'o·lam:
ha·chol v'ha·yam,
rish·rush shel ha·ma·yim,
b'rak ha·sha·ma·yim,
t'fi·lat ha·a·dam.

אֵלִי, אֵלִי,
שֶׁלֹּא יִגָּמֵר לְעוֹלָם:
הַחוֹל וְהַיָּם,
רִשְׁרוּשׁ שֶׁל הַמַּיִם,
בְּרַק הַשָּׁמַיִם,
תְּפִלַת הָאָדָם.

My God, My God,
I pray that these things never end:
the sand and the sea,
the rush of the waters,
the crash of the heavens,
the prayer of the heart.

— HANNAH SENESH

Ei·le·cha A·do·nai ek·ra,
v'el A·do·nai et·cha·nan,
sh'ma A·do·nai v'cho·nei·ni,
A·do·nai he·yeih o·zeir li.

אֵלֶיךָ יְיָ אֶקְרָא,
וְאֶל יְיָ אֶתְחַנָּן,
שְׁמַע יְיָ וְחָנֵּנִי,
יְיָ הֱיֵה עֹזֵר לִי.

To You, Adonai, I call,
and to Adonai, I plead:
hear me, Adonai, be gracious to me,
Adonai, be my helper.

— PSALMS 30:9,11

Im ein a·ni li, mi li?
U·ch'she·a·ni l'atz·mi,
mah a·ni?
V'im lo ach·shav,
ei·ma·tai?

אִם אֵין אֲנִי לִי, מִי לִי?
וּכְשֶׁאֲנִי לְעַצְמִי,
מָה אֲנִי?
וְאִם לֹא עַכְשָׁיו,
אֵימָתַי?

If I am not for myself, who will be for me?
And if I am only for myself,
what am I?
And if not now,
when?

— HILLEL, PIRKEI AVOT 1:14

Im esh·ka·cheich, Y'ru·sha·la·yim,
tish·kach y'mi·ni.
Tid·bak l'sho·ni l'chi·ki
im lo ez·k'rei·chi,
im lo a·a·leh et Y'ru·sha·la·yim
al rosh sim·cha·ti.

אִם אֶשְׁכָּחֵךְ, יְרוּשָׁלַיִם,
תִּשְׁכַּח יְמִינִי.
תִּדְבַּק לְשׁוֹנִי לְחִכִּי
אִם לֹא אֶזְכְּרֵכִי,
אִם לֹא אַעֲלֶה אֶת יְרוּשָׁלַיִם
עַל רֹאשׁ שִׂמְחָתִי.

If I forget you, Jerusalem,
let my right hand wither.
May my tongue stick to my palate
if I do not remember you,
if I do not raise Jerusalem
above all my joys.

— PSALMS 137:5-6

Im tir·tzu,
ein zo a·ga·dah:
lih·yot am chof·shi
b'ar·tzei·nu,
e·retz Tzi·yon viY·ru·sha·la·yim.

אִם תִּרְצוּ,
אֵין זוֹ אַגָּדָה:
לִהְיוֹת עַם חָפְשִׁי
בְּאַרְצֵנוּ,
אֶרֶץ צִיּוֹן וִירוּשָׁלַיִם.

If you will it,
it is no dream:
to be a free people
in our own land,
the land of Zion and Jerusalem.

— THEODOR HERZL AND NAPHTALI HERZ IMBER
— COMBINATION BY DEBBIE FRIEDMAN

E·met A·tah hu ri·shon
v'a·tah hu a·cha·ron,
u·mi·bal·a·de·cha
ein la·nu me·lech
go·eil u·mo·shi·a.

אֱמֶת אַתָּה הוּא רִאשׁוֹן
וְאַתָּה הוּא אַחֲרוֹן,
וּמִבַּלְעָדֶיךָ
אֵין לָנוּ מֶלֶךְ
גּוֹאֵל וּמוֹשִׁיעַ.

True it is that You are the first
and You are the last,
and other than You
we have no ruler,
redeemer, or savior.

— MORNING SERVICE LITURGY

A·na, b'cho·ach
g'du·lat y'min·cha
ta·tir tz'ru·rah.
Ka·beil ri·nat a·m'cha,
sa·g'vei·nu, ta·ha·rei·nu, no·ra.

אָנָּא, בְּכֹחַ
גְּדֻלַּת יְמִינְךָ
תַּתִּיר צְרוּרָה.
קַבֵּל רִנַּת עַמְּךָ,
שַׂגְּבֵנוּ, טַהֲרֵנוּ, נוֹרָא.

Please, with the power
of Your great right hand
free the bound.
Accept the song of your people,
empower us, purify us, Awesome One.

— RABBI NECHUNYA BEN HAKANAH, 2ND CENTURY;
KABBALAT SHABBAT SERVICE

A·nah A·do·nai ki a·ni av·de·cha;
a·ni av·d'cha,
ben a·ma·te·cha,
pi·tach·ta l'mo·sei·rai.

אָנָּה יְיָ כִּי אֲנִי עַבְדֶּךָ;
אֲנִי עַבְדְּךָ,
בֶּן אֲמָתֶךָ,
פִּתַּחְתָּ לְמוֹסֵרָי.

I pray to You, Adonai, for I am Your servant;
I am Your servant,
the child of Your handmaid,
You have opened my bonds.

— PSALMS 116:16

A·ni y'shei·nah v'li·bi eir.
Kol, do·di do·feik!
Pit·chi li a·cho·ti,
ra·ya·ti, yo·na·ti, ta·ma·ti,
she·ro·shi nim·la tal
k'vu·tzo·tai r'si·sei lai·lah.

אֲנִי יְשֵׁנָה וְלִבִּי עֵר.
קוֹל, דּוֹדִי דוֹפֵק!
פִּתְחִי לִי אֲחֹתִי,
רַעְיָתִי, יוֹנָתִי, תַמָּתִי,
שֶׁרֹאשִׁי נִמְלָא טָל
קְוֻצּוֹתַי רְסִיסֵי לָיְלָה.

I sleep, but my heart is awake.
Hark, My beloved knocks!
Open to me, my sister,
my love, my dove, my perfect one,
for my head is filled with dew,
and my locks with the drops of night.

— Song of Songs 5:2

A·ni ma·a·min
be·e·mu·nah sh'lei·mah
b'vi·at ha·Ma·shi·ach,
v'af al pi she·yit·mah·mei·ah,
im kol zeh
a·cha·keh lo
b'chol yom she·ya·vo.

אֲנִי מַאֲמִין
בֶּאֱמוּנָה שְׁלֵמָה
בְּבִיאַת הַמָּשִׁיחַ,
וְאַף עַל פִּי שֶׁיִּתְמַהְמֵהַּ,
עִם כָּל זֶה
אֲחַכֶּה לּוֹ
בְּכָל יוֹם שֶׁיָּבֹא.

I believe
with perfect faith
in the coming of the Messiah,
and though he may tarry,
in spite of all of this,
I expect him
every day, that he will come.

— Adaptation of Maimonides' 12th Principle of Faith

O·rech ya·mim as·bi·ei·hu,
v'ar·ei·hu bi·shu·a·ti.

אֹרֶךְ יָמִים אַשְׂבִּיעֵהוּ,
וְאַרְאֵהוּ בִּישׁוּעָתִי.

With long life I will satisfy him,
and make him behold My salvation.

— Psalms 91:16

E·sa ei·nai el he·ha·rim,
me·a·yin ya·vo ez·ri.
Ez·ri mei·im A·do·nai,
o·seih sha·ma·yim va·a·retz.

אֶשָּׂא עֵינַי אֶל־הֶהָרִים,
מֵאַיִן יָבֹא עֶזְרִי.
עֶזְרִי מֵעִם יְיָ,
עֹשֵׂה שָׁמַיִם וָאָרֶץ.

I lift up my eyes to the mountains,
from where comes my help?
My help comes from Adonai,
Maker of heaven and earth.

— PSALMS 121:1-2

A·shi·rah lA·do·nai b'cha·yai,
a·za·m'rah lEi·lo·hai b'o·di.
Ye·e·rav a·lav si·chi,
a·no·chi es·mach bA·do·nai.
Yi·ta·mu cha·ta·im min ha·a·retz
u·r'sha·im od ei·nam.
Ba·r'chi naf·shi et A·do·nai.
Ha·l'lu·yah.

אָשִׁירָה לַיְיָ בְּחַיָּי,
אֲזַמְּרָה לֵאלֹהַי בְּעוֹדִי.
יֶעֱרַב עָלָיו שִׂיחִי,
אָנֹכִי אֶשְׂמַח בַּיְיָ.
יִתַּמּוּ חַטָּאִים מִן הָאָרֶץ
וּרְשָׁעִים עוֹד אֵינָם.
בָּרְכִי נַפְשִׁי אֶת יְיָ.
הַלְלוּיָהּ.

I will sing to Adonai all my life,
I will hymn to my God as long as I [exist].
Let my prayer be pleasing to God,
for I, I will rejoice in Adonai.
Let sinners disappear from the earth
and the wicked be no more.
Bless, O my soul, Adonai.
Halleluyah.

— PSALMS 104:33-35

Bil·va·vi *mish·kan ev·neh* / בִּלְבָבִי מִשְׁכָּן אֶבְנֶה / In my heart, I will build a sanctuary
la·ha·dar k'vo·do. / לַהֲדַר כְּבוֹדוֹ. / to Your Glorious Presence.
u·va·mish·kan miz·bei·ach a·sim, / וּבַמִּשְׁכָּן מִזְבֵּחַ אָשִׂים / In that sanctuary I will place an altar
l'kar·nei ho·do. / לְקַרְנֵי הוֹדוֹ. / to the rays of Your Splendor.
U·l'neir ta·mid e·kach li / וּלְנֵר תָּמִיד אֶקַּח לִי / For an eternal light I will take
et eish ha·a·kei·dah, / אֶת אֵשׁ הָעֲקֵדָה, / the flame of the binding [of Isaac],
u·l'kor·ban ak·riv lo / וּלְקָרְבָּן אַקְרִיב לוֹ / and for a sacrifice I will offer You
et naf·shi ha·y'chi·dah. / אֶת נַפְשִׁי הַיְּחִידָה. / my precious soul.

— ELEAZAR AZIKRI, SEFER CHAREDIM

Ba·ruch Hu E·lo·hei·nu / בָּרוּךְ הוּא אֱלֹהֵינוּ / Blessed is our God
she·b'ra·a·nu lich·vo·do, / שֶׁבְּרָאָנוּ לִכְבוֹדוֹ, / who created us for God's Glory,
v'hiv·di·la·nu min ha·to·im, / וְהִבְדִּילָנוּ מִן הַתּוֹעִים, / separated us from those gone astray,
v'na·tan la·nu to·rat e·met, / וְנָתַן לָנוּ תּוֹרַת אֱמֶת, / gave us the Torah of truth,
v'cha·yei o·lam na·ta b'to·chei·nu. / וְחַיֵּי עוֹלָם נָטַע בְּתוֹכֵנוּ. / and planted within us life everlasting.

— K'DUSHA D'SIDRA (WEEKDAY SIDDUR)

Ba·ruch ha·Ma·kom, / בָּרוּךְ הַמָּקוֹם, / Blessed is the Presence,
Ba·ruch Hu. / בָּרוּךְ הוּא. / Blessed are You.
Ba·ruch she·na·tan To·rah / בָּרוּךְ שֶׁנָּתַן תּוֹרָה / Blessed is the One who gave the Torah
l'a·mo Yis·ra·eil. / לְעַמּוֹ יִשְׂרָאֵל. / to the people Israel.
Ba·ruch Hu. / בָּרוּךְ הוּא. / Blessed are You.

— PASSOVER HAGGADAH

Ba·r'chei·nu, a·vi·nu,
ku·la·nu k'e·chad, b'or pa·ne·cha.

בָּרְכֵנוּ, אָבִינוּ,
כֻּלָּנוּ כְּאֶחָד, בְּאוֹר פָּנֶיךָ.

Bless us, our Parent,
together as one, with the light of Your face.

— AMIDAH

Da·vid, Me·lech Yis·ra·eil,
Chai v'ka·yam.

דָּוִד, מֶלֶךְ יִשְׂרָאֵל,
חַי וְקַיָּם.

David, King of Israel,
lives and endures.

— TALMUD ROSH HASHANAH 25A

Si·man tov u·ma·zal tov
y'hei la·nu
u·l'chol Yis·ra·eil. A·mein.

סִמָּן טוֹב וּמַזָּל טוֹב
יְהֵא לָנוּ
וּלְכָל יִשְׂרָאֵל. אָמֵן.

May there be a good sign and good fortune
for us
and for all Israel. Amen.

— KIDDUSH LEVANAH CEREMONY

Do·di li *va·a·ni lo,*
ha·ro·eh ba·sho·sha·nim.
Mi zot o·lah min ha·mid·bar,
m'ku·te·ret mor u·l'vo·nah?
Li·bav·ti·ni a·cho·ti cha·lah.
U·ri tza·fon u·vo·i tei·man.

דּוֹדִי לִי וַאֲנִי לוֹ,
הָרֹעֶה בַּשּׁוֹשַׁנִּים.
מִי זֹאת עֹלָה מִן הַמִּדְבָּר,
מְקֻטֶּרֶת מוֹר וּלְבוֹנָה?
לִבַּבְתִּנִי אֲחֹתִי כַלָּה.
עוּרִי צָפוֹן וּבוֹאִי תֵימָן.

My beloved is mine, and I am his;
he tends his flock among the lilies.
Who is that going up from the wilderness,
fragrant with myrrh and incense?
You have ravished my heart, my sister, my bride!
Awake, north wind; come, south wind.

— SONG OF SONGS 2:16, 3:6, 4:9, 4:16

Hei·vei·nu sha·lom *a·lei·chem.*

הֵבֵאנוּ שָׁלוֹם עֲלֵיכֶם.

We have brought peace to you.

Ha·vah Na·gi·lah v'nis·m'chah.   הָבָה נָגִילָה וְנִשְׂמְחָה.   Come, let us rejoice and be happy.

Ha·vah n'ra·n'nah v'nis·m'chah.   הָבָה נְרַנְּנָה וְנִשְׂמְחָה.   Come, let us sing and be happy.

U·ru a·chim b'leiv sa·mei·ach.   עוּרוּ אַחִים בְּלֵב שָׂמֵחַ.   Awake, brothers [and sisters], with a joyful heart.

— Moshe Nathanson (or possibly Abraham Zvi Idelsohn)

Ha·vah na·shi·rah   הָבָה נָשִׁירָה   Let us sing

shir Ha·l'lu·yah.   שִׁיר הַלְלוּיָהּ.   a song of praise to God.

Ho·shi·ah et a·me·cha   הוֹשִׁיעָה אֶת עַמֶּךָ   Save your people

u·va·reich et na·cha·la·te·cha.   וּבָרֵךְ אֶת נַחֲלָתֶךָ.   and bless Your heritage.

u·r'eim v'na·s'eim ad ha·o·lam.   וּרְעֵם וְנַשְּׂאֵם עַד הָעוֹלָם.   Tend them and sustain them forever.

— Psalms 28:9

Hi·neih mah tov u·mah na·im   הִנֵּה מַה טּוֹב וּמַה נָּעִים   Behold, how good and how pleasant it is

she·vet a·chim gam ya·chad.   שֶׁבֶת אַחִים גַּם יָחַד.   for brothers [and sisters] to dwell together.

— Psalms 133:1

Ha·shi·vei·nu A·do·nai Ei·le·cha   הֲשִׁיבֵנוּ יְיָ אֵלֶיךָ   Return us to you, God,

v'na·shu·vah.   וְנָשׁוּבָה.   and we will return.

Cha·deish ya·mei·nu k'ke·dem.   חַדֵּשׁ יָמֵינוּ כְּקֶדֶם.   Renew our days as of old.

— Lamentations 5:21

Hash·mi·i·ni et ko·leich,
ki ko·leich a·reiv u·mar·eich na·veh.

הַשְׁמִיעִינִי אֶת קוֹלֵךְ,
כִּי קוֹלֵךְ עָרֵב וּמַרְאֵיךְ נָאוֶה.

Let me hear your voice,
for your voice is pleasant and your appearance comely.

— *Song of Songs 2:14*

Va·a·ni, t'fi·la·ti
l'cha A·do·nai, eit ra·tzon.
E·lo·him b'rov chas·de·cha,
a·nei·ni be·e·met yish·e·cha.

וַאֲנִי, תְפִלָּתִי
לְךָ יְיָ, עֵת רָצוֹן.
אֱלֹהִים בְּרָב חַסְדֶּךָ,
עֲנֵנִי בֶּאֱמֶת יִשְׁעֶךָ.

As for me, may my prayer
come to You, Adonai, at a time of favor.
God, in Your great kindness,
answer me with Your sure deliverance.

— *Psalms 69:14 and Morning Service Liturgy*

U·va·u ha·o·v'dim
b'e·retz A·shur
v'ha·ni·da·chim b'e·retz Mitz·ra·yim
v'hish·ta·cha·vu lA·do·nai
b'har ha·ko·desh biY·ru·sha·la·yim.

וּבָאוּ הָאֹבְדִים
בְּאֶרֶץ אַשּׁוּר
וְהַנִּדָּחִים בְּאֶרֶץ מִצְרָיִם
וְהִשְׁתַּחֲווּ לַיְיָ
בְּהַר הַקֹּדֶשׁ בִּירוּשָׁלָיִם.

And the strayed
who are in the land of Assyria
and the expelled who are in the land of Egypt
will come and bow down to God
on the holy mountain, in Jerusalem.

— *Isaiah 27:13*

V'ha·eir ei·nei·nu b'To·ra·te·cha,
v'da·beik li·bei·nu b'mitz·vo·te·cha,
v'ya·cheid l'va·vei·nu
l'a·ha·vah u·l'yir·ah et sh'me·cha,
v'lo nei·vosh l'o·lam va·ed.

וְהָאֵר עֵינֵינוּ בְּתוֹרָתֶךָ,
וְדַבֵּק לִבֵּנוּ בְּמִצְוֹתֶיךָ,
וְיַחֵד לְבָבֵנוּ
לְאַהֲבָה וּלְיִרְאָה אֶת שְׁמֶךָ,
וְלֹא נֵבוֹשׁ לְעוֹלָם וָעֶד.

Enlighten our eyes with Your Torah,
attach our hearts to Your mitzvot,
unite our hearts
to love and revere Your Name,
so that we may never be ashamed.

— *Shacharit (Morning Service) Liturgy*

Va·ha·vi·o·tim el har kod·shi
v'si·mach·tim b'veit t'fi·la·ti.
O·lo·tei·hem v'ziv'chei·hem
l'ra·tzon al miz·b'chi
ki vei·ti beit t'fi·lah
yi·ka·rei l'chol ha·a·mim.

וַהֲבִיאוֹתִים אֶל הַר קָדְשִׁי
וְשִׂמַּחְתִּים בְּבֵית תְּפִלָּתִי.
עוֹלֹתֵיהֶם וְזִבְחֵיהֶם
לְרָצוֹן עַל מִזְבְּחִי
כִּי בֵיתִי בֵּית תְּפִלָּה
יִקָּרֵא לְכָל הָעַמִּים.

I will bring them to my holy mountain
and make then rejoice in my house of prayer.
Their burnt offerings and sacrifices
will be well received on my altar
for my house will be called
a house of prayer for all peoples.

— ISAIAH 56:7

V'no·mar l'fa·nav
shi·rah cha·da·shah. Ha·l'lu·yah!

וְנֹאמַר לְפָנָיו
שִׁירָה חֲדָשָׁה. הַלְלוּיָהּ.

Let us sing before the One
a new song. Halleluyah!

— PASSOVER HAGGADAH

U·fa·ratz·ta
ya·mah va·keid·mah
v'tza·fo·nah va·neg·bah.

וּפָרַצְתָּ
יָמָה וָקֵדְמָה
וְצָפֹנָה וָנֶגְבָּה.

And you shall spread out
to the west, and to the east,
and to the north, and to the south.

— GENESIS 28:14

V'ka·reiv p'zu·rei·nu
mi·bein ha·go·yim
u·n'fu·tzo·tei·nu ka·neis
mi·yar·k'tei a·retz.
Va·ha·vi·ei·nu l'Tzi·yon
ir·cha b'ri·nah,
v'liY·ru·sha·la·yim beit mik·dash·cha
b'sim·chat o·lam.

וְקָרֵב פְּזוּרֵינוּ
מִבֵּין הַגּוֹיִם
וּנְפוּצוֹתֵינוּ כַּנֵּס
מִיַּרְכְּתֵי אָרֶץ.
וַהֲבִיאֵנוּ לְצִיּוֹן
עִירְךָ בְּרִנָּה,
וְלִירוּשָׁלַיִם בֵּית מִקְדָּשְׁךָ
בְּשִׂמְחַת עוֹלָם.

Bring our scattered ones near
from among the nations
and our dispersed gather in
from the ends of the earth.
Bring us to Zion
your city, in song,
and to Jerusalem your Temple
in everlasting joy.

— *Musaf Amidah for Festivals*

U·r'eih va·nim l'va·ne·cha.
Sha·lom al Yis·ra·eil.

וּרְאֵה בָנִים לְבָנֶיךָ.
שָׁלוֹם עַל יִשְׂרָאֵל.

May you see your children's children.
Peace on Israel.

— *Psalms 128:6*

U·sh'av·tem ma·yim b'sa·son
mi·ma·ai·nei ha·y'shu·ah.

וּשְׁאַבְתֶּם מַיִם בְּשָׂשׂוֹן
מִמַּעַיְנֵי הַיְשׁוּעָה.

And you shall draw water
from the wells of deliverance.

— *Isaiah 12:3*

V'sha·vu va·nim lig·vu·lam.

וְשָׁבוּ בָנִים לִגְבוּלָם.

And [Your] children shall return to their own borders.

— *Jeremiah 31:16*

V'sa·mach·ta b'cha·ge·cha
v'ha·yi·ta ach sa·mei·ach.

וְשָׂמַחְתָּ בְּחַגֶּךָ
וְהָיִיתָ אַךְ שָׂמֵחַ.

And you will rejoice in your festivals
and you shall be altogether joyful.

— DEUTERONOMY 16:14,15

Chem·dat ya·mim
o·to ka·ra·ta,
zei·cher l'ma·a·seih v'rei·shit.

חֶמְדַּת יָמִים
אוֹתוֹ קָרֵאתָ,
זֵכֶר לְמַעֲשֵׂה בְרֵאשִׁית.

The most coveted of days
You called it,
a reminder of the work of creation.

— SHABBAT AMIDAH

Tov l'ho·dot lA·do·nai
u·l'za·meir l'shim·cha el·yon,
l'ha·gid ba·bo·ker chas·de·cha
ve·e·mu·nat·cha ba·lei·lot.

טוֹב לְהֹדוֹת לַייָ
וּלְזַמֵּר לְשִׁמְךָ עֶלְיוֹן,
לְהַגִּיד בַּבֹּקֶר חַסְדֶּךָ
וֶאֱמוּנָתְךָ בַּלֵּילוֹת.

It is good to give thanks to Adonai
and to sing to your name, Most High,
to proclaim Your kindness in the morning
and Your faithfulness at night.

— PSALMS 92:2

Y'va·re·ch'cha A·do·nai mi·Tzi·yon
u·r'eih b'tuv Y'ru·sha·la·yim.
[Y'va·re·ch'cha A·do·nai mi·Tzi·yon]
kol y'mei cha·ye·cha.
U·r'eih va·nim l'va·ne·cha
sha·lom al Yis·ra·eil.

יְבָרֶכְךָ יְיָ מִצִּיּוֹן
וּרְאֵה בְּטוּב יְרוּשָׁלָיִם.
[יְבָרֶכְךָ יְיָ מִצִּיּוֹן]
כֹּל יְמֵי חַיֶּיךָ.
וּרְאֵה בָנִים לְבָנֶיךָ
שָׁלוֹם עַל יִשְׂרָאֵל.

May Adonai bless You from Zion
And may you see the goodness of Jerusalem.
[May Adonai bless You from Zion],
all the days of your life.
And may you see the children of your children.
Peace on Israel.

— PSALMS 128:5-6

Ya·sis a·la·yich *e·lo·ha·yich*
kim·sos cha·tan al ka·lah.

יָשִׂישׂ עָלַיִךְ אֱלֹהָיִךְ
כִּמְשׂוֹשׂ חָתָן עַל כַּלָּה.

Your God will rejoice over you
as a bridegroom rejoices over his bride.

— L'CHA DODI, KABBALAT SHABBAT SERVICE

Yis·m'chu v'mal·chu·t'cha
sho·m'rei Shab·bat v'ko·r'ei o·neg.
Am m'ka·d'shei sh'vi·i
ku·lam yis·b'u
v'yit·a·n'gu mi·tu·ve·cha.
V'ha·sh'vi·i
ra·tzi·ta bo v'ki·dash·to,
chem·dat ya·mim o·to ka·ra·ta,
zei·cher l'ma·a·seih v'rei·shit.

יִשְׂמְחוּ בְמַלְכוּתְךָ
שׁוֹמְרֵי שַׁבָּת וְקוֹרְאֵי עֹנֶג.
עַם מְקַדְּשֵׁי שְׁבִיעִי
כֻּלָּם יִשְׂבְּעוּ
וְיִתְעַנְּגוּ מִטּוּבֶךָ.
וְהַשְּׁבִיעִי
רָצִיתָ בּוֹ וְקִדַּשְׁתּוֹ,
חֶמְדַּת יָמִים אוֹתוֹ קָרֵאתָ,
זֵכֶר לְמַעֲשֵׂה בְרֵאשִׁית.

They will rejoice in Your rule,
those who observe Shabbat and call it a delight.
The people who sanctify the seventh [day]
will all be satisfied
and will delight in Your goodness.
And the seventh [day],
You found favor in it and sanctified it,
most coveted of days you called it,
a reminder of the work of creation.

— SHABBAT MUSAF AMIDAH

Yis·m'chu ha·sha·ma·yim
v'ta·geil ha·a·retz,
yir·am ha·yam u·m'lo·o.

יִשְׂמְחוּ הַשָּׁמַיִם
וְתָגֵל הָאָרֶץ,
יִרְעַם הַיָּם וּמְלֹאוֹ.

Let the heavens be glad
and the earth rejoice,
let the sea roar, and all that fills it.

— PSALMS 96:11

Yis·ra·eil b'tach *bA·do·nai,*
ez·ram u·ma·gi·nam hu.

יִשְׂרָאֵל בְּטַח בַּיְיָ,
עֶזְרָם וּמָגִנָּם הוּא.

Let Israel trust in Adonai,
who is their help and their shield.

— PSALMS 115:9

SHORT SONGS

Yis·ra·eil v'o·rai·ta
v'Ku·d'sha B'rich Hu chad hu.

יִשְׂרָאֵל וְאוֹרַיְתָא
וְקֻדְשָׁא בְּרִיךְ הוּא חַד הוּא.

Israel, the Torah
and the Blessed Holy One are one.

— ZOHAR

To·rah O·rah, *Ha·l'lu·yah.*

תּוֹרָה אוֹרָה, הַלְלוּיָהּ.

Torah is Light, Halleluyah.

Koh a·mar Adonai:
Za·char·ti lach che·sed n'u·ra·yich,
a·ha·vat k'lu·lo·ta·yich —
lech·teich a·cha·rai ba·mid·bar,
b'e·retz lo z'ru·ah.

כֹּה אָמַר יְיָ:
זָכַרְתִּי לָךְ חֶסֶד נְעוּרַיִךְ,
אַהֲבַת כְּלוּלֹתָיִךְ —
לֶכְתֵּךְ אַחֲרַי בַּמִּדְבָּר,
בְּאֶרֶץ לֹא זְרוּעָה.

Thus spoke God:
I remember the devotion of your youth,
your love as a bride —
how you followed Me in the wilderness,
in a land that was not sown.

— JEREMIAH 2:2

Koh a·mar Adonai:
Ma·tza chein ba·mid·bar
am s'ri·dei cha·rev,
ha·loch l'har·gi·o Yis·ra·eil.

כֹּה אָמַר יְיָ:
מָצָא חֵן בַּמִּדְבָּר
עַם שְׂרִידֵי חָרֶב,
הָלוֹךְ לְהַרְגִּיעוֹ יִשְׂרָאֵל.

Thus spoke God:
The people escaped from the sword
found favor in the wilderness,
when Israel was marching to a resting place.

— JEREMIAH 31:2

Ki v'sim·chah tei·tzei·u
u·v'sha·lom tu·va·lun.
he·ha·rim v'ha·g'va·ot
yif·tz'chu lif·nei·chem ri·nah
v'chol a·tzei ha·sa·deh
yim·cha·u chaf.

כִּי בְשִׂמְחָה תֵצֵאוּ
וּבְשָׁלוֹם תּוּבָלוּן.
הֶהָרִים וְהַגְּבָעוֹת
יִפְצְחוּ לִפְנֵיכֶם רִנָּה
וְכָל עֲצֵי הַשָּׂדֶה
יִמְחֲאוּ כָף.

For in joy shall you go out
and in peace shall you be led forth.
The mountains and the hills
shall burst out before you in song
and all the trees of the field
shall clap their hands.

— ISAIAH 55:12,
SPEAKING OF LEAVING THE BABYLONIAN EXILE

Ki heim cha·yei·nu v'o·rech ya·mei·nu
u·va·hem neh·geh yo·mam va·lai·lah.

כִּי הֵם חַיֵּינוּ וְאֹרֶךְ יָמֵינוּ
וּבָהֶם נֶהְגֶּה יוֹמָם וָלָיְלָה.

For they are our life and the length of our days,
and on them will we meditate day and night.

— EVENING SERVICE LITURGY (AHAVAT OLAM)

Ki mi·Tzi·yon tei·tzei To·rah
u·d'var A·do·nai miY·ru·sha·la·yim.

כִּי מִצִּיּוֹן תֵּצֵא תוֹרָה
וּדְבַר יְיָ מִירוּשָׁלָיִם.

For out of Zion will come forth the Torah
and Adonai's word from Jerusalem.

— ISAIAH 2:3

Ki im·cha m'kor cha·yim,
b'or·cha nir·eh or.

כִּי עִמְּךָ מְקוֹר חַיִּים,
בְּאוֹרְךָ נִרְאֶה אוֹר.

For with you is the Source of Life,
in Your light we see light.

— PSALMS 36:10

Kei·tzad m'rak·dim
lif·nei ha·ka·lah?
Ka·lah na·ah va·cha·su·dah.

כֵּיצַד מְרַקְּדִים
לִפְנֵי הַכַּלָה?
כַּלָה נָאָה וַחֲסוּדָה.

How does one dance
before the bride?
The bride is beautiful and charming.

— *Talmud Ketubbot 16b-17a*

Kol ha·n'sha·mah
t'ha·leil Yah, Ha·l'lu·yah.

כֹּל הַנְּשָׁמָה
תְּהַלֵּל יָה הַלְלוּיָה.

Let all [my] being
praise Yah! Halleluyah!

— *Psalms 150:6*

Kol ha·o·lam ku·lo
ge·sher tzar m'od,
v'ha·i·kar lo l'fa·cheid k'lal.

כָּל הָעוֹלָם כֻּלּוֹ
גֶּשֶׁר צַר מְאֹד,
וְהָעִיקָר לֹא לְפַחֵד כְּלָל.

The whole entire world
is a very narrow bridge,
but the main thing is not to fear at all.

— *Rabbi Nachman of Bratzlav*

Lo i·ra
mei·ri·v'vot am
a·sher sa·viv sha·tu a·lai.
Ku·mah A·do·nai, ho·shi·ei·ni.

לֹא אִירָא
מֵרִבְבוֹת עָם
אֲשֶׁר סָבִיב שָׁתוּ עָלָי.
קוּמָה יְיָ, הוֹשִׁיעֵנִי.

I am not afraid
of the myriad forces
arrayed against me on every side.
Arise, Adonai, and save me.

— *Psalms 3:7-8*

Lo yi·sa goi el goi che·rev,
v'lo yil·m'du od mil·cha·mah.

לֹא יִשָּׂא גוֹי אֶל גּוֹי חֶרֶב,
וְלֹא יִלְמְדוּ עוֹד מִלְחָמָה.

Nation shall not lift up sword against nation,
nor shall they ever again know war.

— *Isaiah 2:4*

Lo a·le·cha
ha·m'la·chah lig·mor,
v'lo a·tah ven cho·rin
l'hi·ba·teil mi·me·nah.

לֹא עָלֶיךָ
הַמְּלָאכָה לִגְמוֹר,
וְלֹא אַתָּה בֶן חוֹרִין
לְהִבָּטֵל מִמֶּנָּה.

It is not up to you
to finish the task,
but neither are you free
to neglect it.

— RABBI TARFON, PIRKEI AVOT 2:21

Leiv ta·hor b'ra li, e·lo·him,
v'ru·ach na·chon cha·deish b'kir·bi.
Al tash·li·chei·ni mi·l'fa·ne·cha
v'ru·ach kod·sh'cha al ti·kach mi·me·ni.

לֵב טָהוֹר בְּרָא לִי, אֱלֹהִים,
וְרוּחַ נָכוֹן חַדֵּשׁ בְּקִרְבִּי.
אַל תַּשְׁלִיכֵנִי מִלְּפָנֶיךָ
וְרוּחַ קָדְשְׁךָ אַל תִּקַּח מִמֶּנִּי.

A pure heart create within me, God,
and a firm spirit renew within me.
Do not cast me from your presence
and do not take your holy spirit from me.

— PSALMS 51:12-13

Lu·lei he·e·man·ti
lir·ot b'tuv A·do·nai
b'e·retz cha·yim.
Ka·veih el A·do·nai!
cha·zak v'ya·a·meitz li·be·cha!
v'ka·veih el A·do·nai!

לוּלֵא הֶאֱמַנְתִּי
לִרְאוֹת בְּטוּב יְיָ
בְּאֶרֶץ חַיִּים.
קַוֵּה אֶל יְיָ!
חֲזַק וְיַאֲמֵץ לִבֶּךָ!
וְקַוֵּה אֶל יְיָ!

If I but trusted
to see the goodness of God
in the land of the living.
Place your hope in God!
Be strong and courageous!
Place your hope in God!

— PSALMS 27:13-14

La·Y'hu·dim ha·y'tah
o·rah v'sim·chah v'sa·son viy·kar.
Kein tih·yeh la·nu.

לַיְּהוּדִים הָיְתָה
אוֹרָה וְשִׂמְחָה וְשָׂשׂוֹן וִיקָר.
כֵּן תִּהְיֶה לָנוּ.

For the Jews there was
light and happiness, joy and honor.
So may it be for us.

— ESTHER 8:16, HAVDALAH

SHORT SONGS

L'chu n'ra·n'nah lA·do·nai,
na·ri·ah l'tzur yish·ei·nu.
N'ka·d'mah fa·nav b'todah,
biz·mi·rot na·ri·a lo.

לְכוּ נְרַנְּנָה לַיְיָ,
נָרִיעָה לְצוּר יִשְׁעֵנוּ.
נְקַדְּמָה פָנָיו בְּתוֹדָה,
בִּזְמִרוֹת נָרִיעַ לוֹ.

Come, let us sing to Adonai,
let us shout to the Rock of our salvation.
Let us receive Adonai's countenance with thanks,
with hymns let us shout out to God.

— PSALMS 95:1-2

La·m'na·tzei·ach shir miz·mor.
Ha·ri·u lA·do·nai kol ha·a·retz!

לַמְנַצֵּחַ שִׁיר מִזְמוֹר.
הָרִיעוּ לַיְיָ כָּל־הָאָרֶץ!

For the leader, a song, a psalm.
Shout to God, all the earth!

— AFTER PSALMS 66:1

Ya·kum A·do·nai, ya·fu·tzu o·y'vav,
v'ya·nu·su m'san·av mi·pa·nav.

יָקוּם יְיָ, יָפוּצוּ אוֹיְבָיו,
וְיָנוּסוּ מְשַׂנְאָיו מִפָּנָיו.

Let God arise, enemies be scattered,
foes flee God's presence.

— AFTER PSALMS 68:2

Hi·neih lo ya·num
v'lo yi·shan Sho·meir Yis·ra·eil.

הִנֵּה לֹא יָנוּם
וְלֹא יִישָׁן שׁוֹמֵר יִשְׂרָאֵל.

Lo, neither slumbers
nor sleeps, the Guardian of Israel.

— PSALMS 121:4

L'ma·an a·chai v'rei·ai
a·da·b'rah na sha·lom bach.
L'ma·an beit A·do·nai E·lo·hei·nu
a·vak·shah tov lach.

לְמַעַן אַחַי וְרֵעָי
אֲדַבְּרָה נָּא שָׁלוֹם בָּךְ.
לְמַעַן בֵּית יְיָ אֱלֹהֵינוּ
אֲבַקְשָׁה טוֹב לָךְ.

For the sake of my kin and friends
Let me pray for your well-being.
For the sake of the House of Adonai, our God,
Let me seek good things for you.

— PSALMS 122:8-9

L'o·lam lo esh·kach
pi·ku·de·cha,
ki vam chi·yi·ta·ni.

לְעוֹלָם לֹא אֶשְׁכַּח
פִּקּוּדֶיךָ,
כִּי בָם חִיִּיתָנִי.

I will never forget
your precepts,
for through them, you have kept me alive.

— PSALMS 119: 93

L'sha·nah ha·ba·ah
biY·ru·sha·la·yim ha·b'nu·yah.

לְשָׁנָה הַבָּאָה
בִּירוּשָׁלַיִם הַבְּנוּיָה.

Next year
in Jerusalem rebuilt.

— PASSOVER HAGGADAH

Mah a·hav·ti To·ra·te·cha!
kol ha·yom hi si·cha·ti.

מָה אָהַבְתִּי תוֹרָתֶךָ!
כָּל הַיּוֹם הִיא שִׂיחָתִי.

How I love your teaching!
All day long, it is my theme.

— PSALMS 119: 97

Mah to·vu o·ha·le·cha Ya·a·kov,
mish·k'no·te·cha Yis·ra·eil.
Va·a·ni b'rov chas·d'cha
a·vo vei·te·cha,
esh·ta·cha·veh
el hei·chal kod·sh'cha b'yir·a·te·cha.

מַה טֹּבוּ אֹהָלֶיךָ יַעֲקֹב,
מִשְׁכְּנֹתֶיךָ יִשְׂרָאֵל.
וַאֲנִי בְּרֹב חַסְדְּךָ
אָבוֹא בֵיתֶךָ,
אֶשְׁתַּחֲוֶה
אֶל הֵיכַל קָדְשְׁךָ בְּיִרְאָתֶךָ.

How beautiful are your tents, Jacob,
Your Dwelling Places, Israel.
And I, through Your great kindness,
will enter Your house,
to worship
in Your holy sanctuary, in awe of You.

— NUMBERS 24:5, PSALMS 5:8

Mah ga·d'lu ma·a·se·cha A·do·nai,
m'od a·m'ku mach·sh'vo·te·cha.

מַה גָּדְלוּ מַעֲשֶׂיךָ יְיָ,
מְאֹד עָמְקוּ מַחְשְׁבֹתֶיךָ.

How great are your deeds, Adonai,
your thoughts are very profound.

— PSALMS 92:6

Mah na·vu al he·ha·rim
rag·lei m'va·seir,
mash·mi·a sha·lom, m'va·seir tov,
mash·mi·a y'shu·ah.

מַה נָּאווּ עַל־הֶהָרִים
רַגְלֵי מְבַשֵּׂר,
מַשְׁמִיעַ שָׁלוֹם, מְבַשֵּׂר טוֹב,
מַשְׁמִיעַ יְשׁוּעָה.

How welcome on the mountain
are the footsteps of the herald,
announcing peace, heralding good tidings,
announcing salvation.

— ISAIAH 52:7-8

Mi ha·ish he·cha·feitz cha·yim,
o·heiv ya·mim lir·ot tov.
N'tzor l'shon·cha mei·ra,
u·s'fa·te·cha mi·da·beir mir·mah.
Sur mei·ra va·a·seih tov,
ba·keish sha·lom, v'rod·fei·hu.

מִי הָאִישׁ הֶחָפֵץ חַיִּים,
אֹהֵב יָמִים לִרְאוֹת טוֹב.
נְצוֹר לְשׁוֹנְךָ מֵרָע,
וּשְׂפָתֶיךָ מִדַּבֵּר מִרְמָה.
סוּר מֵרָע וַעֲשֵׂה טוֹב,
בַּקֵּשׁ שָׁלוֹם וְרָדְפֵהוּ.

Who is the man who desires life,
who loves years of good fortune?
Keep your tongue from evil,
your lips from speaking deceit.
Avoid evil and do good,
seek peace and pursue it.

— PSALMS 34:13-15

Mal·chu·t'cha
mal·chut kol o·la·mim,
u·mem·shal·t'cha
b'chol dor va·dor.

מַלְכוּתְךָ מַלְכוּת
כָּל עֹלָמִים,
וּמֶמְשַׁלְתְּךָ
בְּכָל דֹּר וָדֹר.

Your reign is a reign
for all ages,
and your dominion
for all generations.

— PSALMS 145:13

Min ha·mei·tzar ka·ra·ti Yah.
a·na·ni va·mer·chav Yah.

מִן הַמֵּצַר קָרָאתִי יָהּ.
עָנָנִי בַמֶּרְחָב יָהּ.

From a narrow place I called to Yah.
Yah answered me in a wide-open place.

— PSALMS 118:5

Mitz·vah g'do·lah
lih·yot b'sim·chah ta·mid.

מִצְוָה גְדוֹלָה
לִהְיוֹת בְּשִׂמְחָה תָּמִיד.

It is a great mitzvah
to be joyful at all times.

— NACHMAN OF BRATZLAV

Mi·ko·lot ma·yim ra·bim,
a·di·rim mish·b'rei yam,
a·dir ba·ma·rom A·do·nai.

מִקֹּלוֹת מַיִם רַבִּים,
אַדִּירִים מִשְׁבְּרֵי יָם,
אַדִּיר בַּמָּרוֹם יְיָ.

Above the sounds of many waters,
mighty breakers of the sea,
Adonai is supreme on high.

— PSALMS 93:4

M'ki·mi mei·a·far dal.

מְקִימִי מֵעָפָר דָּל.

You raise the poor from the dust.

— PSALMS 113:7

Si·man tov u·ma·zal tov
y'hei la·nu u·l'chol Yis·ra·eil. A·mein.

סִמָּן טוֹב וּמַזָּל טוֹב
יְהֵא לָנוּ וּלְכָל יִשְׂרָאֵל. אָמֵן.

May there be a good sign and good fortune
for us and for all Israel. Amen.

— KIDDUSH LEVANAH CEREMONY

Iv·du et A·do·nai b'sim·chah,
bo·u l' fa·nav bir·na·nah.

עִבְדוּ אֶת יְיָ בְּשִׂמְחָה,
בֹּאוּ לְפָנָיו בִּרְנָנָה.

Serve Adonai with gladness,
Come before the One rejoicing.

— PSALMS 100:2

Od ya·vo sha·lom a·lei·nu
v'al ku·lam.
Sa·lam, a·lei·nu v'al kol ha·o·lam.
Sa·lam.

עוֹד יָבוֹא שָׁלוֹם עָלֵינוּ
וְעַל כּוּלָם.
סָלָאם, עָלֵינוּ וְעַל כָּל הָעוֹלָם.
סָלָאם.

Peace will yet come for us
and for everyone.
Peace, for us and the whole world.
Peace.

— MOSH BEN-ARI

Od yi·sha·ma b'a·rei Y'hu·dah
u·v'chu·tzot Y'ru·sha·la·yim
Kol sa·son v'kol sim·chah,
kol cha·tan v'kol ka·lah.

עוֹד יִשָּׁמַע בְּעָרֵי יְהוּדָה
וּבְחֻצוֹת יְרוּשָׁלַיִם
קוֹל שָׂשׂוֹן וְקוֹל שִׂמְחָה,
קוֹל חָתָן וְקוֹל כַּלָּה.

Again will be heard in the cities of Judah
and the streets of Jerusalem
the sound of joy and the sound of happiness,
the voice of the groom and the voice of the bride.

— *Based on Jeremiah 33:10, cf. Sheva B'rachot*

U·ri Tzi·yon, hoi, u·ri
liv·shi u·zeich,
u·ri Tzi·yon, hoi, u·ri.
Liv·shi big·dei tif·ar·teich,
Y'ru·sha·la·yim ir ha·ko·desh.

עוּרִי צִיּוֹן, הוֹי, עוּרִי
לִבְשִׁי עֻזֵּךְ,
עוּרִי צִיּוֹן, הוֹי, עוּרִי.
לִבְשִׁי בִּגְדֵי תִפְאַרְתֵּךְ,
יְרוּשָׁלַיִם עִיר הַקֹּדֶשׁ.

Awake, Zion, O Awake,
Clothe yourself in splendor
Awake, Zion, O Awake.
Put on your beautiful garments,
Jerusalem, the holy city.

— *Based on Isaiah 52:1*

O·zi v'zim·rat Yah
va·y'hi li liy·shu·ah.

עָזִּי וְזִמְרָת יָהּ
וַיְהִי לִי לִישׁוּעָה.

Yah is my strength and my might,
and has become my salvation.

— *Exodus 15:2, Hallel*

Al na·ha·rot Ba·vel,
sham ya·shav·nu gam ba·chi·nu
b'zoch·rei·nu et Tzi·yon.

עַל נַהֲרוֹת בָּבֶל,
שָׁם יָשַׁבְנוּ גַּם בָּכִינוּ
בְּזָכְרֵנוּ אֶת צִיּוֹן.

By the rivers of Babylon,
there we sat and we wept
as we recalled Zion.

— *Psalms 137:1*

Al sh'lo·shah d'va·rim
ha·o·lam o·meid:
al ha·To·rah, v'al ha·a·vo·dah,
v'al g'mi·lut cha·sa·dim.

עַל שְׁלֹשָׁה דְבָרִים
הָעוֹלָם עוֹמֵד:
עַל הַתּוֹרָה, וְעַל הָעֲבוֹדָה,
וְעַל גְּמִילוּת חֲסָדִים.

On three things
the world stands:
on the Torah, on worship,
and on deeds of loving kindness.

— PIRKEI AVOT 1:2

Am Yis·ra·eil chai.
Od a·vi·nu chai.

עַם יִשְׂרָאֵל חַי.
עוֹד אָבִינוּ חַי.

The People of Israel lives.
Our father [Jacob] still lives.

— SHLOMO CARLEBACH

Eitz cha·yim hi la·ma·cha·zi·kim bah
v'tom·che·hah m'u·shar.
D'ra·che·ha dar·chei no·am
v'chol n'ti·vo·te·ha sha·lom.
Ha·shi·vei·nu A·do·nai, Ei·le·cha v'na·shu·vah.
cha·deish ya·mei·nu k'ke·dem.

עֵץ חַיִּים הִיא לַמַּחֲזִיקִים בָּהּ
וְתֹמְכֶיהָ מְאֻשָּׁר.
דְּרָכֶיהָ דַרְכֵי נֹעַם
וְכָל נְתִיבוֹתֶיהָ שָׁלוֹם.
הֲשִׁיבֵנוּ יְיָ, אֵלֶיךָ וְנָשׁוּבָה.
חַדֵּשׁ יָמֵינוּ כְּקֶדֶם.

It is a Tree of Life for those who grasp it
and its supporters are happy.
Its ways are ways of pleasantness
and all its pathways are peace.
Take us back, Adonai, to You, and we will come back.
Renew our days as of old.

— PROVERBS 3:18, 17; LAMENTATIONS 5:21; TORAH SERVICE

O·seh sha·lom bim·ro·mav
hu ya·a·seh sha·lom
a·lei·nu v'al kol Yis·ra·eil,
[v'al kol yo·sh'vei tei·veil],
v'im·ru a·mein.

עֹשֶׂה שָׁלוֹם בִּמְרוֹמָיו
הוּא יַעֲשֶׂה שָׁלוֹם
עָלֵינוּ וְעַל כָּל יִשְׂרָאֵל,
[וְעַל כָּל יוֹשְׁבֵי תֵבֵל],
וְאִמְרוּ אָמֵן.

May the Maker of peace in the heavens
make peace
for us and for all Israel,
[and for all who dwell on earth,]
and say Amen.

· — LITURGY

Pit·chu li sha·a·rei tze·dek,
a·vo vam o·deh Yah.
Zeh ha·sha·ar lA·do·nai,
tza·di·kim ya·vo·u vo.

פִּתְחוּ לִי שַׁעֲרֵי צֶדֶק,
אָבֹא בָם אוֹדֶה יָהּ.
זֶה הַשַּׁעַר לַיְיָ,
צַדִּיקִים יָבֹאוּ בוֹ.

Open for me the gates of justice,
I will enter them, I will thank Yah.
This is the gate of Adonai,
the just shall enter through it.

— PSALMS 118:19-20

Tza·m'ah naf·shi
lEi·lo·him l'Eil chai.
Da·v'kah naf·shi a·cha·re·cha,
Bi ta·m'chah y'mi·ne·cha.

צָמְאָה נַפְשִׁי
לֵאלֹהִים לְאֵל חָי.
דָּבְקָה נַפְשִׁי אַחֲרֶיךָ,
בִּי תָּמְכָה יְמִינֶךָ.

My soul thirsts
for God, the living God.
My soul clings to You,
Your right hand has supported me.

— PSALMS 42:3, 63:9; COMBINATION BY DVEYKUS

Kol do·di hi·neih zeh ba,
m'da·leig al he·ha·rim,
m'ka·peitz al ha·g'va·ot.
Hash·mi·i·ni et ko·leich,
ki ko·leich a·reiv
u·mar·eich na·veh.

קוֹל דּוֹדִי הִנֵּה זֶה בָּא,
מְדַלֵּג עַל הֶהָרִים,
מְקַפֵּץ עַל הַגְּבָעוֹת.
הַשְׁמִיעִינִי אֶת קוֹלֵךְ,
כִּי קוֹלֵךְ עָרֵב
וּמַרְאֵיךְ נָאוֶה.

Hark! My beloved is approaching,
skipping over mountains,
jumping over hills.
Let me hear your voice,
for your voice is pleasant
and your appearance comely.

— SONG OF SONGS 2:8, 14; COMBINATION BY DVEYKUS

Ro·m'mu A·do·nai E·lo·hei·nu,
v'hish·ta·cha·vu l'har kod·sho.

רוֹמְמוּ יְיָ אֱלֹהֵינוּ,
וְהִשְׁתַּחֲווּ לְהַר קָדְשׁוֹ.

Exalt Adonai our God,
Bow towards God's holy mountain.

— PSALMS 99:9

S'u sh'a·rim *ra·shei·chem*
v'hi·na·s'u pit·chei o·lam,
V'ya·vo me·lech ha·ka·vod. Selah.

שְׂאוּ שְׁעָרִים רָאשֵׁיכֶם
וְהִנָּשְׂאוּ פִּתְחֵי עוֹלָם,
וְיָבוֹא מֶלֶךְ הַכָּבוֹד. סֶלָה.

Lift up, O gates, your heads
and be lifted, eternal doors,
that the Glorious Ruler may enter. Selah.

— PSALMS 24:7

Si·su et Y'ru·sha·la·yim,
gi·lu vah, kol o·ha·ve·ha.
Al cho·mo·ta·yich ir Da·vid
Hif·ka·d'ti shom·rim
kol ha·yom v'chol ha·lai·lah.
S'i sa·viv ei·na·yich u·r'i,
ku·lam nik·b'tzu va·u lach.
V'a·meich ku·lam tza·di·kim,
l'o·lam yir·shu a·retz.

שִׂישׂוּ אֶת יְרוּשָׁלַיִם,
גִּילוּ בָהּ, כָּל אֹהֲבֶיהָ.
עַל חוֹמֹתַיִךְ עִיר דָּוִד
הִפְקַדְתִּי שֹׁמְרִים
כָּל הַיּוֹם וְכָל הַלַּיְלָה.
שְׂאִי סָבִיב עֵינַיִךְ וּרְאִי,
כֻּלָּם נִקְבְּצוּ בָאוּ לָךְ.
וְעַמֵּךְ כֻּלָּם צַדִּיקִים,
לְעוֹלָם יִירְשׁוּ אָרֶץ.

Rejoice with Jerusalem,
be glad with her, all who love her.
On your walls, City of David,
I have set watchmen
all day and all night.
Raise your eyes and look about,
they have all gathered, come to you.
And your people, all of them righteous,
shall possess the land for ever.

— BASED ON ISAIAH 66:10, 62:6, 60:4, 60:21

Shif·chi cha·ma·yim *li·beich*
no·chach p'nei A·do·nai.

שִׁפְכִי כַמַּיִם לִבֵּךְ
נֹכַח פְּנֵי יְיָ.

Pour out your heart like water
before God's presence.

— LAMENTATIONS 2:19

To·rah tzi·vah la·nu *Mo·sheh,*
mo·ra·shah k'hi·lat Ya·a·kov.

תּוֹרָה צִוָּה לָנוּ מֹשֶׁה,
מוֹרָשָׁה קְהִלַּת יַעֲקֹב.

The Torah, commanded to us by Moses,
is the inheritance of the Congregation of Jacob.

— DEUTERONOMY 33:4

Y'hi ra·tzon mil·fa·ne·cha, A·do·nai E·lo·hei·nu,	יְהִי רָצוֹן מִלְּפָנֶיךָ, יְיָ אֱלֹהֵינוּ,	May it be Your will, Adonai our God,
vEi·lo·hei a·vo·tei·nu [v'i·mo·teinu],	וֵאלֹהֵי אֲבוֹתֵינוּ [וְאִמּוֹתֵינוּ],	and God of our ancestors,
she·to·li·chei·nu l'sha·lom,	שֶׁתּוֹלִיכֵנוּ לְשָׁלוֹם,	to lead us in safety,
v'tatz·i·dei·nu l'sha·lom,	וְתַצְעִידֵנוּ לְשָׁלוֹם,	to direct our steps in safety,
v'tad·ri·chei·nu l'sha·lom,	וְתַדְרִיכֵנוּ לְשָׁלוֹם,	to guide us in safety,
v'ta·gi·ei·nu lim·choz chef·tzei·nu	וְתַגִּיעֵנוּ לִמְחוֹז חֶפְצֵנוּ	and enable us to reach our destination
l'cha·yim u·l'sim·chah u·l'sha·lom	לְחַיִּים וּלְשִׂמְחָה וּלְשָׁלוֹם	in life, in joy, and in peace
[v'ta·cha·zi·rei·nu l'vei·tei·nu l'sha·lom].	[וְתַחֲזִירֵנוּ לְבֵיתֵנוּ לְשָׁלוֹם].	[and bring us back home in peace].
V'ta·tzi·lei·nu mi·kaf	וְתַצִּילֵנוּ מִכַּף	Rescue us from the hand of
kol o·yeiv v'o·reiv ba·de·rech,	כָּל אוֹיֵב וְאוֹרֵב בַּדֶּרֶךְ,	every enemy that lurks along the way,
u·mi·kol mi·nei fu·r·a·nu·yot	וּמִכָּל מִינֵי פֻּרְעָנִיּוֹת	and all kinds of disasters
ha·mit·rag·shot la·vo la·o·lam.	הַמִּתְרַגְּשׁוֹת לָבוֹא לָעוֹלָם.	that threaten the world.
V'tish·lach b'ra·chah	וְתִשְׁלַח בְּרָכָה	Send a blessing
b'chol ma·a·seih ya·dei·nu,	בְּכָל מַעֲשֵׂה יָדֵינוּ,	to all the work of our hands,
v'tit·nei·nu l'chein u·l'che·sed u·l'ra·cha·mim	וְתִתְּנֵנוּ לְחֵן וּלְחֶסֶד וּלְרַחֲמִים	and grant us favor, kindness, and mercy
b'ei·ne·cha, u·v'ei·nei chol ro·ei·nu.	בְּעֵינֶיךָ וּבְעֵינֵי כָל רוֹאֵינוּ.	in Your eyes, and in the eyes of all who see us.
v'tish·ma kol ta·cha·nu·nei·nu,	וְתִשְׁמַע קוֹל תַּחֲנוּנֵינוּ,	Hear the voice of our supplications,
ki Eil sho·mei·a t'fi·lah	כִּי אֵל שׁוֹמֵעַ תְּפִלָּה	for You are the God who hears prayer
v'ta·cha·nun A·tah.	וְתַחֲנוּן אָתָּה.	and supplication.
Ba·ruch A·tah A·do·nai, sho·mei·a t'fi·lah.	בָּרוּךְ אַתָּה יְיָ, שׁוֹמֵעַ תְּפִלָּה.	Blessed are You, Adonai, who hears prayer.

— TALMUD B'RACHOT 29B

Index